An
Introduction to
Design and Culture
in the
Twentieth Century

An Introduction to Design and Culture in the Twentieth Century

Penny Sparke

ICON EDITIONS

1817

HARPER & ROW, PUBLISHERS, New York
Cambridge, Philadelphia, San Francisco, Washington
London, Mexico City, São Paulo, Singapore, Sydney

Published by arrangement with Allen & Unwin (Publishers) Ltd.

FIRST U.S. EDITION

Library of Congress Cataloging-in-Publication Data

Sparke, Penny.
  An introduction to design and culture in the twentieth century.
  (Icon editions)
  Bibliography: p.
  Includes index.
  1. Design—History—20th century. 2. Design, Industrial. I. Title.
NK1390.S63 1987   745.4'442   86-46214
ISBN 0-06-430170-2 (pbk.)

---

87 88 89 90 MPC 10 9 8 7 6 5 4 3 2 1

For John

Contents

Contents

Contents

List of Illustrations

page

xi

List of Illustrations

Preface

This book sets out to explore the parameters of a new subject – the cultural history of twentieth-century design – in terms both of its related areas and its essential subject-matter. It also aims to introduce students of design and of design history, as well as anybody who has an interest in the environment, to examples of the kind of material that needs to be researched and documented if a composite picture of design in this century is to emerge.

To write a book which tells its readers all they need to know about twentieth-century design in its cultural context would be an impossible task. Problems of definition; of the sheer mass of essential contextual material; and of the growing bulk of information on modern design, renders it a subject for several books, each one written, preferably, from a different perspective.

This study sets out, therefore, to act as an introduction to design and culture since 1900. In order to present both the story of design in this period and the complexity of its allegiances, I have opted for a combination of a chronological and a thematic case-study approach: as a result, the structure of the book needs some preliminary explanation.

Available definitions of design are varied, complex, contradictory and in a state of permanent flux. Most would agree, however, that as a cultural concept design is determined by the outside forces that have shaped it and by the contexts within which it has manifested itself, as well as by the numerous faces it has presented to the world. It is these which have determined the basic structure of this book.

Where chronology is concerned, I have divided this century into three main periods. Part One of the book concentrates on the formative years of modern design – 1900–17 (with numerous inevitable forays back into the previous century to explain the background to the period); Part Two focuses on the years 1918–45 – the period of consolidation and heroism for modern design; and Part Three – 1945 to the present – concerns itself with design's absorption into society and culture at large. These specific periods are explored most fully in the first chapters to each section, Chapters 1, 5 and 9 – which provide a background for the evolution of modern design.

All three introductory chapters stress the relationship between economics and design but, in each case, from a different perspective. While Chapter 1, 'Mass Production and the Mass Market', examines the link between economics, technology and design, Chapter 5, 'Democracies and Dictatorships', describes the ways in which various political regimes have influenced the relationship between the economy and design, and Chapter 9, 'The Admass Society', focuses on the interdependence between economics, design and social change. Between them, these three chapters introduce the main subject areas which have generated most of the material in this book – the histories of economics, technology, politics and society, all of which impinge upon that multidisciplinary subject the history of design and, together, provide an essential framework for it.

While Chapters 1, 5 and 9 present both a chronological and con- textual base-line, the remaining nine chapters of the book concentrate on a number of more specifically design-related themes. Many issues characterize design in the twentieth and, to some extent, the nine- teenth centuries which distinguish it as a concept from its definition in the past. They include the professionalism of the designer as a problem-solver for industry; the state support of design; the penetra- tion of designed artefacts into the mass environment; the growth of design education; the designer's response to new materials and technologies; the emergence of new products with a technological bias; the mass-manufacturing company as the patron of innovative design; the emergence and subsequent rejection of a design philosophy and aesthetic determined by the machine; and, most recently, a sense of disillusion with design as an adjunct of big business. It is these themes which have determined the subject-matter of the rest of the book and which have inspired the case-studies which make up the bulk of the text.

Each theme has been placed within the historical section from which its most extensive case-studies have been selected. These nine chapters are not, however, limited to the historical boundaries of the section which houses them but embrace the whole century, albeit in a necessarily sketchy manner. Thus, for example, Chapter 3, which examines the evolution of modern design theory, stresses the early decades of the century but also freely discusses the interwar and postwar period. I have tried, in this way, to enable the readers to see both the broad 'horizontal' and the more specific 'vertical' forces that have shaped design in this century. As a result, the picture of design thus presented emerges as the sum of its parts rather like the way that a picture 'painted by numbers' only makes sense when it is finished even though glimpses of the final image can be grasped along the way. My method resembles that which W. H. Walsh calls 'colligation', an approach to history which assumes that 'different historical events can be regarded as going together to constitute a single process, a whole of which they are all parts'.[1] I have used the 'painting by numbers' approach not in order to be deliberately evasive but rather to show that design is so deeply rooted within the structure and evolution of society that an account of its history in this century almost involves recounting that of modern civilization as a whole.

Inevitably, in working out this complicated grid structure, some repetition has occurred and a number of design case-studies re-emerge to illustrate different themes. The example of design in the USA in the interwar period is used, for instance, to illuminate the story of the professional consultant designer, the impact of new materials, and the evolution of a mass style. This helps to emphasize both the importance of the example and the way in which the themes overlap each other.

While the main text of the book provides an overview of the progress of design and culture through this century, more detailed information about that story is contained within the end-of-chapter notes, the appended glossary of proper names, and the captions to the illustrations.

In addition to listing the sources of quotations used within the text, the notes also contain useful information about a number of twentieth-century design movements and styles, as well as explaining the meaning of specialist vocabulary and describing seminal modern products. The glossary of proper names is intended as a guide to major designers, design critics and manufacturing companies committed to twentieth-century design and can be consulted whenever (q.v.) or (qq.v.) follows a name or names in the text; and the captions to the illustrations describe and contextualize a number of both seminal and representative objects and images, with an emphasis upon visual analysis.

This range of additional material is as important as the main text as it serves as a necessary factual adjunct to the general, more discursive backbone provided by the latter. The bibliography is also intended to be an intrinsic part of the text, for with its guidance the reader will be able to pursue in more detail any interests that this introductory text may generate.

In addition to explaining the book's structure and purpose I should also declare my bias where its subject-matter is concerned. As I am dealing solely with the period after 1900, and with design in its most democratic sense, my main concern is with the relationship of design with mass-production industry. As a result, the neighbouring areas of craft, architecture and fine art which in previous centuries were more closely linked with the development of design have been largely ignored.

I also decided to focus on consumer rather than on capital goods[2] and I have chosen to exclude advertising and graphic design, environmental design and fashion design, except in those instances where their inclusion illuminates the evolution of industrial or, more specifically, product design. This is not because these areas are irrelevant or unimportant but, on the contrary, because they are so vital that to discuss them in adequate depth would necessitate a book at least twice the length of this one. It has, therefore, been necessary to leave these areas out in the hopes that they will be dealt with fully elsewhere.

Although a great deal of the material in the book derives from my own research, much of the information and many of the ideas it contains are not new. They have, however, not been drawn together in this way before and it is the sum of the parts which is, therefore, breaking new ground.

The book is a synthesis of much of the material I have amassed over a period of about twelve years spent researching and teaching the history of design and my thanks go to the many people with whom I have, over this period, discussed the issues involved: to friends and family; to colleagues in the Department of Art History at Brighton Polytechnic and in the Department of Cultural History at the Royal College of Art; to fellow-members of the Design History Society; to many of the students I have worked with – both designers and historians – in both of the above institutions and elsewhere; to friends and colleagues in the countries where I have done most of my research, namely, Italy, Scandinavia and the USA; and, especially, to the group of friends who patiently bore with me while I wrote most of the final draft during the summers of 1982 and 1983 in the heat of Southern Italy.

Penny Sparke
1985

Notes: Preface

1   W. H. Walsh, *An Introduction to Philosophy of History* (London: Hutchinson 1967), p. 24.
2   This book concentrates on the function of design as a quality of 'consumer goods' – that is, products which are openly available through retail outlets – rather than of 'capital goods' which are more specialized products, available only to a specialist market direct from the manufacturer or wholesaler. In the former context, design plays a part in the 'sales appeal' of the product, whereas in the latter area it is much more involved with its utilitarian qualities.

Introduction:
The Contexts of
Modern Design

Now that 'Design' is understood from Tokyo to Moscow, from Buenos Aires to Montreal, it is obvious that each country according to its politics, its economics, its sociology, its industry, uses 'Design' in a different way; but one must add that a universal language is being constructed daily.[1]

This book is about design and culture in the twentieth century. The word 'culture' is used throughout the text in its most democratic sense, that is, as a concept which embraces the ideas and values expressed by modern society as a whole, rather than one which only touches one level of human endeavour. In parallel, design is understood here as a phenomenon which affects everybody.

This definition of culture has to be considered within a broad context which subsumes economics, politics and technology as these are the forces which have determined the dominant cultural patterns in modern society. Design is also formed and sustained by these forces and, as a result, designed artefacts act as cultural ciphers. In this book, I have set out to examine both the way in which culture has influenced design in this century and the manner in which design has, in its turn, played a part in creating culture through the objects, institutions, personalities and the patterns of behaviour and thought that have accompanied it. Since 1900 design and culture, in this wide sense, have become increasingly interdependent and the implications of this relationship will re-emerge constantly in the following chapters.

My main thesis is that, within the framework of industrial capitalism which created it and continues to dominate it in contemporary Western society, design is characterized by a dual alliance with both mass production and mass consumption and that these two phenomena have determined nearly all its manifestations. Like Janus, design looks in two directions at the same time: as a silent quality of all mass-produced goods it plays a generally unacknowledged but vital role in all our lives;

xix

as a named concept within the mass media it is, however, much more visible and generally recognized. In this latter guise design becomes an extension of marketing and advertising. The 'designer-jeans' phenomenon, which persuades us to buy a product because it has been designed, is, culturally speaking, totally distinct from the activity of the anonymous designers within industry who resolve the problems of cost, appearance and use in consumer products. The way in which design as an adjunct of marketing has grown out of design as an aspect of mass production is a major theme within the story of modern design and the focus of this book. It is a change which directly mirrors the way in which the model of mass-production industry, as presented by Henry Ford, which dominated American ideas about industrial organization in the early twentieth century, has been challenged by an alternative model which stresses batch production, a smaller scale of operations (or set of operations), and, at times, a fair amount of hand or skilled work. This latter model – best expressed by Sloane's work at General Motors in the USA in the 1920s and by contemporary developments in Japan and Italy – puts the demands of the marketplace above those of the logic of mechanized mass production and tends, as a result, to value the diversification of products rather than, or as well as, standardization. These two models of industry coexist in this century and have different implications for the meaning of design. An important sub-theme is the way in which the aesthetic of designed artefacts has swung repeatedly backwards and forwards from production to consumption as sources of metaphorical inspiration.

While this book concentrates on design as it has come to be defined and understood since the advent of mechanization, and emphasizes those themes which have made it part of recent history, it is also important to remember that the concept has an earlier history which is largely responsible for the way we comprehend it today. Design has always been one aspect of a larger process – whether of manufacturing, in the craft or mechanized sense, or, from the consumer's point of view, of participating in social or economic life – and its definition has, from the moment the word entered the English language, been in a state of constant flux due, primarily, to the changes in the socio-economic framework which has sustained it. Thus the difference between a seventeenth-century pattern-maker and a modern industrial designer is less one of the nature of their respective creative activities than of the economic, technological and social constraints within which the activity is performed. What have remained constant are the visualizing and humanizing aspects of the design process as even today the designer's input into the manufacture of an electronic calculator, for example, focuses on the aesthetic and ergonomic aspects of that product.

The most significant and powerful constraining factor on design in the last two centuries has, however, been its growing alliance with mass production and mass consumption. This, more than any other historical event, has determined the special characteristics we associate with its role in modern society. In recent decades, manufacturing industry has removed design from its original, humble and largely anonymous backstage position as an element in the production process and pushed it into the limelight as an important aspect of the saleability and desirability of consumer products. The French Marxist writer, Laurent Wolf, explains that it has become merely 'a new way of elaborating products linked to the "profound mutation" of the production process'.[2] Design, in the 'old' sense, has not disappeared however. It remains as central to the process of production as it ever did but tends, at least in terms of its cultural image, to be overshadowed by the more sales-oriented concept.

The ambiguity created by the co-existence of these two faces of design has been the greatest stumbling-block in a satisfactory analysis of it. It is a difficulty which is exacerbated by the confusion and ideological assumptions which have been made by many of this century's critics and historians of design. It was those critics, among them Nikolaus Pevsner, Lewis Mumford, Herbert Read and Siegfried Giedion (qq.v.) – all of whom supported the functionalist ideals of the Modern Movement[3] in the interwar years – who helped to perpetrate the myth that 'good design' is synonymous with the machine aesthetic,[4] who ignored the meanings that society was to come to associate with that particular design movement, and who thereby turned design into a heroic rather than an everyday concept. The critical tradition established by these writers has been hard to supersede and it is only recently, as a result of the growing dissatisfaction with the Modern Movement, that their views have been questioned.

It has become increasingly difficult also to extricate the propaganda of design from its real manifestations and to separate sales talk from fact. One way of avoiding this impasse is to move beyond the Modern Movement critics and to consider design within the context of social life. From this perspective, design simply becomes one of the forms of mass communication in modern society inasmuch as it plays a fundamental role, both practical and psychological, within daily life.

In understanding many of the changes in the meaning of modern design it is important to grasp the modifications that have been effected by changing social patterns to which the designer, like everybody else, can only respond as best he or she can. The changing role of women in this century, for example, has influenced the appearance and image of the so-called labour-saving devices in the home needed to minimize housework. Conversely, design initiatives can modify social behaviour, as is the case, for example, with the Sony Walkman, the miniature tape-cassette player which has encouraged a new attitude towards such solitary activities as jogging and travelling on the underground.

While the relationship between social change and design change remains a chicken and egg problem it is equally difficult to decide whether economic necessity, public taste, available technology, or social need came first as causes for design innovation. For example, the emergence in this century of new materials and production techniques, such as die-casting in plastics manufacture, has been highly influential in determining the appearance of many of the products which surround us but, at the same time, those objects would never have entered the mass environment if they did not fulfil an earlier need, whether practical, economic, political, social, or psychological. In many ways the stories of design 'failures' – such as that of the Ford Edsel in the early 1950s[5] – reveal more about the meaning of design in contemporary society than those of the 'successes' as one can isolate a single factor as a cause for failure while 'success' depends upon an inextricable combination of forces.

The social and psychological necessity for design is easily justified by the fact that we only need to buy, for example, one set of plastic crockery which would last us a life-time. That we continue to buy expendable products made of fragile materials, and often, indeed, to invest in duplicate examples which only vary stylistically, because of the demands of social status or ritual emphasizes the fundamentally symbolic role that design plays in our consumption and use of objects. While this tendency may be minimized at the more technical end of the spectrum – most of us do not, for example, need more than one micro-wave oven – even in goods of this nature there are signs that pluralism[6] is increasingly the norm. The socio-cultural argument is reinforced by the economic demands of industrial capitalism which depends on the constant consumption of goods. Together they locate design in the centre of the picture as it is design that provides the variation that is so essential to modern society.

Design decisions are constantly being made everywhere, whether by designers or consumers. They all focus on the aesthetic of the product whether, in the designer's case, defined as a creative resolution of the joint demands of technology, price, function and social symbolism or, in the case of the buying public, as the fulfilment of the requirements of taste, practicality and social and economic needs.

Design is, more often than not, therefore, manifested in tangible and visible form and objects are, therefore, an important point of entry for the design critic or historian. They are not always, however, the final word as design is, ultimately, a cultural phenomenon whose effects are as abstract as they are physical. Objects play a significant role in this book – particularly those like the Italian Vespa motor-scooter[7] which encapsulate many of the important aspects of modern design and culture – but most of them are included as examples or illustrations rather than as the main substance of my text.

As Patrix implies in the quotation at the beginning of this introduction, it is the nature of design in the modern world to be international as it depends increasingly on the structure of the world market for its very existence. The English word 'design' is currently used widely in countries such as Japan, Italy, France, the Scandinavian countries and the USA, a fact which indicates that its meaning in contemporary society has moved away from its definition in previous centuries when it was interchangeable with the Italian *il disegno* and the French *le dessin*. The fact that these countries have abandoned these native terms in favour of 'design' suggests that more than just a mere shift in meaning has taken place and that what has occurred is, in fact, the emergence of an entirely new concept. It is the nature of this concept and the way in which it has evolved in this century that I aim to explore.

Notes: Introduction

1 G. Patrix, *Design et environnement* (Paris: Casterman, 1973), p. 23.
2 L. Wolf, *Idéologie et production: le design* (Paris: Editions Anthropos, 1972), p. 10.
3 The term 'Modern Movement' is used by architectural and design critics and historians to describe the movement in architecture and design which succeeded Victorian eclecticism and ornament and which dominated the first half of the twentieth century. It was an international movement with high social ideals – expressed in the writings of Le Corbusier, Walter

Gropius (qq.v.) and others – and is recognized, in the buildings and objects it engendered, by the elimination of decoration and an emphasis on geometric simplicity and a minimal use of colour.

4　The expression the 'machine aesthetic' is used to describe the style of the products – at first, furniture, metalwork, ceramics and glass and, later, machines themselves – which were designed in the general spirit of the Modern Movement. The reference to the 'machine' was more metaphorical than literal, however, giving rise to such epithets as 'simple', 'rational' and 'standardized'. It was an aesthetic which penetrated the worlds of painting and sculpture as well, and which formed an important part of the 'modern' sensibility in the early years of this century.

5　The Ford Edsel automobile, named after Edsel Ford, was designed in 1958 but, due to its rather dated, awkward styling and the fact that 1958 was a recession year, it only remained on the market for two years. As the Ford Company had invested $250 million in it, it proved a massive financial disaster.

6　The term 'pluralism' is used to describe the multiple values held and expressed simultaneously within contemporary society. Mass-produced, designed artefacts reflect that multi-valency and there has been a tendency, in recent years, to reject the univalent, 'modern' design philosophy of the early century. Eclecticism, or the simultaneous use of several different styles in the man-made environment, is one of the inevitable results of this recent tendency.

7　The Vespa motor-scooter, manufactured by the Italian engineering company Piaggio, is an example of a consumer product which has become a strong cultural symbol. Since the late 1940s it has been a highly visible object in the everyday environment symbolizing, in Italy, the post-fascist society and, in Britain, the newly emergent youth culture of the 1960s.

PART ONE

Proto-Design, 1900–1917

1

Mass Production and the Mass Market

Physically industrialisation liberated man by overcoming the barrier of distance, by cheapening commodities, and by diversifying social experiences. Politically it helped to release him from the encumbrance of prescriptive privilege and traditional inequality.[1]

Although mass production and mass consumption have their roots in the years before 1800, it was not until the beginning of the last century that the word 'mass' took on any real meaning. Rapid developments in production mechanization, accompanied by huge increases in population and the wealth of the masses, provided such new scales of manufacturing and consumption that 'design' took on a new and unprecedented significance in contemporary life.

While the division of labour, and the developments in mass production that resulted from this earlier organizational change, had already determined the emergence of the design process as we now know it, mechanization provided new constraints for it and mass consumption turned it into a tangible and ubiquitous feature of everyday life. This double-edged role for design characterizes it in the contemporary world and distinguishes it from the way the concept was understood in the pre-industrial context.

The Technological Revolution
in Britain

During the so-called Industrial Revolution which took place in Britain at the end of the eighteenth century, the discovery of steam-power and its multiple uses had inspired the invention of numerous new machine-tools and production techniques, among them Nasmyth's steam

3

hammer[2] and Watts's steam pump.[3] In turn the new tools and techniques were responsible for the production of new consumer machines – without them, for example, the manufacture of the sewing machine and the typewriter would not have been possible. Soon both the factory and the everyday environment were radically transformed by the arrival of objects hard to imagine before the technological revolution. The steam train, for example, conceived in the 1830s as a means of transporting coal to industrial centres before it was thought of as a means of public mobility, transformed the landscape and modified the life-style of a large sector of the population by providing a new form of communication between the town and the countryside.

Another result of the work of the steam pump was the discovery of a new material, cast-iron, that was to alter radically the manufacturing techniques and appearance of many new products in the environment and was thus responsible for a huge revolution in design, making possible new feats of engineering and new kinds of architectural and product decoration.

Changes in production and in design were felt most strongly in the traditional 'applied art' industries in Britain in the early nineteenth century. Technological progress, and its influence on the mechanization of production, was a dominant force behind the rapid expansion of industrialization in this period. Harnessed to commercial ends, it advanced in leaps and bounds and made otherwise complex tasks simple. In textile production, for example, the Spinning Jenny[4] and the Jacquard loom[5] revolutionized the way textiles were both conceived and made and intensified the changes in the process of design that the division of labour had already instigated. No longer could the craftsman make spontaneous decisions about the appearance of the final product during its manufacture but, as in, for example, the case of production with the Jacquard loom, the desired pattern had to be fully planned and broken down into its component parts before manufacture began. This method of designing prior to production was echoed in fabric printing with the use of the mechanical roller, and in ceramics production where moulds were used increasingly in the mass-production sector. The effects of these organizational changes in production methods were felt both in the appearance of the final products, which was influenced increasingly by the constraints of technology, and in the structure of labour patterns within the factory, with the emergence of a new breed of 'art-workers' who translated the ideas of fine artists into mass production.

4

Mass Production and
Design in the USA

While Britain led the way in the first half of the nineteenth century in the application of new technologies to the mass production of goods within the traditional applied art sector, across the Atlantic, in the USA, huge advances were being made in the efficient organization of labour and production; in the development of specialized machine-tools; and in the manufacture of new consumer products with a technological bias. In the USA mechanized mass production was encouraged even more enthusiastically than in Europe where manual labour was cheaper and more available, and the US system which evolved is, as a result, referred to as 'The American System of Manufacture'. In its early phase, in the mid-nineteenth century, it had radical implications for the appearance of products and is often heralded as the first influence on design in what came to be known as the 'Functionalist tradition', that is, the design theory that claims that manufacturing methods determine not only the means of production but also the forms of the products.

The first American apologist of this theory was the sculptor Horatio Greenough who wrote a short treatise entitled *Form and Function* in its support. Among the thoughts he elaborated was a fear that the new simple aesthetic the Americans had achieved in engineering structures such as their ships and bridges, was under threat from the market-oriented approach favoured in Britain. This latter approach, according to Greenough, encouraged the union of sophisticated fine-art principles with the manufacture of mass-produced goods at one end of the spectrum but, at the other end, also produced excessive and ill-conceived ornamentation, particularly in those goods exported to new markets such as the USA. He felt that while the graduates of the new British design schools, established in the 1930s, enhanced one aspect of manufacture, 'the lower talents fill the factory, the foundry and the atelier, to fashion fabrics for ourselves'[6] and expressed his hope that this tendency would not be emulated in the USA: 'I am aware of the economic sagacity of the English, and how fully they understand the market; but I hope that we are not so thoroughly asphyxiated by the atmosphere they have created as to follow their lead in our own creation of a higher order.'[7] The US exhibits at the 1851 Crystal Palace Great Exhibition in London showed how the USA's approach to manufacture affected the nature and appearance of a number of their

5

1 Singer sewing machine. First patent model, 1851.
Isaac Merritt's patent model, the No. 1 Standard, was invented in 1851. It was a lock-stitch machine, made of cast-iron. Its simple aesthetic reflected its means of production and its function, that is, the cogs and other parts of the mechanism were all exposed and the cast-iron components undecorated. Even the packing case it arrived in was used as the sewing-table. This machine demonstrates clearly that brief moment in US design which preceded the time when the new machines became decorative items aimed at the female consumer and destined for the home and office. In 1958 Singer introduced its Family Machine which fulfilled this latter role much more adequately.

products. Where the new mechanical objects were concerned, it was an approach which took little heed of market preferences, and the machines which emerged in these early days of US mass production, like Singer's first sewing machine [1] in which all the mechanical parts were exposed, were technically advanced but visually very simple, like the engineered structures that Greenough admired so much.

The form of the Colt revolver exhibited at the 1851 Exhibition, and subsequently manufactured in Britain for a few years, was also the visible result of the USA's advanced system of mass manufacture. The components of the revolver were all standardized and interchangeable and, in the 1849 model, no attempts were made to conceal the fact that its appearance was simply the result of the combination of its assembled, machine-made parts. This was an approach to design which had more in common with the vernacular craft tradition than with the application of marketing ideas to mass production, which Britain was busy developing in this period.

In the catalogue to the Philadelphia Centennial Exhibition of 1876, a German Commissioner 'urged Germany to follow the example of American industry which had succeeded in raising both the quantity and quality of production by a proper application of machinery',[8] and there seemed to be a consensus among the other industrialized countries that this was indeed the case. Where 'design', in the traditional sense of 'applied art' or 'taste' in goods which had a craft heritage was concerned, however, Europe was definitely still the trend-setter and the USA was the first to acknowledge this. Again a writer in the Philadelphia catalogue noted that in this context 'Few American pieces were fully equal, in point of elegance and artistic finish and design, to any of the English or even the French exhibits in the same line'.[9] While US products in the sphere of the applied arts, like the Union Porcelain Works vase of 1876 [2], attempted to emulate the European vogue for narrative decoration, others, in the area of machine-tools and agricultural machinery, suggested that design might be seen simply as a question of 'problem-solving' in the light of technological and organisational constraints, rather than, in the traditional sense, as elegant decoration applied by a fine artist. The undecorated McCormick reaper, for example – a piece of US agricultural machinery also exhibited in 1851 – was aesthetically unacceptable to the British taste-conscious public who described it as a 'cross between a chariot, a wheelbarrow and a flying machine',[10] but as a piece of equipment whose appearance was dictated solely by the nature of its production

2 Vase. Union Porcelain Works 1876.
Many of the ceremonial items manufactured in the USA during this period by traditional
companies looked to European models for their aesthetic inspiration. This vase, which is
22¼ in. high, was the best known of Karl Müller's pieces and is in the collection of the
Brooklyn Museum. It employed the narrative, decorative tradition well established in
similar products in Europe by this time. Made to celebrate the American Centennial of
1876, its decorative motifs are, however, specifically American in origin. They include a
relief portrait of George Washington, scenes from American historical and contemporary
life – both agricultural and industrial – as well as a number of American symbols, including
American bison and the American eagle. The stylistic idiom is one of nineteenth-century
eclecticism.

and its function, it was well in advance of its time. Although the professional designer for industry was not to emerge for another half a century, the constraints upon the industrial design process were beginning to become apparent. In the USA a kind of technological determinism operated for a brief period before the sudden growth of mass consumption from the 1860s onwards caused that country to emulate the British example of designing to suit market needs.

The symbolic and aesthetic needs of the market were slow, however, to affect some new US products, as the example of the Ford automobile reveals. Standardization in mass production had reached a highly sophisticated level in the USA long before it was emulated elsewhere. It appeared first in fire-arms production when Eli Whitney (q.v.) had, half a century before Colt, initiated the manufacture of a musket made from interchangeable parts. The unskilled workers he employed were all taught to make each of the musket's fifty individual components which were made to uniform standards and were thus identical. Whitney built a factory outside New Haven in Connecticut where he worked on his machine-tools, among them special moulds, jigs, gauges and, eventually, a milling machine. His concept of uniform parts was adopted for the manufacture of other products, among them clocks and sewing machines, by the middle of the century.

A little earlier, Oliver Evans (q.v.) had invented the assembly line in his flour mill, due to the shortage and high cost of labour in the USA, but the combination of this idea with the concept of standardization needed the arrival of a mechanically complex object which was assembled from components and which could be directed, if low-cost production were achieved, at the mass market. This was to be provided by the automobile, through the pioneering work of individuals like Henry Leland and Henry Ford (qq.v.).

Ford had been struggling since the 1890s to get his production line established. In 1903 he made his famous statement about standardization, in which he referred to Adam Smith's theories about mass production: 'The way to make automobiles is to make one automobile like another automobile, to make them all alike, to make them come from the factory all alike, just like one pin is like another when it comes from a pin factory.'[11] From that year onwards, he set about both designing a car that would be suitable for the mass market and finding ways of lowering the cost of its manufacture. With his Model T, or Tin Lizzie as it came to be called, Ford succeeded in designing a car which was right for the mass market. He also organized its mass production so that the price was right – it cost $850 at first but went down to $360 in 1916 – which he achieved through his invention, in 1914, of a moving line system for the chassis assembly. Experiments had been taking place in the Ford factory for a number of years with this end in sight. These included working out details such as the best speed for the line, the correct height of the work and the correct positioning of the workmen. Combined with some aggressive marketing, Ford's moving assembly line resulted in the mass production and mass acceptance of his new car and by 1920 every other car in the world was a Model T Ford [3].

Ford's deep commitment to Adam Smith's principles led him to believe that a standardized aesthetic was needed for the mass market as he felt that mass taste could be educated to agree to the acceptance of a standard, functional product. As a result the black Model T remained visually uniform for almost twenty years. With the onset of the Depression, however, in the late 1920s, and increasing competition from rival companies, Ford was forced to revise his earlier theory and to introduce the principle of stylistic variation and expendability into his product, a direction in which his competitor, General Motors, had already been moving for a number of years.

The Expansion of the British Market

Like the mechanization of the traditional industries, mass consumption was a British phenomenon first. The main reasons for the expansion of the market in Britain in the nineteenth century were the growth of the population,[12] an increase in its spending power,[13] and shifts in public taste which encouraged people to transfer their spending from one set of goods to another, following the principle of 'upward emulation'. This set of factors combined to revolutionize man's relationship with the material world as it enabled more people both to be able and to want to purchase more, different objects. In turn, it created its own set of accompanying developments which included changes in industrial production methods in order to increase output to meet the demands of the new, expanded market, new kinds of retailing outlets to make the newly desired goods readily available, the growth of advertising to stimulate demand and disseminate information about the new products,

3 Ford Model Ts at Highland Park Factory, 1915.
This picture shows the chassis assembly at the Ford Highland Park plant and focuses on the 'Body Chute' which was located in John R. Street. It was an intrinsic part of Ford's system of standardized mass production at this time. The 'endless belt' was controlled by the man at the lever at the extreme right of the platform. The rest of the men were occupied in sending the next body down the chute and in putting the slings, which hang from the gallows cross-bar, around the body. The chassis were driven to this part of the plant and positioned ready to receive the bodies.

and the increasing significance of design as a factor within marketing and social relationships.

Although not yet a subject for general discussion, design was, none the less, becoming increasingly important as an aid to the mass consumption of goods. Whereas it was still, where the manufacturer was concerned, linked inextricably to the technological and organizational constraints of mass production, it was beginning to move into the public arena and as well as being a measure of public needs and aspirations, reflected public taste and social status.

The growth of the relationship of design to marketing is contained in the history of the expansion of mass consumption in this period. The period begins at the time which Lewis Mumford calls the 'third stage of industrialization'[14] – that is, the age of electricity which occurred in the second half of the nineteenth century. At that time Britain underwent a period of mechanization in a number of consumer areas, like furniture manufacturing, which, untouched by the changes in the early part of the century, now reorganized some of its production methods. This coincided with a number of social changes which took place at the same time. A higher proportion of the population, for example, now had homes of its own and needed furnishings for them. For these new consumers appearance and life-style were becoming increasingly important and this pointed the way to products becoming a means of offering them style and social status which, in turn, called for increased product elaboration.

Many more goods were available to the British consumer in the second half of the nineteenth century than ever before. In the 1860s there was, for example, a fall in the price of gas and, as a result, more gas stoves became available on a hire basis. By 1914 objects like the US Bissell carpet sweeper were available on the British market; following its success in the US market, the domestic vacuum cleaner had made an appearance at the turn of the century [4]; sewing machines transformed the clothing industry and entered the domestic arena; and the bicycle and automobile became common appendages of the urban scene by the first decade of the new century.

The strategies involved in catering for, sustaining and expanding this new mass market subsumed the question of design, and many marketing decisions were made which had implications for design. The textile industry of the early century had, for example, located its different markets not only through price differentiation but through design variation.[15] Conscious that the majority of the new market, at

Sweep With Electricity For 3c a Week

You Can Afford *This* Electric Suction Sweeper As Easily As You Can Afford a Sewing Machine

No more dirt or dust! No more back-aches on cleaning day! This wonderful little machine takes up all the dust, scraps and dirt from carpets, furniture, curtains and portieres more perfectly than any of the big vacuum cleaners for the services of which you pay $35 to $50.

It works like magic. Simply attach the wire to an electric light socket, turn on the current and run the machine over the carpet as you would an ordinary carpet sweeper. Its rapidly revolving brushes loosen the dirt, and the strong suction pulls it into the dirt bag in the twinkling of an eye. Nothing escapes its marvelous cleaning influence.

So simple a child can do it.

So economical anyone can afford it.

Have your cleaning finished in one-fourth the time and with one-tenth the labor!

HOOVER Electric SUCTION SWEEPER

For All Houses Wired for Electricity. Price $70; Extra Attachments, $15 per Set

Hoover Electric Sweeper Co., New Berlin, Ohio

4 Advertisement for Hoover electric suction sweeper, 1909.

Hoover first advertised its sweeper in 1908 in the *Saturday Evening Post*, offering a ten-day free trial of the cleaner in people's own homes. This first full-page advertisement appeared in *Collier's Magazine* a year later. Like many of the manufacturers dealing with the new products, the company needed to put a lot of energy into advertising and into explaining the uses and potential of its product to the new consumers, most of whose homes were still not wired for electricity at this early date. Many sweepers were, in fact, returned, unsold, to the Hoover factory. During the following decade Hoover developed a policy of training all sweeper salesmen to answer consumer questions and, eventually, of creating the Hoover man who travelled from door to door on a bicycle.

home and abroad, had no visual training and therefore was easily persuaded to buy what was available, manufacturers largely ignored questions of 'taste' on this level of production and concentrated instead on speed of production and low cost. Thus the patterns they presented to this sector of the market were simple ones, largely modified from traditional designs and produced in a minimum of colours. This contrasted dramatically with the textiles aimed at the other end of the market where 'artistic' quality and visual innovation were pre-requisites.

Retailing and advertising were obvious ways of both satisfying and stimulating demand and both these areas expanded rapidly around the turn of the century. In the field of retailing fixed shops took over from the street market, multi-branch retailing firms emerged and, in general, shops expanded both in size and variety, catering for a broader range of customers and providing more goods than ever before. The department store was a product of this period, catering at first for the top end of the market only but gradually, as time went on, expanding the range of its goods. In London department stores grew from establishments such as Peter Robinson,[16] which had set itself up as a linen drapers in Oxford Street in 1833, and Gamages,[17] which opened in Buckingham Palace Road in 1858; in Paris the Bon Marché store opened in 1852 and Macy's began business in New York in 1860. They aimed their goods at middle-class customers who were eager to acquire what has been called the 'paraphernalia of gentility', and they provided many facilities for their shoppers, including rest rooms and writing rooms.

Advertising, organized by agencies, also increased its strengths in the 1880s. There were signs between 1900 and 1914 that supply was beginning to outstrip demand in some industrial sectors and advertising expanded as a result. US selling techniques, which had developed more quickly, were beginning to be emulated in Britain by this time and the role of advertising as a means not just of building a market but of outselling the competition was becoming established as the norm. Design was already becoming an extension of advertising, that is, a means of selling by modifying the product itself.

The manufacture of consumer goods met the demands of the mass market through changes in scale and the adoption of new production techniques. Where the 'applied art' industries were concerned, manu-facturers expanded their output but at a slower pace than in either the USA or Germany. Britain had, however, been well ahead in discovering a mass market for ceramics as a result of the pioneering work of Josiah Wedgwood (q.v.) at the end of the eighteenth and beginning of the nineteenth centuries. Sheffield-based cutlery production also became increasingly mechanized and moved downmarket in the second half of the century, but many other products, particularly those with a technological bias, had to be bought from abroad to meet the demands of the market. The first threat was from Germany but, increasingly, towards the end of the century, the USA dominated the picture. The USA was the country where all the new patents came from and it was well ahead in the mass-manufacturing game.

With increased wealth came a growing need for status symbolism and the middle classes in Britain began to concern themselves with buying luxuries, previously a privilege of the upper middle classes and the aristocracy. By the end of the century, status symbolism was beginning to move down into the working-class life-style and, inevitably, it looked to the class immediately above it for inspiration.

Art and Industry

Although as a public concept design was absent from the picture of consumption in the second half of the nineteenth century, 'art' as applied to industry was a much-discussed and fashionable topic. There had been much debate in British Establishment circles, about the fear of foreign competition and worry, in the mid-century, about the low standard of British taste and manufactured goods. This fear inspired publications on the subject of artistic taste which implored the British public and the manufacturer to consider more carefully the whole complex issue of taste. It was thought that lessons from fine art would reform the British eye and museums were set up and design schools opened in an effort to improve standards at home and hopefully, as a result, on the foreign market.[18]

Towards the end of the century the movement called Art Manufacturing[19] consciously set out to inject art into one range of its products by commissioning a well-known artist, craftsman, or architect of the day to provide the product's artistic content. This usually took the form of a surface pattern in the case of textiles and ceramics or, in the case of decorative ironwork and cutlery, a decorative shape. This conscious injection of 'art' into manufactured objects, undertaken as a means of making them more desirable as status objects, was initially the prerogative of the traditional applied art industries and of a wealthy market, but gradually it also began to penetrate the world of the new technological goods and to affect the mass market. Consumer machines began to boast surface patterns but it was to be some time before 'name' designers were to be employed in this sector of production.

By the end of the nineteenth century, all the factors necessary for the emergence of industrial design in the twentieth-century sense had surfaced. In both Europe and the USA the requirements for the expansion of mass production – mechanization, standardization, and the emergence of the mass market, and the emergence of a whole new range of products which made new demands on the manufacturer and transformed the life-style and expectations of the consumer, had become realities. The pre-industrial, pre-capitalist system of supply neatly fitting demand was by now completely defunct and, in addition, the rule of aristocratic taste was over and a new set of taste values were emerging, with the public looking to the manufacturer to fulfil its symbolic needs. While in the early stages the new production machinery and techniques dictated the forms and general appearance of the new technological products, this soon proved insufficient to convince the new consumer, with his new-found wealth, that he could not live his life without, for example, possessing a typewriter. In their attempts to market their goods, the manufacturers of the new products inevitably emulated the model of the applied art industries.

As yet the 'designer', defined as a professional as distinct from the fine artist, the architect and the craftsman, had not emerged, although new labour roles were of necessity being formulated as a result of the increased division of labour brought about by mechanization. By the early years of the twentieth century, however, the models of production and the market that were current at that time were, more or less, the same ones that were to prevail later in the century and the world was therefore ready for the emergence of twentieth-century design.

Notes: Chapter 1

1   C. Harvie, G. Martin and A. Scharf, *Industrialization and Culture 1830–1914* (London: Macmillan, 1970), p. 11.
2   James Nasmyth (1808–90) perfected his steam hammer in 1838, thereby facilitating the mechanization of industrial production.

3   Dependent upon the use of steam as a power source, James Watts's (1756–1819) pumping engine was first introduced in 1783, thereby replacing the water-wheel as a means of driving machinery.

4   The principle of the Spinning Jenny was invented by James Hargreaves in 1764 but it was 1769 before it was being sold and made. It had sixteen spindles, thus speeding up the spinning process enormously. The first jennies were used by spinners in their own cottages.

5   The Jacquard loom, invented in the early 1800s, speeded up the textile weaving process. It depended on a mechanism involving cards with holes punched into them which selected the warp threads to be lifted and so wove a pattern into the cloth.

6   It was on the basis of ideas expressed in the sculptor, Horatio Green-ough's book *Form and Function* – first published in the USA in the first half of the nineteenth century – that the theory of architectural Func-tionalism emerged in the early twentieth century. Greenough defined it as a principle which meant designing a building from the inside outwards, and letting the essential structure dictate the form and therefore its external appearance. In his book he praises the work of American engineers in the design of ships, machines and bridges, and is critical of architecture with false façades. His ideas remained the basis of Functionalist thinking right up until the 1930s and the phrase 'Form follows Function', borrowed from the American architect Louis Sullivan at the turn of the century, echoed Greenough's ideas exactly. Functionalism became the dominant design philosophy and language of the first half of this century, interchangeable stylistically with the 'Machine Aesthetic'.

7   H. Greenough, *Form and Function* (Berkeley, Calif.: University of California Press, 1947), p. 6.

8   J. D. McCabe, *The Illustrated History of the Centennial Exhibition: Philadelphia 1876* (Philadelphia, Pa: National Publishing Company, 1975), p. 14.

9   ibid., p. 108.

10   N. Pevsner, *High Victorian Design* (London: Architectural Press, 1951), p. 38.

11   This statement was made by Henry Ford in 1903 and is quoted in J. B. Rae, *The American Automobile: A Brief History* (Chicago: University of Chicago Press, 1965), p. 59.

12   W. Hamish Fraser in his book *The Coming of the Mass Market* (London: Macmillan, 1981) explains that 'by 1911 there were 18 million more bodies to house and clothe and tastes to satisfy and demands for fashion to pamper than there had been in 1851 in Britain' (p. 3).

13   Fraser also gives details of the increases in spending power 'taking 1850 as a base year at 100, G. H. Wood's index shows a rise to 180 by 1900 where money wages were concerned' (ibid., p. 15).

14   In his book *Technics and Civilization* (London: Routledge and Kegan Paul, 1934), Louis Mumford gives names to the different technological periods in history. He calls the most recent period, the 'neotechnic' age.

15   More details about the way in which the British textile industry used designers in the first half of the nineteenth century can be found in Hazel

Clark's PhD thesis, 'The role of the designer in early mass-production industry' (Brighton Polytechnic, 1982).

16 Peter Robinson first set up as a linen designer in Oxford Street, London, in 1833.

17 Frederick Gamage opened his store in Buckingham Palace Road, London, in 1858.

18 The Design Reform Movement in Britain in the middle of the nineteenth century inspired a number of initiatives by the Establishment of the day to improve the general level of public taste. In 1832 Sir Robert Peel had blamed falling exports on incompetent design and the National Gallery was built as part of his attempt to remedy this. In 1835 Mr Ewart's Select Committee was set up to examine the state of British design. As a result of its findings, a Normal School of Design was set up in 1937 by the Board of Trade in London and by 1846 eleven other design schools had also been established throughout the country. Henry Cole's *Journal of Design and Manufacture*, first published in 1949, also had a quality of reforming zeal about it. As President of the Society of Arts, Prince Albert was also highly active in this campaign.

19 The movement of the second half of the nineteenth century, referred to as Art Manufacturing or the Aesthetic Movement, involved a number of companies from the applied arts sector bringing in 'name' architects and designers to work on their products in order to give them 'art' appeal. It was, in essence, a commercial version of the earlier Arts and Crafts Movement which, although full of social idealism at its outset, had ended up by simply encouraging the middle-class consumption of decorative items with a 'fine art' content. The fashion for 'art-jewellery', art-ceramics and glass, and art-furniture, reached its peak in the 1870s and 1880s and well-known designers of the day, such as E. W. Godwin, Christopher Dresser (q.v.), Bruce Talbert, Lewis F. Day, and others were approached by numerous manufacturing companies to design their goods for them.

2

New Products for New Life-Styles

At 14, in Paris where I was born, I had seen the birth of the telephone, the aeroplane, the automobile, electricity in the home, the phonograph, the cinema, the radio, elevators, refrigerators, X-rays, radioactivity, and not the least, modern anaesthesia.[1] (Raymond Loewy)

Creating an object *ex novo* is, inevitably, a very different process from modifying one that is already in existence. In the former case, it is not simply a matter of finding new forms to suit new needs and new markets, but rather of defining new functions and of harnessing new technologies and scientific discoveries. While the inventor is involved with the creation of an object-concept, rather than with its adaptation to mass production and its commercial viability, his work and that of the designer have, in the past, frequently overlapped. In the contemporary world, however, with the emergence of technologically complex objects, the two have become separated and have moved into different spheres of activity. Invention belongs increasingly to the world of science and technology rather than to that of manufacture and sales, and the development of new products has, for the most part, been superseded by the invention of new technical components – such as the transistor – which have to be integrated into new products – such as the transistor radio – by the designer.

In the nineteenth century when most of the modern mechanical, electrical and electronic products with which we now surround ourselves – the typewriter, the bicycle, the sewing machine, the food mixer – were invented, the distinctions between invention and design were less clearcut. These new products did not appear suddenly, however, but emerged gradually as the result of a process of experimentation and refinement. In the evolution of any new product a period of gestation is involved during which time the details are slowly perfected and the concept gradually defined. The process does not stop there, however, as redesign and improvement are continually applied to all objects as a response both to changing technological discoveries and to the dictates of commerce and fashion. There is, none the less, a moment when the evolution of any product reaches a peak of conceptual consolidation and we can say with confidence that, for example, the typewriter has been invented.

Economic, technical and social forces influence invention although the relationship between them differs in the case of every new object. During the nineteenth century radical changes in these three areas of human endeavour resulted in the emergence of a plethora of new inventions, the mass production of which was made possible by parallel advances in precision machine-tooling, materials technology and, later, the discovery of electricity. Invention succeeded invention as technological discoveries were joined by the demand for new machines to facilitate many areas of human work and to increase the options available for leisure.

Innovation and the Applied Arts

By the late nineteenth century most of the traditional art industries had expanded from their craft backgrounds into larger production units and had increased the size of their markets accordingly. There was no question, however, of having to reinvent the soup tureen, the chair, or the knife and fork but rather of having to manufacture and sell these items in greater quantities than ever before.

Thus in these otherwise traditional areas innovation was needed both to facilitate their production and to attract new markets. In the USA this was the period of the folding and revolving table (1878), the sofa-bed (1876) and the platform rocker (1872), as well as of furniture made of new materials like cast- and wrought-iron. Technical innovation in conventional objects such as these was one means of providing the novelty and flexibility that the new consumers increasingly wanted from their furniture. This did not amount to true invention, however, as David A. Hanks explains in his book *Innovative Furniture in America*:

Although innovation implies originality, it does not always imply discovery or invention of an entire form. The concept of the folding chair, for instance, can

20

be traced back to ancient times. Yet the form may be considered innovative in the period we are surveying, having been discovered anew (rather than merely revived) in the nineteenth century.[2]

According to Hanks the factors that influenced these remarkable innovations in furniture design were new techniques and materials combined with the social demand for portability, flexibility and comfort.

In spite of these US advances in the application of new technology and new ideas to traditional objects, many of the modifications made to craft-based products in this period were of a more superficial nature. Stylistic and decorative variation were widely incorporated by many manufacturers into production as a means of satisfying the taste requirements of the new markets. For the new nineteenth-century consumer, social status became increasingly associated with applied decoration and, for a large proportion of the market, the more elaborate the pattern the greater was the status symbolism of the product. In spite of the attempts made to control the rampant eclecticism that ensued and to make decoration more subservient to the form and function of the product, stylistic innovation ruled the day and a series of alternative styles, from Gothic Revival[3] to Art Nouveau,[4] dominated the applied arts in the second half of the nineteenth century.

The Age of Electricity

The harnessing of electrical power was one of the major technological advances to influence the new consumer machines in the second half of the nineteenth century. Like coal before it, the advent of electricity also modified production methods and facilitated the distribution of the new products, but its main impact was upon the environment facilitating activities and helping to create products that we now take for granted.

In the home, electricity helped to make everything cleaner and faster. The harnessing of electrical power for domestic purposes went through several preliminary stages but it was with the electric lamp that the impact of this new power source was most generally felt. The electric lamp, like the electric pen and phonograph which preceded it, was a discovery of Thomas Alva Edison who had predicted in 1884 that: 'With electricity you will be able to drive sewing machines, shoe-cleaning machines and washing machines. You will be able to light your

5   Hoover Model O electric suction sweeper, 1908.
This electric suction sweeper was invented by Murray Spangler in 1908, the year in which he formed the Electric Suction Sweeper Company soon to be taken over by the Hoover family. This first model combined unsophisticated iron castings, a sheet steel body and basic construction techniques with Art Nouveau decoration which was highly fashionable internationally at that time. In the following year Hoover introduced its Senior sweeper. This was a lighter model, with aluminium main castings and no decoration.

house and cook your food.'[5] In the USA, where labour was short and labour-saving devices much in demand, Edison's ideas found a ready environment. In 1886 George Westinghouse decided to enter the electric-lighting field and in 1892 the General Electric Company was formed as a merger of Thomson-Houston with the Edison Companies. Thus by the end of the nineteenth century the USA was equipped with a highly developed electrical industry which was ready to manufacture consumer goods dependent upon that particular power source.

While one early application of the electric motor was in the field of transportation, the electric fan also made its appearance in the late 1880s. The electrically powered elevator arrived shortly after, and soon many other machines and tools began to be supplied with motors. With these developments the concept of the electrical appliance emerged, ready to move into the hands of the designer who was to give it a form and an identity.

Whilst at first the new goods openly displayed both their mechanisms and their motors, gradually cast-iron housings were added for reasons of cleanliness and safety and, as mass consumption increased, surface decoration was applied in emulation of practice in the more traditional 'art' industries. One explanation for this phenomenon was the need to sell products such as sewing machines and vacuum cleaners to women who, it was claimed, responded more readily to decorated surfaces [5]. While it was common practice for the inventor or an engineer to decide on the form of the product, men or women with an 'artistic' background were often brought in to deal with the applied decoration.

The New Products and Society

Between 1790 and 1900, 600,000 patents were registered in the USA and although some of these inventions were British or European in origin, it was in the USA that most of them were developed. As Sigfried Giedion commented in his book *Mechanization Takes Command*, published in 1948, 'In America, inventive fantasy and the instinct for mechanization were the common property of the people'.[6] Among the many reasons for this explosion of inventions was the fact that the shortage of cheap manual labour in the USA meant that it was dependent upon mechanization to keep up with Europe. This was coupled with a shortage of manual help in the home which encouraged the development of labour-saving devices. Thus it was in US homes

6 Singer sewing machine, 1911.
The Singer Company led the field in the USA in the manufacture of sewing machines in the latter half of the nineteenth century. By 1865 the image of the Family Machine, with its curvilinear, gilt decoration applied to the surface of its shaped, black, cast-iron body-shell, and its wooden sewing-table which doubled as a piece of furniture, had been consolidated. All the changes that occurred from that time onwards were merely modifications to this basic model. In 1911, for example, an electric motor was added to drive the treadle and cabinets were built into the table to store sewing aids.

that objects like cookers, washing machines, refrigerators, sewing machines [6] and dish washers first flourished and the US office was the first to exploit the advantages of new products such as the typewriter, the adding machine, the cash register, the dictaphone and the telephone. This tremendous thirst for invention was a result both of technology capturing the popular imagination and of sheer necessity, both economic and social.

By 1900 many of the mechanical and electrical goods that we use today had not only been invented but were reasonably widely used. In 1880 50,000 Americans had a telephone; in 1883 a number of electrical domestic appliances – among them hot-plates, kettles, cooking pans and hot blankets – were shown at the Vienna Exhibition; and by 1910 the vacuum cleaner, the washing machine with spin-drying system and the electric dish washer were also in existence. The majority of these new consumer goods were aimed at replacing diminishing manual labour, thereby providing more time for leisure activities which, in turn, were catered for by other new products such as the camera, the wireless and the phonograph.

One impetus behind the widespread acceptance of such domestic appliances as the vacuum cleaner, the cooker and the washing machine was the attempt, made in the early twentieth century predominantly in the USA, to rationalize household labour along the lines of scientific management, and thereby to align housework with factory labour.[7] This tendency, paralleled by the general movement of female emancipation in this period, was part of the general desire to systematize and mechanize as much work as possible in the effort to expand the USA's production and improve its position in world trade. While Britain had begun its foray into industrialization with the mechanization of the simple crafts – spinning, weaving and iron-making – the USA had applied the same principle to more complicated factory activities such as bread-making and meat-processing. These developments had as much impact on the household as they did on the factory floor and the development of such processes as factory canning, for example, which also took place in these years, was as labour-saving to the housewife as the advent of the domestic vacuum cleaner.

Britain lagged behind in such developments but gradually began to emulate US advances. One of the reasons for the increased use of electrical products in the British home after 1914 was the electricity supply companys' need to increase the number of consumers and the range of uses to which electricity could be put in order to reduce their production costs. Everybody was therefore encouraged to use electrical appliances and direct links were established between the sale of electricity and the promotion of domestic appliances. By 1914, according to the results of research undertaken by Adrian Forty, 'Almost all the domestic applications of electricity that we now know had been envisaged and a wide variety of appliances (many of them US made) were on the market, although not in any great quantity'. In Britain, however, it was only after 1945, Forty claims, that 'the decision to spend surplus wealth on appliances for the home has been a noticeable characteristic'.[8]

The situation was very different in the USA where the developments in 'household technology' had been extremely rapid. In the mid-nineteenth century household work had been labour-intensive, but by the end of the century technology had noticeably reduced the amount of manual labour in nearly every household task in the USA. A. E. Kennelly has described one highly eccentric example of a labour-saving device of 1880 which involved the mechanization of table service:

the dishes, as electrically signalled for the hostess, are laid on little trucks filled with tiny motors, and are started out from the pantry to the dinner-table. They stop automatically before each guest who, after assisting himself, presses a button at his side and so gives the car the impetus and right of way to his next neighbour.[9]

At the same time, linoleum floors, porcelain and copper sinks and tiled lavatories also helped minimize household labour, and washing machines made laundering much easier: in the kitchen gas and electric ovens replaced the dirty coal- or wood-burning ranges. The curve of progress continued to rise into the years after the First World War. While 3,000 washing machines were produced in 1909, this rose to 70,000 in 1916; there were 500,000 coming off the production line in 1919 and in 1925 the figure was 882,000. The same picture of accelerated growth was echoed in the production and sales of vacuum cleaners and gas ovens and, as a result, technology took over from the servant in the USA and the housewife took on the household work aided by her new labour-saving devices.

If technical, economic and social factors were responsible for the development and dissemination of the new products, their design was the result of the dictates of the production processes, individual inventive genius, gradual modification from use and market requirements. Once the concept of the product was established, it was still necessary to provide it with a visual identity, to improve its production and function, and to direct it at the appropriate market. In tracing the development of a few of this century's new products, it is interesting to see how invention and design often worked very closely together in the early stages, while later on the designer became increasingly responsible for modifications and for new forms.

THE VACUUM CLEANER
Invented by an Englishman, H. Cecil Booth, in 1901, the vacuum cleaner started life as a device for drawing air through a cloth on which dust was deposited. Booth went on to found the British Vacuum Cleaner Company which used pumps, driven either electrically or by petrol, which were mounted on horse-drawn carts. Vacuuming was done by passing the hose through the window of the house while the cart was parked outside. Around 1904 smaller domestic cleaners appeared which functioned on the same principle: one model was mounted on a trolley, while another was hand-operated by two servants. With the increasing use of the small electric motor, the forerunner of today's upright vacuum cleaner emerged in 1908. The idea of a basic box with a hose attached to it was the principle behind the cylinder vacuum cleaner of a decade later, although since then numerous designers, including the American Raymond Loewy, the Swede Sixten Sason (qq.v) working for Electrolux, and the American Henry Dreyfuss (q.v.) working for the Hoover Company have given this well-known object a variety of guises. In the 1950s the Castiglioni brothers (q.v.) in Italy transformed the vacuum cleaner into a piece of organic sculpture with their innovative Spalter model, which could be fixed by a strap to the user's back and dragged easily across the floor.

Once the technical problems were solved and the market had been persuaded that it needed vacuum cleaners, the problem for the designer was one of finding an appropriate consumer symbolism and imagery for a machine which would not be out of place in a domestic setting but which looked, nonetheless, technically impressive, confidence-inspiring, efficient and easy to clean.

THE RADIO
The problem of finding a visual identity for a product which consists of a vast number of mechanical and electrical components is one which also beset the designers of radios in the twentieth century. Growing out of the success of wireless telegraphy, the crystal set was an early form of

what came to be called the 'wireless' (so-called because it did not need headphones). It was during the First World War, however, that the advantages of using broadcasting as a public service were realized, but it was not until the 1920s and 1930s that any efforts were made to render the wireless both attractive and efficient. Because it was usually put in the domestic parlour, the wireless was thought of as a piece of furniture, and the idea of the radio cabinet emerged as a result of this natural assumption. What emerged was an early instance of a designer putting all the mechanical components of an object into a box and styling it appropriately. While, back in the early 1920s, the radio had been little more than a collection of crystals and wires, the valve, the battery and the loudspeaker were soon added and all these components were packaged neatly into the cabinet. From being a plain wooden box which simply served to house the parts safely the radio cabinet was soon transformed into an object of aesthetic interest as rival manufacturers hired designers to style their sets for them. In exactly the same way as the Art Manufacturers had brought in fine artists to work on the appearance of their traditional products back in the 1870s and 1880s so, in the 1930s, radio companies set about revamping their sets. Murphy's consulted the furniture company Gordon Russell Limited (q.v.) in its attempt to give its radios a striking, visual identity, while E. K. Cole (of the Ekco Radio Company) hired two architects, Serge Chermayeff and Wells Coates (qq.v.), who were to provide more radical versions of the 'modern' radio cabinet than Russell's. Wells Coates presented a round radio with a body-shell made of Bakelite, simple dials and carefully composed controls: it was a striking design which symbolized the future rather than the past. By the end of the 1930s an image of the radio as a modern machine had emerged which superseded its dependence on the earlier furniture model [30]. This was reflected particularly well in the Castiglionis' Phonola radio of 1939 which borrowed its modern imagery from the telephone, already by then a familiar modern domestic machine. Following the Second World War, the discovery of the transistor transformed the radio into a miniature object – an inconceivable achievement before that particular technological step forward, putting an end to the idea that the radio was a piece of furniture once and for all.

THE TYPEWRITER
The typewriter is among the many products which early adopted a particular visual identity which has remained fundamentally unchanged

7 Remington Rand typewriters, 1875 and 1949.

Sholes and Glidden's typewriter, built by Remington & Sons Ltd in 1875, was the first commercially successful model on the market and it was rapidly succeeded by many other models which improved on this original design. It only printed in capital letters and the typing was invisible to the operator. In design terms it was rather tall and somewhat box-like in shape, determined entirely by the arrangement of the internal mechanisms and the forms and assembly method of the metal castings which made up its body-shell. Its black surface was covered with complex ornamentation derived from natural forms and intended to appeal to the new consumers of those years. In contrast, the 1949 model was lower, undecorated apart from a few visual accents, more compact and more visually unified. It was built on a unit construction and could thus be disassembled for cleaning. The improvements in metal-casting technology of this later period made a smoother, more sculptural form possible for this model which was available in two-tone grey with a chromium-plated finish.

since the nineteenth century. Along with the adding machine, the dictaphone and the telephone, the typewriter radically changed the organization of the office. In 1714 the first patent for a 'writing machine' had been given to a certain Henry Mill and in 1829 the first model known to have worked appeared. Invented by an American, William Burt, it was called the 'Typographer', but it was not until the late nineteenth century that the idea of using a typewriter to speed up office work was put into practice. The first commercially successful type-writer was invented by C. L. Sholes and C. Glidden and mass produced by E. Remington & Sons who manufactured the first models in 1875 [7]. These already had many of the visual characteristics of a modern machine including a body-shell which was necessary for keeping dust out of the mechanism. Many other designs appeared on the market after the Remington machine and in 1887 it was estimated that 60,000 typists were employed in the USA.

Some inevitable technical innovations took place as the machine evolved through the late nineteenth and early twentieth centuries and in 1896 F. X. Wagner's Underwood No 1 typewriter appeared, looking even more like more modern models as it had less decoration on its body than the earlier Remington. Gradually portability and electricity influenced the typewriter and its modern appearance evolved accord-ingly. Among the companies to 'style' the typewriter most successfully in the post Second World War period was the US firm IBM, which hired the architect Eliot Noyes (q.v.) to work on its range of electric, electronic and manual models, while the Italian office-machinery company Olivetti developed, with the help of architects Marcello Nizzoli, Ettore Sottsass and Mario Bellini (qq.v.), some of this century's most sophisticated typewriter shells. In recent years elec-tronics have modified many of the components and mechanisms of the typewriter and its appearance has, inevitably, changed as a result, but because of its constant ergonomic requirements, the modifications have been fairly minimal compared with other products. It remains, in essence, the same object that emerged over a hundred years ago.

THE BICYCLE
The example of the bicycle demonstrates an interesting feature of the production and design of mechanical consumer goods, that is, the way in which manufacturers have often transferred their production from one object to another according to the dictates of the market. In the late nineteenth century, for example, a British company called Rowley

Turner moved over from producing sewing machines to bicycle manufacture when the company's Paris agent brought over a Michaux velocipede which had been on display at the Paris Exhibition of 1867, and persuaded the company to manufacture 400 similar machines for him to take back and sell in Paris. Similarly, when cycling went out of fashion at the end of the century and automobiles became the new means of transport, many companies left bicycle production as a consequence and went over to car production.

The form of the bicycle has survived, for the most part, the vagaries of fashionability and styling. Three main factors – lightness, stability and comfort – dictate its visual form and once these elements had been satisfactorily combined in the 1890s [8] the problem was as good as solved for all time. It had taken, in fact, about a hundred years to find that particular solution and the bicycle had already gone through several transformations before it arrived at the form we recognize today. Invention and design had gone hand in hand in search of the right solution, facilitated by technical innovations – such as the pneumatic tyre, first discovered and patented in 1898 by J. B. Dunlop – and the emergence of a mass market created by the fashion for cycling in the 1890s. Aided by propaganda put out by the popular press about the benefits of fresh air, exercise and travelling into the countryside, the market for bicycles expanded enormously at the turn of the century.

Britain was at the forefront of bicycle technology and introduced the high-wheeled bicycle to the USA at the Centennial Exhibition of 1876 in Philadelphia. Impressed by what he saw there, a certain Albert A. Pope of Boston came to London and Coventry to study bicycle construction, after which he returned to the USA and, in 1878, bought a sewing machine factory which he proceeded to convert into a bicycle factory.

For a while, in the 1890s, the bicycle was a firm status symbol and society ladies painted their machines to suit their dress. For them, cycling represented a new-found freedom and independence. In the USA the cycling craze reached its peak in about 1899, by which time about 312 factories had been set up to manufacture bicycles. During the first two decades of the new century, however, the impact of the bicycle was completely overpowered by the arrival of the horseless carriage. Between 1900 and 1905 more than three-fifths of the US bicycle manufacturers went out of business as a result of the increasing emphasis on that new product. The British designer-inventor Alex Moulton's small-wheeled bicycle of the 1960s provided one of the few

8 Dursley-Pedersen bicycles, 1907.
Pedersen, a Danish engineer living in Britain, patented a bicycle in 1893 which had a new frame construction consisting of small metal tubes triangulated in pairs. It weighed 23 lb. and steered better than previous models. Another of its new features was a hammock seat. It was made in the Humber Works in Beeston between 1897 and 1902 and subsequently at the Lister Works in Dursley until 1914. In 1897 it cost £25, but became cheaper later on, and it was available in enamel, nickel-plated, or copper-burnished finishes. Pictured here are the male and female versions of this advanced bicycle which had, in common with other contemporary models, rubber tyres, a metal chain cover and many other features of the modern bicycle.

examples of a bicycle redesign which had a significant impact on the popular image of the object.

THE AUTOMOBILE
Ironically, the bicycle industry provided the facilities for the growth of its main rival, the automobile industry. It is impossible to isolate a single individual or a single date for the invention of the automobile. It emerged from experiments made in the mid-1880s in Germany by both Benz and Daimler and, subsequently, went through several trans-formations, notably being powered, in turn, by gasoline, electricity and steam until the advantages of petrol were universally acknowledged. A number of factors, such as road improvements and the abolition of the road toll, combined to encourage the advent of the horseless carriage and by the 1890s there was a blossoming automobile industry in France, Germany, Britain and the USA.

In Europe driving was an upper-class activity and both the pro-duction methods and design of the automobile reflected this fact. Production was small-scale and labour-intensive and cars were extremely expensive items in the early days. Visually they evolved in a logical manner from the image of the horseless carriage into a more self-contained object with its own visual identity. Up until the late 1920s, however, the car remained an object clearly composed of many different component parts and little attempt was made to integrate them into a visual whole. The boot, for example, was often a suitcase or picnic hamper strapped on to the rear of the body, and the mudguards and running-boards were isolated units attached to the body where possible.

In the USA the story was rather different, for here the automobile had to be reinvented and it was the Duryea brothers who read about Benz's car in *Scientific American* and emulated his discoveries. By the late 1890s the horseless carriage was making a place for itself in US life and several firms, many of them previously cycle manufacturers, started up at that time – an example of free, competitive enterprise in action. Whereas in the first decade of this century it was usual for chauffeurs to drive the car in Europe, this was not the case in the USA and, as a result of the pioneering work of Henry Ford and his use of full-scale assembly-line production, the automobile rapidly became a democratic object on that continent – 'a new form of personal trans-portation for the common man'.[10]

Between 1900 and 1910 in the USA all the services peripheral to the automobile industry – among them sales and repair facilities and the petroleum and rubber industries – expanded rapidly, but after the First World War there was a rapid shrinkage in the number of minor automobile producers and only the large companies – General Motors, Ford and Chrysler – survived. Others simply vanished or turned their attention to other goods. In the early 1930s the Hupp Motor Company, for instance, the company for whom Raymond Loewy designed his 'Hupmobile' in 1932, moved into the production of kitchen appliances and electronics. In 1926 Ford abandoned production for a year and emerged at the end of this period with the Model A and his decision that stylistic innovation rather than technical and aesthetic standardization was the order of the commercial day. This radical change of policy on the part of Henry Ford was of tremendous significance for the development of modern design as it showed that, in the end, it is form rather than function which sells a consumer product within our particular economic climate. By the 1920s the automobile had come to stay. People were using them to go to work in, farmers came into the city in them, car advertising expanded and filling stations and roadside restaurants grew apace. By the 1930s the automobile had succeeded in bringing design into the street and in making the USA design-conscious.

The technological advances of the nineteenth century were so numerous that not only could an object be perfected technically and functionally through a process of experimentation and the test of time, but it could also be produced in mass and disseminated to an increasingly large sector of the public. Design played a part in this process at several different stages. It formed an intrinsic element in the original invention, part of the modification process for mass production, and part of the sales policies of the mass manufacturers. Between 1880 and 1930 the new products had not only transformed society but, through their mass presence, caused design to become part of everyday life for the vast majority of people, influencing their buying habits, their life-styles and their social relationships.

Since that period continued and accelerated technical and technological advances have meant that invention is still a reality although, in the production of consumer goods, it occupies a smaller part of engineers' and designers' time than the improvement of existing products and redesign. Occasionally, as in the case of relatively rare products like the Vespa motor-scooter and the Sony Walkman, a new product 'type'[11] emerges, as if out of nowhere, which bears little relationship to its immediate forebears. Such innovation usually derives from the application of a technology or an idea which originated in quite a different sphere of activity. By moving sideways into a new evolutionary development this technique or idea results in radical change or design innovation. With the Vespa, it was the early experiences of its engineer, Corriado D'Ascanio, in helicopter design which when transferred into the area of motor-scooter design resulted in a totally new image for that piece of transport machinery. In the case of the Walkman radical innovation came about as a result of the fact that it was Sony's design team rather than, as is usually the case, its engineers or marketing men who created the initial concept for the product.

Since the Second World War innovation has taken precedence over invention in the area of the design and manufacture of consumer products and the packaging of objects has tended to dominate design activity. This has coincided, historically, with the rise of giant corporations and the concentration of power and resources into larger and larger units. With the advent of electronics and the technological opportunities that the microchip has brought with it, design has taken one step further in this same direction. In the area of domestic and office equipment the designer has, increasingly, become a packager and his role has diverged dramatically from that of the engineer whose job it is to provide the designer with a set of increasingly small components and to work on product development. As a result, the processes of invention and design have tended to move further apart from each other and, within the contemporary industrial and economic context, it is unlikely that these two tasks will be recombined in the immediate future.

Notes: Chapter 2

1 R. Loewy, *Never Leave Well Enough Alone* (New York: Simon & Schuster, 1951), p. 33.
2 D. Hanks, *Innovative Furniture in America from 1800 to the Present* (New York: 1981), p. 29.
3 The Gothic Revival was an important architectural and design style of the early to mid-nineteenth century which celebrated the cultural unity of Christian beliefs with decorative design which had existed in the medieval period. A. W. N. Pugin was its main exponent in Britain and he evolved, in his support of that style, a number of protofunctional tenets for design.
4 Art Nouveau was an international architectural and design movement and style which reached its peak at the turn of the century. It was char-

acterized both by a stylized curvilinear aesthetic – most evident in France and Belgium – which took its cue from the stems and tendrils of plant life, and by a more rectilinear style – most evident in Scotland and Austria – which was at once more abstract and more concerned with structure than surface decoration. It was a movement which sought to reject the historism of the nineteenth century and to move afresh into the new century.

5   T. A. Edison in D. Fredgant, *Electrical Collectibles: Relics of the Electrical Age* (San Luis Obispo, Calif.: Padre Productions, 1981), p. 14.

6   Hanks, *Innovative Furniture*, p. 17.

7   See F. Taylor *The Principles of Scientific Management* (New York: Harper, 1961. First published 1911).

8   A. Forty, 'Electrical appliances 1900–1960', in *Design 1900–1960: Newcastle Polytechnic Design History Conference Papers* (Newcastle Polytechnic, 1976), pp. 104–5.

9   A. E. Kennelly, quoted in David M. Katzman, *Seven Days a Week: Women and Domestic Service in Industrializing America* (Champaign, Ill.: University of Illinois Press, 1981), p. 127.

10   J. B. Rae, *The American Automobile: A Brief History* (Chicago: University of Chicago Press, 1965), p. 63.

11   The term 'product type' is used to describe the idea that particular functions – for example, mechanical letter-writing – have, in our culture, become so intrinsically linked with particular forms – for example, an object which sits on a desk-top, has keys and a roller around which paper is fitted – that the forms and functions are inextricably interconnected in our minds. Thus 'the typewriter' is a twentieth-century 'product type' which, while it is constantly modified, is unlikely to be totally superseded in the foreseeable future. Our environment is densely populated by such 'types', some of which have a long life-span, others of which are still in the process of being defined.

3

Theory and Design in the Twentieth Century

We realised that the product made by machines could possess an 'aesthetic' properly derived from a confrontation between function and form.[1]

One of a designer's major tasks in whichever field he specializes – be it electrical products, ceramics, glass, silver or engineering structures – is to bestow form upon an otherwise formless material or set of materials. Whether the intention is to facilitate production or to seduce the consumer through visual sophistication, the process of form-giving is a constant problem for the designer and has inspired many and varied approaches through this and the last centuries.

Before the emergence of the design profession in the 1930s, it was individuals from related areas – craft, architecture and the fine arts – who first applied their minds and hands to this problem. After that time design theory tended to move away from the specific problem of form-giving and became the preserve, primarily, of non-practitioners, among them design propagandists and, later, sociologists, anthropologists, cybernetic theorists and semiologists. The latter were more concerned with the meaning of the designed artefact than with its aesthetic dimension, however, and it was not until the 1960s and 1970s that ideas about object appearance began to surface again.

By the turn of the century a substantial amount of design theory relating to form had already been expounded. Most nineteenth-century ideas were, however, esoteric in nature and had little effect upon the mass of objects produced and consumed at that time. A filtering process was soon in operation, however, which ensured that what was desired by a small elite group today was made available for a much wider market tomorrow. In this context, it is therefore useful to trace the origins of some nineteenth-century attitudes towards form in design in order to understand the problems and prejudices inherited by the following century.

Architects and Engineers in the Mid-Nineteenth Century

The architectural historian, John Gloag, has said that there were two kinds of form-givers in Britain in the mid-nineteenth century, architects whom he calls 'putters-on of styles' and engineers or 'putters-up of structures',[2] and that the energy generated by the dialogue between these two approaches inspired most of the design theory of that period. Opinions varied greatly in the architectural camp about whether 'Gothic' or 'Classical' style, in the sense of applied ornamentation, was correct, while the engineers were, on the whole, unconcerned about the aesthetic implications of their technical problems. It was Isambard Kingdom Brunel (q.v.), creator of the Clifton Suspension Bridge among many other well-known engineered structures, who said dismissively that 'for detail of ornament I have neither knowledge nor time'.[3] For him the mathematical resolution of structural problems was the route to correct form; function, not aesthetics, inspired all his designs.

While the engineer wanted to transform new materials – notably iron and steel – into new machines and structures, the architect was creating styles for the new affluent, status-conscious consumer, aware that qualities like novelty and comfort were closer to the hearts of the Victorian *nouveau riche* market than conventional good taste. It was the question of taste, however, and its ever-lowering threshold, that inspired a number of individuals in the mid-century to rethink the basic principles of design, from both aesthetic and social perspectives, and to generate a mood of reform which was to gain a strong foothold by the second half of the century. Henry Cole (q.v.) thus described the stylistic eclecticism which was rife at that time: 'There is no general agreement in principles of taste. Everyone elects his own style of art. Some take refuge in a liking for pure Greek, others believe only in Pugin, others lean upon imitations of modern Germans.'[4]

Design reform in the nineteenth century was approached from two fundamental perspectives: one looked to tradition for a design method while the other sought new ways of solving the problem of style. The first was to lead to a re-evaluation of the implications of the craft process and of man's relationship with the natural world while the other looked to the aesthetic implications of mass production. The former movement focused on William Morris (q.v.) and his somewhat romantic evocation of the medieval workshop [9], while the latter took a more realistic look at modern manufacturing. Both parties agreed, however, on the same basic premise that although ornament was essential to design, indiscriminate eclecticism should be discarded in favour of a more soundly based, structured and systematic approach towards the subject. The traditionalists, prominent among them John Ruskin (q.v.), sought 'truth', claiming that unless ornament was 'visible, natural and thoughtful'[5] it was invalid and dishonest. Ruskin was a strong supporter of the Gothic Revival for its ability to combine realistic natural ornament with a frank display of structure and materials, and he cried out energetically against new materials and the deceptive concealment of structure and cast- or machine-made ornament. The Crystal Palace symbolized for him all the atrocities of the modern age[6] and he attacked Henry Cole (q.v.) vociferously for his support of mass production. Ralph Wornum (q.v.) summed up the feelings of all the reformers when he wrote that 'ornament is essentially the accessory to and not the substitute of the useful ... it can have no independent existence practically'.[7]

In his book *The Roots of Modern Design*,[8] Herwin Schaefer has pointed out that, in addition to the over-decorated, status objects produced for the new middle classes in this period, there was also another level of production in existence which stressed utilitarian rather than aesthetic values and which was largely unselfconscious in its design. It was to the 'honest', 'simple' qualities of these vernacular products that many reformers began to look, and words like 'function' and 'structure', derived from the vocabulary of the engineer, began to permeate their writings and speeches in an attempt to reduce the aesthetic anarchy of Victorian mass-produced goods. In his report on the 1851 Exhibition Richard Redgrave (q.v.) wrote that 'where use is so paramount that ornament is repudiated, and fitness for purpose being the end sought, a noble simplicity is the result',[9] and Gottfried Semper (q.v.), a German staying in London in the 1850s who was closely associated with the Cole group, proposed a system of classification of ornament based on function. In his attempt to provide a systematic categorization which would help solve the problem of

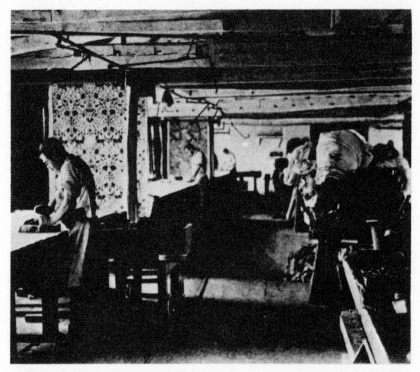

9 Hand-printing chintzes at Morris & Company Workshops, Merton Abbey, Surrey, c. 1900.
This scene of men printing William Morris-designed chintzes with hand-held wooden blocks was taken from a Morris & Company catalogue of 1909. It shows the medieval-inspired, craft manufacturing base which Morris had advocated so frequently in his writings as a means of avoiding 'alienation' in work. The pattern on the fabric hanging to dry is one of Morris's more stylized designs and is characteristic in its relative flatness and in its debt to natural forms.

appropriate ornmament, he tried to link together objects with common utilitarian functions, such as 'pouring out' and 'containing'.[10] In the same spirit of rationalization Owen Jones, and later Christopher Dresser (qq.v.) worked out their ideas about ways of controlling arbitrary ornament and published treatises on the subject. In 1852 Jones had advocated, 'an intelligent and imaginative eclecticism'.[11] And in his *Grammar of Ornament* of 1856 he wrote that: 'All ornament should be based upon a geometrical construction. In surface decoration, all lines should flow out of a parent stem. Every ornament, however distant, should be traced to its branch and root',[12] thus providing a set of rules for the designer to bear in mind when applying decoration to objects. He based his propositions upon patterns and theories from other periods and cultures, stressing, as did Dresser, oriental practice.

While many attempts were made to control and limit the nature and scale of Victorian ornament, there was never any question of its fundamental relevance to the applied arts. There was no real diminution in the chasm between the practice of the applied arts and engineering in this period and the architect retained the role of taste-maker *par excellence*. The design of the new machinery, however, remained predominantly in the hands of the engineer and the manufacturing team and did not in this period form part of the concerns of the more progressive designers. It was to be some time before the machine aesthetic – formulated, ironically, first for architecture, then for the decorative arts and applied finally to machines themselves – was to become the dominant design style of the day. First, a strange process had to occur which involved making conscious and theoretical that which had previously been unconscious and determined by forces outside man's direct control, that is, the role of the technology of materials and production in the aesthetic of mass-produced objects.

Individualism and Standardization at the Turn of the Century

It was William Morris (q.v.), that master of nineteenth-century decoration, who claimed that 'the more mechanical the process, the less direct should be the imitation of natural forms'.[13] In stylistic terms, the move from the nineteenth to the twentieth centuries was simply a matter of leaving behind the natural world and the individual as the symbolic sources of the language of mass-produced objects and of adopting, instead, the metaphor of the machine and the mechanized environment as the stimuli for a new theory of form. The transition was, however, a gradual one. While the engineer continued to treat technology as a fact, the architect, seeking a new aesthetic, began to see it as a source of symbolic inspiration and to inject it, metaphorically at least, into his designs. Thus terms like 'function', 'materials', 'standardization' and others referring to the necessary, internal properties of the machine-made, mass-produced artefact, took on a quasi-mystical significance for the generation of architects who set out to evolve the machine aesthetic.

The years around the turn of the century were transitional ones and Art Nouveau – a style which spread, internationally, through architecture and the applied arts between 1890 and 1910 – provided a platform from which it was possible to look both backwards and forwards simultaneously. While Nikolaus Pevsner, writing later, saw it as the last stronghold of nineteenth-century individualism,[14] others, impressed by its use of new materials, namely glass and wrought-iron, and its structural integrity represented by the strong unification of form and decoration – such as was found, for example, in the work of Hector Guimard (q.v.) in Paris – saw within Art Nouveau the seeds of a new approach towards mass-produced form. For them, the style concentrated less on an object's symbolic relationship with the rest of the environment than on its intrinsic structural and functional qualities. Otto Wagner (q.v.), an architect and protagonist of Viennese *Jugendstil*[15] – a late and predominantly rectilinear manifestation of Art Nouveau – wrote in 1895, representing this view, that 'All modern forms must correspond to new materials and the new requirements of our time, if they are to fit modern mankind'.[16] The Viennese *Jugendstil* designers were themselves heavily influenced by the Scotsman, C. R. Mackintosh (q.v.), who was amongst the first to combine curvilinear forms with a more 'rational' aesthetic based upon structure as well as decoration [10]. But however radical it may have been in its attitude towards new materials and its rejection of historicism, Art Nouveau finally reached a cul-de-sac, less through its decorative aesthetic than its social limitations. It thus remained an exclusive style aimed at a metropolitan, wealthy market and never fully penetrated the mass market.

The problems involved in the search for a new aesthetic for the new century were highlighted in the confrontation that took place between

10 C. R. Mackintosh, DS4 armchair, 1918 (reproduced by Cassina, 1975). Mackintosh's lounge chair of 1918, which has an ebonized ashwood frame, inlaid with mother-of-pearl, and a sea-grass seat, is part of a set of dining-room furniture designed in 1918 which also comprises a sideboard and a dining-table. The chair is 75 cm. high and displays Mackintosh's love of rectilinear form. Along with Josef Hoffmann and Frank Lloyd Wright (who also made extensive use of the Japanese-derived grid in their designs for furniture) he was one of the most radical designers from the first part of the twentieth century and an inspiration for many early Modern Movement protagonists. He remains, however, in his use of materials and commitment to craft traditions, a turn-of-the-century designer.

the Belgian architect-designer, Henri Van de Velde (q.v.), and the German diplomat, Hermann Muthesius (q.v.). Both men were members of the Deutscher Werkbund, a body set up in Germany in 1907 to promote the collaboration between artists and manufacturers in that country.

Van de Velde established many of the theoretical foundations for Art Nouveau. With his knowledge of British art theory, he articulated a number of proto-functionalist ideas, among them that 'utility can generate beauty', 'ornament should be structural and dynamographic', and 'ornament and form should appear so intimate that the ornament seems to have determined the form'[17] which underpinned one wing of that movement. While the advocates of nineteenth-century symbolism had defined ornament in terms of the natural world, Van de Velde developed a theory of object symbolism in which it was the object's own internal structure which was expressed by the ornament. A fine artist by training, Van de Velde left Belgium for Germany in 1900 and was invited to Weimar to head the city's new School of Decorative Arts. During his time in Germany he developed his ideas fully and built some of his most famous buildings, including the Maison Hohenhof of 1907 and the theatre for the Werkbund Exhibition in Cologne in 1914. This was also the year in which his ideas were to clash so violently with those of Muthesius.

Muthesius had visited Britain at the end of the nineteenth century on behalf of the Prussian Board of Trade to investigate British domestic architecture. He was hugely impressed by the aesthetic simplicity of the work of Arts and Crafts architects and, in 1904–5, published a book entitled *Das Englische Haus* in which he outlined his impressions of their work. Speaking, for example, of their services, water pipes and electric lighting, he wrote:

Form developed purely from purpose is by itself so ingenuous and expressive that it evokes a feeling of aesthetic well-being that differs in no way from a feeling of artistic pleasure. Here we have a really new art based on actual modern conditions and modern achievements, and which perhaps, one day . . . will be seen as the most eloquent expression of our age.[18]

Muthesius's approach to form was highly abstracted and, unlike Van de Velde, he saw standardization as the chief aesthetic determinant of objects produced in the modern age.

Van de Velde, on the other hand, firmly defended his defence of the individual in the face of the mass: 'so long as there are artists within the [Deutscher] Werkbund, and so long as they are able to influence its fate, they will protest against the imposition of orders or standardization'.[19] The ideological conflict between the two centuries where architectural form was concerned was thus completely formulated. While Van de Velde continued to support the freedom of the artist to create form according to the dictates of his own intuition, albeit taking into account the requirements of the modern age, Muthesius was wholly committed to the principle that the laws of mechanized mass production dictate both the appearance and the symbolic and cultural function of the mass-produced, machine-made object. While his purpose in developing these ideas was primarily practical, that is, to ensure the possibility of a high standard of mass production to meet the needs of the German export trade, the effect of his words was to encourage the development of standard types, both in architecture and industrial design.

Whatever the outcome of the 1914 debate, in terms of a new base for a new design aesthetic, huge advances had been made. The possibility of design moving into line with technology and production rather than subject to the whims of the individualistic fine artist had been aired and discussed: it was during the subsequent two decades that these ideas were to be more fully defined and to become a reality.

The Machine Aesthetic

By the 1920s many architects had looked not only to the work of the engineer and to the machine as sources of symbolic inspiration but also to the technological advances in building construction in formulating their new aesthetic. In the USA the steel-framed building placed the priority upon structure rather than decoration and a number of architects advocated, as a cultural necessity,[20] the removal of decoration. Increasingly, also, they began to look to modern architecture to provide an aesthetic for mass-produced consumer goods as well.

The fine arts, painting and sculpture, also became machine-conscious in this period and, like architecture and design, began investigating their own internal properties, in the search for a new aesthetic which would ally itself, metaphorically at least, to the newly mechanized mass environment.

In product design the main constraints were still the problems of technology and the mass market but some aesthetic advances were made in this period which paralleled the developments in architecture.

45

One notable example was the work of the architect, Peter Behrens (q.v.). Although previously enthralled by the decorative curves of Art Nouveau, Behrens went on to design a number of small electrical appliances, kettles [13], fans, and so on for the A.E.G. Company in Germany, paying careful attention both to the rationalist base of their production and to their utilitarian function as the base for his aesthetic decisions. Although vestiges of Art Nouveau were visible in the kettles, their appearance also owed much to the anonymously designed, technically determined products of early mass-production industry. The machine aesthetic had come full circle and was now being consciously manipulated by architects, still the major form-givers at that time, and applied to consumer machines themselves.

The interwar movement in architecture and design, which generally is referred to as the Modern Movement or by the label 'Modernism', and which embraced work produced in Holland, the USSR, Germany, France, the USA, Austria and a number of other countries, was characterized by its fascination with the machine and the industrialized environment. At the turn of the century the German furniture designer and craftsman, Richard Riemerschmid (q.v.), had already betrayed that particular obsession, looking to the man-made forms in the urban environment as a source of inspiration.

A fascination with 'type forms', such as bridges, grain-silos and mass-produced objects also characterized the work of Le Corbusier (q.v.) in France in the 1920s. He based his architectural principles upon the assumptions of mechanization, referring frequently in his writings to the mass-production practices of the automobile industry and the aesthetic 'purity' of standardized artefacts: 'We postulated that mechanisation is based on geometry, that it is our very language, by which I mean that geometry denotes order and that mankind expresses itself only through order.'[21] The philosophical leap from the idea of the machine to that of simple, geometrical form was made by all the Modern Movement protagonists. It was a leap of faith rather than fact but one which, nevertheless, underpinned all aspects of the machine aesthetic, both in theory and practice. For Le Corbusier and others, the machine implied undecorated geometric form as well as being an abstract force with a strong visual, cultural and spiritual symbolism attached to it. In social terms, commitment to the machine aesthetic implied a democratic approach to design, while nineteenth-century naturalism was equated with conservatism and elitism.

Until the 1930s these ideas failed to influence the design of mechanical and electrical consumer goods which lay outside the scope of the architect-designer. It was only 'architectural accessories' (that is, furniture, glass, ceramics and textiles – all products, ironically, with a craft tradition behind them) that were transformed by the unmistakable stamp of the machine aesthetic in the years following the First World War.

Because of its close affiliations with architectural space, its relative ease of manufacture and its potent symbolism, the chair, that 'sitting-object', was used by most of the architect-philosophers of the Modern Movement to articulate, in material form, their ideas about materials, construction and space. The Dutchman, Gerrit Rietveld's (q.v.) Red–Blue wooden chair of 1917/18, for example, was an exercise in abstract form in which the sculptural manipulation of construction and space created a particular visual formula which was to inspire many other similar experiments. All the joints of the chair overlapped each other to emphasize its essential structure and Rietveld painted the planes in different colours to stress their separateness from each other.

At the Bauhaus[22] in Germany in the 1920s, the director, Walter Gropius's (q.v.) aim was to create an understanding of 'basic' or 'elementary' form which could be applied to mass-produced goods and, finally, to architecture. Wassily Kandinsky and Paul Klee (qq.v.) taught foundation-year students how to articulate the language of geometric form and elementary composition in two and three dimensions and to reject all memories of naturalistic realism and historicism.

Marcel Breuer (q.v.), a graduate from the Bauhaus course, went on to teach at that institution and to create items of furniture which reflected the aesthetic ideas he had imbibed as a student. Principles of 'objectivity' and 'universality' formulated by the De Stijl Movement in Holland[23] influenced Breuer's work, as did the aesthetic ideas of Russian and East European Constructivism,[24] and he evolved in response a highly formal approach towards the problem of chair design. Although the Bauhaus was strongly craft oriented in the objects produced in its workshops, many of Breuer's designs were highly suitable for mass production and were indeed later mass produced in large numbers. Inspired by the strength and lightness of the bicycle, Breuer became fascinated by the possibilities of tubular steel and found in this material the technical solution to the aesthetic question that he had been asking himself for some time. Breuer's reworking of the traditional club armchair of 1926 has become an icon of the Modern

11 Mies van der Rohe, tubular-steel side-chairs, 1927.

Mies's famous cantilevered side-chair made of tubular steel with a leather, or cane, seat and back was first shown in the interior schemes which he created, with Lilly Reich for the Werkbund exhibition in Weissenhof and for the Silk Exhibit at the Exposition de la Mode in Berlin. It was marketed by the Berliner Metallgewerbe, which was taken over by Thonet in 1932, as the MR 534. Mies was the most uncompromising of the Modernist architects and this chair, which was followed by a model with arms, a stool and a coffee table, was the most visually exciting of the cantilevered chairs of the 1920s. It shows clearly how, for the Modernist designers, materials and construction became symbols in their own right. It has been reproduced by Knoll International.

Movement, a classic reinterpretation of an existing chair type which aligns itself completely with the Modern Movement's commitment to lightness rather than weight and to space rather than mass.

The tubular-steel chair – the inevitable result, according to Breuer, of 'the functional requirements of the object and the necessities of modern machine production'[25] – paved the way for many other experiments with new materials and abstract form by many Modern Movement protagonists through the 1920s and 1930s, thereby succeeding, perhaps more than any other domestic object, in popularizing the machine aesthetic. The work of Mies van der Rohe (q.v.) at the Bauhaus [11], also in tubular steel, has had a similar effect on the twentieth-century environment, making Modernism a reality as well as an abstract idea.

While the transference of the architecturally dominated machine style into machines themselves was slow, once mass consumption of domestic equipment became widespread, many manufacturers began to realize the commercial advantages of the 'modern style'. By the early 1930s automobiles and domestic and office machinery began to look like integrated objects rather than a set of disparate, mechanical parts – a result both of new production technologies and the desire for a 'modern' look [28]. The US industrial designers, who were responsible for styling the new products, were all committed, at least in their writings, to the purist ideas about form established in Europe. The leading member of this group, W. D. Teague (q.v.), expressed his emotional debt to the European Modern Movement when he wrote in his book of 1940, *Design This Day*, that 'Factories of steel and glass are buildings in forms that are triumphs of rational planning and of the sense of the objectives of industry'.[26] The US designers lacked, however, the political and social idealism that inspired their European counterparts and soon their slogan 'styling follows sales' had replaced the more purist 'form follows function', and the machine aesthetic had been transformed from a philosophy into a marketing device.

'Good Form'

By the end of the Second World War, the practice of styling mechanical and electrical goods to make them appear clean, crisp, geometrical and, above all, modern, had become commonplace. Cars, electric razors, radios, food-mixers, typewriters, cameras, washing-machines, and so on, were all given body-shells, at first rather bulbous due to the fashion for streamlining and the limitations of production technology, but moving increasingly in the direction of the simple black and white boxes which dominated product design in the 1960s and 1970s. Dubbed either the 'efficiency style', or the 'New Functionalism',[27] designers had finally transferred the machine aesthetic from architecture and the applied arts into product design, thereby creating one of the dominant visual languages of the second half of the twentieth century.

At the forefront of the postwar movement towards 'good form', as it came to be known internationally, the German electrical company, Braun, set out, after 1951, to create an image of electrical consumer goods which would consciously reflect the spirit of the age. Committed to the geometric forms associated poetically with the rationalism of machine production, Braun went as far as to name its products accordingly. Thus their Kitchen-Machine, an elegant electric food mixer of 1957, is composed of a set of parallel lines created by the outline, the seamings of the housing and the carefully placed ventilation holes. The whole object is an exercise in harmonious composition and geometric simplicity in which no extraneous details are added to the machine's essential features.

Design formalism[28] reached its zenith in the objects manufactured in Germany in the years after the war [38] and England, Japan, Italy and the USA obsessively emulated, albeit with subtle national variations, the German style. The kind of purist sensitivity that led Piet Mondrian, the De Stijl painter, to travel in trains with the window blinds down so that he would not be disturbed by the chaos of the natural landscape, and that now makes Dieter Rams (q.v.), Braun's chief designer, want to live in an environment made up of white tiles, was a symptom of artists and designers taking the machine aesthetic to a logical conclusion and finding there the impasse of pure geometry. Where mass-produced, consumer machines were concerned, it was, inevitably, the style rather than the philosophy of Modernism that was, on the whole, adopted.

The Crisis of Modernism

While we can speak of a 'true' or 'honest' form for a simple, traditional object which has a craft manufacturing base, it is not so easy to apply the same criteria to design of a complex product such as a food mixer which is made of numerous components and whose outward appearance is dependent upon a body-shell rather than its internal structure. The problem that emerged from the transference of a craft-based aesthetic theory into the area of mass manufacturing did not reach a crisis point until the years after the Second World War, when a number of individuals began to articulate their doubts about the relevance of Modern Movement theory to industrial design and to contemporary society.

A decade after the end of the Second World War a new set of ideas emerged which questioned the autocracy of the Modern Movement as the dominant twentieth-century design aesthetic and which replaced architecture as a model for design with that of mass culture. It defined design as an essentially popular expendable phenomenon in contrast to the exclusive universal ideas with which Modernism was associated. The British critic and historian Reyner Banham (q.v.) challenged the machine aesthetic vociferously, claiming that mass production is, in the end, determined by economic and technological change rather than by abstract notions of rationalism and order. In 1955 he wrote that 'the illusion of common "objectivity" residing in the concept of function, and in the laws of Platonic aesthetics has been a stumbling block to product criticism',[29] and pointed out that the Modern Movement protagonists had created a confusion between the meaning of objectivity in mechanical engineering laws and its meaning in the laws of aesthetics, and that the concept of standardization had been misunderstood in its equation with an ideal rather than a momentary norm. The raising of these confusions to the level of a creed had resulted, claimed Banham, in the creation of a dominant twentieth-century design aesthetic which was based on fallacy rather than fact. Other critics and designers picked up Banham's points and suggested that there are many potential sources of product form besides that of the machine alone. Banham summarized such feelings when he stated that: 'We live in a throwaway economy, a culture in which the most fundamental classification of our ideas and worldly possessions is in terms of their relative expendability.'[30]

According to Banham, objectivity and universality needed to be replaced by expendability and he suggested that designers should turn their attentions to the formulation of a new, symbolically determined aesthetic which would meet the psychological requirements of the mass consumer. This aesthetic was best expressed, according to Banham, in the American automobile of the 1950s [12]. This new attitude had radical implications, and soon the floodgates were open for

51

12 Buick Roadmaster, 1951.
It was to US cars of the early 1950s, like this Roadmaster Model 76-c convertible, that the Independent Group looked in its search for designed objects with iconographic potency and mass-market appeal. Among the details they isolated were the sensuous curves of the headlight housings, the aggressive 'cow-catcher' grill, the chrome finish, the bulbous curve of the bonnet and the 'speed-lines' on the side, all of which contributed to the automobile's message of 'power and sex'. In this decade the US automobile became the ultimate symbol of anti-Modern Movement thinking and of consumer-oriented design.

a reconsideration of eclecticism, revivalism, pattern and colour – all those aesthetic qualities of objects which the Modern Movement, in its search for absolute laws, had suppressed. The problem for the designer shifted from one of a search for appropriate form to one of appropriate symbolism, and the consumer moved back into the centre of the picture replacing the machine as the major symbolic source for the mass-produced object. It was a volte-face which mirrored the growing emphasis on marketing within manufacturing industry and the movement's principal theorist was the American architect, Robert Venturi, who published his treatise on the subject, *Complexity and Contradiction in Architecture*, in 1966. The effects of this theoretical reversal were slow to be felt but by the end of the 1970s and early 1980s it was possible to talk about 'Post-Modern design',[31] especially in the areas of architecture, furniture and interior design. As always, it was late to penetrate the area of product design, but even so there were growing signs that the 'black box'[32] [49] had had its day – an event which Banham had predicted when, in 1955, he had written that 'the aesthetics of consumer goods are those of the popular arts'.[33]

Ideas about form-giving in design had come full circle. From an idealistic rejection of nineteenth-century ornament and eclecticism to the evolution of a full-blooded twentieth-century design theory which modelled itself on an idea of the machine and its contribution to modern life – and which was imposed on a largely uncomprehending public – designers and design theorists had come back to the idea that the role of the market and consumer psychology were important influences on the object and that these must therefore be reflected in its aesthetic.

Notes: Chapter 3

1   G. Dorfles, *Introduction à l'industrial design* (Paris: Casterman, 1974), p. 15.
2   J. Gloag, *Victorian Taste: Some Social Aspects of Architecture and Industrial Design from 1820–1900* (Newton Abbot: David & Charles, reprint 1972), p. 3.
3   C. Harvie, G. Martin and A. Scharf, *Industrialization and Culture 1830–1914* (London: Macmillan, 1970), p. 257.
4   F. McCarthy, *A History of British Design 1830–1970* (London: Allen & Unwin, 1979), p. 8.
5   ibid., p. 24.
6   In his book *High Victorian Design* (London: Architectural Press, 1951), Nikolaus Pevsner describes Ruskin's antagonism to the Crystal Palace

which the latter saw as a heathen structure and described as 'a green-house, bigger than a greenhouse was ever built before' (p. 44).

7   J. Gloag, op. cit., p. 137.

8   H. Schaefer, *The Roots of Modern Design: Functional Tradition in the Nineteenth Century* (London: Studio Vista, 1970).

9   McCarthy, *History of British Design*, p. 16.

10 P. Steadman, *The Evolution of Designs* (Cambridge: Cambridge University Press, 1979), p. 33.

11 S. Durant, *Victorian Ornamental Design* (London: Academy Editions, 1972), p. 17.

12 ibid., p. 22.

13 W. Morris, 'The lesser arts', in A. Briggs (ed.), *William Morris: Selected Writings and Design* (Harmondsworth, Middx: Penguin, 1973), p. 103.

14 In his various accounts of the subject, Nikolaus Pevsner frequently repeated that, for him, Art Nouveau was the last manifestation of nineteenth-century individualism. See, for example, 'Art Nouveau', in *The Sources of Modern Architecture and Design* (London: Thames & Hudson, 1968), p. 113.

15 Jugendstil was the Northern European version of Art Nouveau. It had manifestations in Germany, Austria and the Scandinavian countries and tended to be less visually extravagant than its southern European counterparts.

16 G. Naylor, *The Arts and Crafts Movement* (London: Studio Vista, 1971), p. 184.

17 S. Tshudi-Madsen, *Art Nouveau* (London: Weidenfeld & Nicolson, 1967), pp. 54–5.

18 T. and C. Benton and D. Sharp, *Form and Function: A Source Book for the History of Architecture and Design, 1890–1939* (Milton Keynes, Bucks: Open University Press, 1975), p. 115.

19 N. Pevsner, *Pioneers of Modern Design* (Harmondsworth, Middx: Penguin, 1960), p. 37.

20 Adolf Loos, for example, wrote that 'ornament is no longer an expression of our culture'. Quoted in K. Rowland, *History of the Modern Movement* (Wokingham, Berks: Van Nostrand Reinhold, 1973), p. 76.

21 Le Corbusier, *Towards a New Architecture* (London: Architectural Press, 1974), p. 255.

22 Set up by Walter Gropius in Weimar in 1919 the Bauhaus was an educational establishment where the study of the Machine Aesthetic was encouraged wholeheartedly. The curriculum was planned in such a way that all students spent time looking at the 'elements of form' before they went on to learn craft skills.

23 The De Stijl Movement in Holland took its name from the periodical of that name which was launched in 1917. Piet Mondrian was the painter associated with the group which also included, among others, the painter/architect Theo Van Doesburg and the designer/architect Gerrit Rietveld. The work produced by the De Stijl group, in the ten or so years in which they worked together, focused on the articulation of basic plastic elements – lines, squares and oblongs, and planes, combined with the use

of the primary colours and black and white. Also referred to as Neo-Plasticism the movement contributed enormously to the evolution of the machine aesthetic in the twentieth century.

24   The movement referred to as Constructivism, which covered a spectrum of artistic activities from painting to sculpture to design and architecture, emerged in post-revolutionary Russia. It is best known through the work of the designers Vladimir Tatlin, Alexander Rodchenko and El Lissitzky (qq.v.) who evolved an abstract language of two-dimensional and three-dimensional form, based on the principle of building up simple geometric units into complex structures, in imitation of the work of the anonymous engineer. Their work contributed significantly to the European machine aesthetic of the 1920s.

25   C. Wilk, *Marcel Breuer: Furniture and Interiors* (New York: Museum of Modern Art, 1981), p. 66.

26   W. D. Teague, *Design This Day: The Technique of Order in the Machine Age* (London: Studio Publications, 1946), p. 29.

27   The term 'New Functionalism' was used after the Second World War to describe the revived use in product design of the purist style of the 1920s. In its second incarnation the style tended to emphasize form rather than a philosophical or social approach to design and it became, as a result, just another visual option available to mass-production industry at that time.

28   The term 'formalism' derives from fine-art criticism and describes the tendency of some painters and sculptors to focus entirely on the internal formal properties of their artworks at the expense of their socio-cultural context. Many designers, in the post-Second World War period, manifested similar preoccupations and, as a result, many products developed a strongly sculptural identity, displaying great attention to formal detail.

29   Reyner Banham, 'A throwaway aesthetic' (March 1960), reprinted in P. Sparke (ed.), *Reyner Banham: Design by Choice* (London: Academy Editions, 1981), p. 90.

30   ibid., p. 90.

31   Post-Modernism is the name used to describe the tendency in recent architecture, and to a lesser extent in design, to reject the visual purism of the Modern Movement, felt to have resulted in empty formalism. The Post-Modernists have experimented with an alternative aesthetic or sets of aesthetics which accept eclecticism, bad taste, decoration, complexity and ambiguity.

32   The term 'Black Box' is used to describe that neo-functionalist aesthetic in postwar design which, in its search for a minimal language, has tended to reduce design's visual options to the simple cube and to the basic colours, black and white. It is a design language which has dominated the area of electronic consumer equipment since the 1950s, but is now being superseded by experiments with expressive form and evocative colours.

33   Banham, 'A throwaway aesthetic', p. 93.

4

Promoting Design

As soon as 'design' had become generally accepted as an intrinsic part of the systems of mass production, marketing and consumption, many of the countries which depended on it increasingly for successful trading, saw the need both to consolidate its role within industry and to communicate its benefits to as wide an audience as possible in order to guarantee its future. By the middle of the twentieth century, a number of organizations and institutions had been formed for this specific purpose, some, as in Britain, Sweden and Japan, government-sponsored and others, as in Denmark, are independent. While some were established to protect the interests of the newly formed design profession, others set out to inform the manufacturer and the public about the advantages, both in terms of profit and the quality of life, of becoming 'design-conscious', and yet others were devoted to the task of establishing their country's products on the world market. Some, like the Council of Industrial Design[1] which was set up in Britain by the Board of Trade of the Coalition Government in 1944 'to promote by all practicable means, the improvement in the products of British industry'[2] performed all three functions simultaneously. The Council's primary motive was, typically, to help in the national effort of re-establishing Britain as a force in world trade, and to compete with those countries which had shown, in the years before the Second World War, that they were aware of the advantages of selling their products to the rest of the world in the name of design.

Design promotion has, in the twentieth century, played an important role in the economic expansion of those countries which make up the industrialized world, as an awareness of design has come to represent a country's ability to compete on the world market. It has also provided a strong channel of communication through which a number of ideologies have been transmitted. Notable among these are economic and political nationalism, the supremacy of industrial capitalism, and middle-class taste values.

In the promotion of design, the roles of exhibitions and of the mass media have proved to be vital means of communicating to a mass audience the complex function that design plays within the economy and culture as a whole. Without the support of the public and the manufacturer, design can penetrate neither consumption nor production and cannot, as a result, become part of a nation's export identity. It is, therefore, primarily as a means of persuading these parties of the necessity of design, both to everyday life and to the national economy, that so many bodies have made so many efforts.

As part of the programme of communicating the general benefits of design many of the organizations involved in design promotion have set themselves up as arbiters of taste, intent on the task of improving design standards. Aesthetic reform was at the forefront of the minds of individuals like Prince Albert and Henry Cole when, in the mid-nineteenth century, they made their pioneering efforts to improve the standards of design through the establishment of museums and by training the 'designer' in the skills of the fine artist. Their efforts represented their concern about Britain's position on the world market in the face of the high standards of taste and design of their major competitor, France. They failed, however, to set up an official government body to promote design and it was not until a century later, with the formation of the Council of Industrial Design, that such a body was created in Britain, many years after similar organizations had been formed elsewhere.

The Arts and Crafts Heritage

The roots of most twentieth-century design promotion organizations lie in the craft revival movements of the second half of the nineteenth century. During that period a large number of craft organizations emerged which defined themselves as support systems for the maintenance of high standards in design. The Scandinavian countries were among the first to feel the need for such an organization and the Swedish Design Society (the Svenska Slöjdforeningen) was formed, in 1845, to protect the crafts during and after the abolition of the old guild system. This was followed by the Finnish Society of Crafts and Design founded thirty years later, mainly as a result of the efforts of C. G. Estlander (q.v.) who then headed the new craft school in Helsinki.

Britain followed fast on the heels of the Nordic countries, and with the expansion of the Arts and Crafts Movement in the last quarter of the century a number of societies and workshops emerged, all of which felt the need for a united front on which to confront the degeneration of aesthetic standards brought about by unbridled mass production. Mackmurdo's Century Guild of 1882, the Art Workers' Guild of 1884, the Arts and Crafts Society of 1888, and C. R. Ashbee's (q.v.) Guild and School of Handicraft of the same year were all, in effect, early private design pressure groups, aiming to protect designers, to encourage a high level of aesthetic and moral standards in the objects in the environment, and to act as publicity machines organizing exhibitions at home and abroad.

It was through such exhibitions that the model of the craft workshop was both received and emulated in a number of other countries in the years around the turn of the century. The best-known derivatives were the German examples, centred mainly in Munich and Dresden,[3] the Viennese Werkstätte founded by Josef Hoffmann and Koloman Moser (qq.v.) in 1903, and similar organizations formed in Denmark and the USA. Hoffmann described the British origins of these guild-like workshops in his programme of the Viennese Werkstätte of 1904: 'We have founded our workshop ... it should become a centre of gravity surrounded by the happy noise of the handicraft production and welcomed by everybody who truly believes in RUSKIN and MORRIS.'[4]

The Deutscher Werkbund

In Germany the craft workshops acted as breeding grounds for the first design organization which was to aim its attentions at industry rather than the handicrafts. The Deutscher Werkbund was set up in Munich in 1907 and its aim was clearly set out in its first programme as being 'to improve the design and quality of German goods'.[5]

In many ways, the Werkbund stands as a model for subsequent developments. Not only have its aims been frequently reiterated but its constitution, its policy and its tactics all provided examples for many later organizations. It was formed initially as a result of the efforts of Hermann Muthesius (q.v.), with the strong support of the Belgian, Henri Van de Velde (q.v.), and the politician, Friedrich Naumann, and its aims – to restore unity and national identity to German culture through the medium of improved industrial production and to assert

Germany's predominance on the international market – were explicitly nationalistic in emphasis.

Germany was the third European country to industrialize after Britain and France and it needed both to compete with these countries and to develop a sense of national identity on the world market. To ascertain the way in which the competition operated, Hermann Muthesius had been sent to England to examine the basis of the British architectural aesthetic. He returned to Germany convinced that he had found the answer and persuaded a number of associates, including manufacturers, architects and politicians, that an organization should be formed to bring about the necessary reform of German mass-produced goods.

The Werkbund's role was essentially two-fold. First of all it acted as a co-ordinating body or forum which enabled industrialists, artists, architects, craftsmen and other individuals interested in the link between the artistic and the economic aspects of mass production, to meet and discuss issues and tactics relevant to this end. Secondly, it functioned as a pressure group in the task of evolving high aesthetic standards in the German mass production of consumer goods. Among the projects it admired was the alliance between the German designer, Peter Behrens (q.v.), and the Allgemeine Elektricitäts-Gesellschaft (AEG) which resulted in one of the first corporate identity schemes for a modern company. Behrens worked on a whole range of products for AEG, among them fans and kettles [13], as well as designing the factories and all the graphics.

The first Werkbund meeting, held in Munich in 1907, was attended by about a hundred people and Theodor Fischer, a professor of architecture, was elected the first president. By 1909 there were 731 members of whom just over half were artists and just under half were manufacturers. Their programme was one of action which included attempting to raise the level of taste of the general public through publications and exhibitions; implementing a programme of public education, particularly through public lectures; putting pressure upon retailers and manufacturers to sell and make Werkbund-approved products; and doing surveys of consumer goods available on the market. The scope of its interest was wide and it gradually moved further and further away from the applied arts in the direction of the new mechanical and electrical products and objects of transport. The Werkbund was also deeply concerned with the question of the home, particularly workers' housing and minimal dwellings – an interest which

13 Peter Behrens, kettles for AEG, 1909.

This page from the Allgemeine Elektricitäts-Gesellschaft's (General Electric Company's) sales brochure illustrates three versions of an electric kettle manufactured by the company and designed, as the sales blurb tells us, by Peter Behrens. The kettle which was available in three finishes – matt steel, nickel-plated steel, or hammered copper – was just one element in the 'corporate' scheme that Behrens produced for AEG which included the design of its buildings and all its graphic material, as well as the electrical products themselves. The style used throughout was one which rejected nineteenth-century ornamentation and eclecticism (although there are vestiges of tradition in the kettle's woven-cane handle and the ornate knob on the lid) and espoused the new aesthetic implications of rationalism, mechanization and standardization. This is reflected in the ordered nature of the page layout and in the clarity of the typeface selected.

reflected the ideals of social democracy which illuminated so much of its work.

Among the successes that the Werkbund boasted in the first phase of its programme was the establishment of a Museum of Industrial Design in Hagen, and the organization of a number of travelling exhibitions, including one which went to Newark in the USA in 1912. It also succeeded in encouraging a new 'rational' aesthetic in German goods which was manifested in, for example, Walter Gropius's (q.v.) interior of a train sleeping compartment and Grenander's (q.v.) coaches for an underground train.

In spite of the pioneering work undertaken by individuals associated with the Werkbund, such as Richard Riemerschmid (q.v.) who was applying the new principles of standardization to furniture and working towards the idea of the *typenmöbel*,[6] the new aesthetic was best received by manufacturers for whom no aesthetic tradition existed. It appeared most frequently, therefore, in electrical appliances, objects of transport and functional buildings like railway stations and factories.

In 1914 a major Werkbund exhibition was held in Cologne and a number of pavilions were built to house the industrial products to be displayed there. In spite of the subsequent decline of the German economy and its manufacturing strength the Werkbund continued its programme of propaganda and education through the First World War and into the 1920s, publishing its yearbooks and a magazine called *Form* which ran from 1925 to 1933. The second major exhibition sponsored by the Werkbund was the huge international housing project of 1927 held at Weissenhof at which all the principal International Style[7] architects were represented. In the years leading up to its eclipse by the Nazi regime in 1933 the Werkbund's main emphasis was upon architecture and the domestic habitat, the initial enthusiasm for product design having gradually diminished.

At the end of the Second World War efforts were made to reconstitute the Werkbund and to this end a number of small groups emerged in various parts of Germany – Düsseldorf, Baden, Hessen, Bodensee and Berlin – peopled by familiar names from the pioneering period, among them Otto Bartnung, Hans Scharoun, Max Taut and Lilly Reich (qq.v.). In 1947 the Werkbund was formally re-established and adopted a forward-looking, post-Nazi approach inspired by the slogan 'A new form for a new life-style (*Lebensform*)'.[8] The first postwar exhibition was held, nostalgically, in Cologne in 1950 and one of its first projects was the constitution of a new German design organization called the Rat für Formgebung.

Established by the German government in 1951, the Rat's aesthetic policy emulated that of the Werkbund in its emphasis upon rational, functional form. It concentrated its efforts on new products – electronic equipment, laboratory apparatus and transport – rather than on the more traditional applied arts, and the Neo-Functionalist aesthetic it promoted characterized the German approach to design in the postwar period which was clearly demonstrated in their exhibits at the Milan Triennales of the 1950s.

Apart from its clear influence upon German mass-produced goods, the Deutscher Werkbund's main function in the twentieth century has been to inspire other countries to follow its lead in establishing bodies both to support and promote design. Unlike the Scandinavian and British craft bodies which had preceded it the Werkbund was more explicitly concerned to bridge the gap between art and industry, and its efforts and successes encouraged a number of other countries to attempt that same gargantuan task.

The first countries to follow Germany's lead were two of its neighbours – Austria and Switzerland. The pioneering work undertaken by Hoffmann and Moser in the craft-based Wiener Werkstätte was continued by the Austrian Werkbund which was founded in 1910 to emulate the aims of the German organization. In 1912 an exhibition of applied arts was held in Vienna and in 1914 Hoffmann was represented at the Cologne Exhibition. His name, along with that of Josef Frank (q.v.), a Viennese architect, were the ones most closely associated with the Austrian Werkbund. Frank was represented at the Weissenhof Exhibition in 1927 and in 1932 he contributed to the Viennese Siedlung Exhibition, the Austrian equivalent of the earlier German project. In 1934 Frank went to Sweden to live and the Austrian initiative was soon eclipsed by the rise of Hitler and the imminence of war.

The Swiss Werkbund was established on the German model in 1913. In the following year the first issue of its mouthpiece, *Werk*, was published and in 1918 an exhibition was held in Zurich. The Swiss body aimed to establish a national design policy and style in a country which was essentially multicultural. By the 1930s, through the efforts of the Werkbund, Swiss technical exhibitions and graphic design had all come to be acknowledged internationally as fine examples of good, functional design.

The Design and Industries Association

Like the other design organizations established on the Werkbund model, the British version – the Design and Industries Association (DIA) – also went a long way towards imitating both the ideals and the practice of the German example. It failed ultimately, however, to radically change the attitudes of either the British manufacturers or the public towards the role of design in mass production and everyday life. This was due to a number of complex factors, among them their deep-seated commitment to the late nineteenth-century craft ideal.

The DIA was formed in 1915 as a direct result of the Werkbund's success in Germany. Four founder members of the Association had visited the 1914 Cologne exhibition and returned greatly impressed by the standard of the German goods they had seen displayed there. When war was declared in 1914 and the importation of German and Austrian goods ceased, these pioneers were determined that British aggression against Germany should not mean that the quality of German goods was undermined. They managed to mount a small exhibit of German goods at the Goldsmiths' Hall in 1915 to show British designers the progressive nature of the Werkbund's work, and the decision was made to form a similar organization in Britain which came as a direct result of the exhibition's impact. In order to demonstrate its commitment to the future the DIA described itself as 'A new body with new aims' determined to 'instil a new spirit of design into British industry'.[9] Early members included the retailer and furniture designer Ambrose Heal (q.v.); his cousin and the architect of his store in Tottenham Court Road, Cecil Brewer (q.v.); the silversmith and director of the Poole Pottery, Harold Stabler (q.v.); and the director of the Dryad Furniture Company, Harry Peach (q.v.). But the guiding spirit behind the group's early aesthetic theories was, without doubt, the architect C. R. Lethaby (q.v.) whose Arts and Crafts-based philosophy of 'the well doing of what needs doing'[10] permeated all DIA discussions about industrial aesthetics. Individuals who joined later in the 1920s included the design propagandists, Noel Carrington and John Gloag; the Cotswolds furniture designer, Gordon Russell (q.v.); and Frank Pick (q.v.) who was to revolutionize London Transport's design policy in a way similar to that in which Grenander had worked on the Berlin Railway. Pick's Werkbund-like concerns differed, however, from those of his fellow DIA members who tended, in spite of their commitment to modernity, to remain within the limits of the traditional 'art industries' – especially ceramics, textiles and furniture. The Arts and Crafts Movement's involvement with the domestic habitat had established a firm British design tradition which was perpetuated, unquestioningly, by the DIA and the industries it influenced – among them the Dryad Furniture Company, the ceramics firms, Poole & Carter, Stabler & Adams, and the textiles firms, Warner's and, later, Morton Sundour and Edinburgh Weavers – were all manufacturing concerns with a traditional craft base and an established market.

In imitation of the Werkbund, however, the DIA organized a programme of consumer education through exhibitions and publications in the 1920s and 1930s: its magazine was called, in turn, *Design in Industry, Design Today*, and *Trend*[11] and it planned numerous lectures and discussion groups on the subject of design, all of which were well attended. Its exhibitions, including the 1920 display of 'Household Things' which consisted of eight rooms fitted out with furniture, pottery and glass with a few concessions made to hardware in the form of brooms and brushes, reflected a preoccupation with both the domestic environment and with what the DIA referred to as the 'Efficiency Style'.[12] In the formulation of this aesthetic it was the simple, modest forms of the Scandinavian applied arts which were emulated, however, rather than the tougher rationalism of the German-inspired International Style which, in the end, it came to mistrust. The DIA remained throughout its lifetime an elitist institution, supporting Modernist ideals which never really took commercial realism into account. Its effects on mass-production industry in Britain were, in the end, fairly negligible.

The Council of Industrial Design

In spite of the initiatives made in Britain during the 1930s to promote design, only a few tangible advances were actually made. In 1931 the Board of Trade appointed a Committee on Art and Industry under Lord Gorell who made his report on that subject the following year; and in 1933 the Council for Art and Industry was constituted under the chairmanship of Frank Pick (q.v.).

It was not until after the Second World War that the British government finally intervened to sustain the pioneering work of the DIA. Like its predecessor, however, the new government body soon encountered the problem of resolving the contradiction between

Britain's deep-rooted craft traditions and the need for increased mass production. When the Council of Industrial Design (later the Design Council) was set up in 1944 by the Board of Trade, the main stimulus behind its formation was fear of foreign competition from countries like the USA, Czechoslovakia, Sweden and Switzerland, all of which were reaping huge successes on the world market with their manufactured goods. Both the first and the second directors of the council, S. C. Leslie and Gordon Russell, were acutely conscious that Britain was trailing its feet in its late recognition of the significance of design as a factor in industrial and commercial operations and, in attempts to correct this, they implemented programmes of 'catching-up', sending teams of people to Sweden and elsewhere to investigate how those countries had arrived at their designs for mass production. At the same time, they initiated a policy of public design education through TV and radio programmes, exhibits in cinema foyers, travelling exhibitions, and a series of books on design published by Penguin Books[13] – all aimed at familiarizing the public with that new concept, 'design'.

The council's first piece of major design propaganda took the form of an exhibition. Held at the Victoria and Albert Museum in 1946, it was called, confidently, 'Britain Can Make It', and it reflected a world which succeeded the grey austerity of wartime design. The exhibition had a number of messages for the visitors who crowded enthusiastically into it, among them the fact that Britain had got back on its feet very rapidly after the devastation of war; that it had produced a whole new exciting range of designs, from furniture to fashion to garden equipment; and that industrial design was here to stay. This last claim was conveyed most effectively by one particular exhibit entitled the 'Birth of an Egg-Cup' [23] which set out to 'demonstrate how the designer works when he is designing an article for mass production and how different materials and different processes influence his design'.[14] Another section entitled 'Designers Look Ahead' underlined the importance of industrial design to the future of British society by showing the public some visionary products, like an air-conditioned bed and a streamlined sewing machine by F. H. K. Henrion (q.v.). The Council's determined wish to raise the level of public taste as a means of creating a market for the new 'contemporary' design was evident in the form of a quiz at the exhibition which encouraged visitors to formulate their preferences and vote for the designs they favoured.

14 Design for Eating Exhibition poster, late 1940s.
In the years following the end of the Second World War, the Council of Industrial Design held a number of exhibitions and initiated a programme of propaganda in an attempt to persuade the public of the benefits that 'good design' can bring to everyday life. This poster, designed by the Design Research Unit for the Council in a whimsical Surreal style typical of British display graphics of the period, advertised the advantages of eating in 'pleasant surroundings'. It shows Britain's debt at this time to Scandinavian social ideals and to their commitment to the roles of tradition and pattern in contemporary design. Ercol furniture is featured in the domestic interior.

'Good Design'

The dual, Werkbund-inspired policy of promoting design for industry and attempting simultaneously to raise the standards of public taste characterized the Council's programme of activities through the postwar years. It emerged clearly from the pages of *Design* magazine, first published in 1949; in the exhibitions it both mounted and sponsored [14]; at the Design Centre in the Haymarket which opened in 1956; and in its system of giving annual awards to a number of selected products which conformed to the council's criteria for 'good design'.

A problem which had beset all the design promotion organizations established since the Werkbund was that of defining 'good design'. By the 1950s there was a more or less international consensus on the issue which derived, in theory at least, from the Arts and Crafts principles of 'fitness to purpose' and 'truth to materials'. Britain remained, however, more committed to the craft ethic than West Germany in its understanding of the concept. Gordon Russell had been brought up in the Cotswolds and was steeped in the craft traditions of men like C. R. Ashbee, E. Gimson and the Barnsley brothers (qq.v.). In his book about furniture written for Penguin after the Second World War, Russell betrayed his preference for traditional values: 'There is much to stimulate a sensitive designer who will remember that there is no necessity to discard all old materials and methods. English oak remains a glorious material, if rightly used.'[15]

Unlike the Werkbund, the British design bodies were ultimately unable, both practically and emotionally, to bridge the gap between the hand and the machine. The Werkbund's emphasis upon social democracy and the importance of standardization as a means of producing cheaply for the masses had saved that particular organization from the cul-de-sac of elitism which the Council of Industrial Design encountered very early on. By the 1960s, when mass production and mass consumption had become strong forces in British society, the Council found itself overwhelmed by the quantity of products which appealed to popular taste and which offended its craft-based sensitivity and it was forced to compromise its principles in the face of this pressure from the marketplace.

In the USA, in the years following the Second World War, the design department at the Museum of Modern Art[16] in New York also took upon itself the task of defining and exhibiting 'good design' in an attempt to reform mass taste, epitomized in those years by the streamlined, finned extravagancies that crowded the US highways. It was also an attempt to put US design on the world map and to compete with the high design standards shown by countries like Sweden, Denmark and Italy.

The idea of using a design collection as a means of promoting 'good design' was in a direct line of descent from Henry Cole's (q.v.) Museum of Decorative Arts established in South Kensington in the mid-nineteenth century and which had been emulated by many other European countries, particularly Germany, around the turn of the century. When the Museum of Modern Art in New York was founded in 1929 Alfred H. Barr Jr (q.v.), its first director, had proposed 'that standards be defined and history be written for architecture and design just as for painting and sculpture',[17] and to these ends the museum both collected and exhibited architecture and design from 1923 onwards. From the start, the collection was concerned with 'mass-produced useful goods' rather than with the 'decorative arts' but tended, none the less, to concentrate on products from the traditional art industries – furniture, textiles and ceramics. Objects were selected according to two main criteria: 'quality' and 'historical significance'.

Until the early 1960s very few mechanical appliances were included in the collection because the curator of design, Arthur Drexler (q.v.), felt that 'too often their design is determined by commercial factors irrelevant, or even harmful, to aesthetic quality'.[18] Although the gap was soon to be filled, mostly by Italian and German products, the high-minded 'art'-based criteria remained the ones according to which all objects, whether traditional or new, were selected.

The MOMA collection has tended to be associated with the more European-oriented aspects of US design in this century, like the furniture of Charles Eames and Eero Saarinen (qq.v.) which was first shown at the museum in 1940 in an exhibition called Organic Design in Home Furnishings organized by Eliot Noyes (q.v.). In the 1950s Edgar Kaufman Jr (q.v.) organized a series of Good Design exhibitions at the museum which set out to persuade wholesale buyers, manufacturers and designers that design was indeed a marketable commodity. In defining 'good design' Kaufmann did little more, however, than reiterate the same Arts and Crafts values that had been voiced by so many Modern Movement spokesmen before him, emphasizing, once again, the well-known tenets of truth to materials, the unification of form and function, aesthetic simplicity, and expression of the modern age.[19] The discrepancy between good design and popular values was now wider than ever before.

By the early 1950s, an international language of 'good design' had emerged which was defined, upheld and promoted by all the design organizations whose task it was to expand trade, both at home and abroad. It was widely disseminated in periodicals, exhibitions[20] and at conferences[21] in spite of a growing awareness that alternative attitudes were emerging from other sectors of society – whether from the manufacturer with his eye on the mass market, or from the growing pressure of mass taste – and were beginning to have an influence upon the relationship of design to everyday life.

The Scandinavian Ideal

Another of the countries influenced directly by the work of the Deutscher Werkbund was Sweden. The Swedish Design Society (the Svenska Slöjdforeningen) had already been in existence for sixty years at the time of the Werkbund's formation, but had tended, throughout the nineteenth century, to stress handicrafts rather than machine production. Knowledge of German design reform came to Sweden in the early twentieth century. In 1912 Gregor Paulsson (q.v.), soon to become the society's director, visited Berlin, talked to Werkbund members and returned to Sweden, as the DIA members had to Britain, full of enthusiasm for Werkbund ideals. In 1909 the society had organized an Art and Industry Exhibition in Stockholm, emphasizing the design of workers' and one-family housing. This exhibition initiated a series of debates about the society's real role and, as a result, in 1916 it was radically reorganized on Werkbund lines.

The Swedish society also took on the role, at this time, of a kind of employment agency, putting fine artists in touch with manufacturers and vice versa, and it was as a direct result of this scheme in 1916 that the ceramics company, Gustavsberg [15], employed the artist, Wilhelm Kåge (q.v.), and, in 1916 and 1917, the glass manufacturer, Orrefors, took on the artists Simon Gate (q.v.) and Edward Hald (q.v.) respectively. Although trained as fine artists all three men were quick to learn craft techniques and were soon working on mass-produced wares, in close co-operation with the other members of the production team.

In 1917 the society organized an Exhibition of the Home in

15 Plate-making at the Gustavsberg Ceramics Works, 1895.
The artist, Gunnar Wennerberg, worked at the Gustavsberg ceramics works from 1895
to 1908. He brought the company into the modern era as far as design was concerned by
developing a light, Swedish version of the international *Jugendstil*. Although he was
primarily a decorator he also worked as a craftsman in the factory and can be seen here
making plates. Wennerberg was succeeded at Gustavsberg, in 1917, by Wilhelm Kåge
who took the company even further into the twentieth century by working on designs for
cheap, mass-produced wares aimed at the working-class market.

Stockholm which emphasized decent and inexpensive furniture that was within reach of everybody's pocket and would fit into the simplest of dwellings. Then in 1919 Gregor Paulsson (q. v.) published a pamphlet entitled *More Beautiful Everyday Things* in which he stressed that the new direction for Swedish design was to be one in which individualism was to be replaced by collectivism in the pursuit of 'a culture of form on a broad social basis'.[22]

A dual emphasis upon a simple life-style and form for the product has characterized the Swedish society's approach towards design in this century. Like the Werkbund and the DIA it pursued, after 1916, a programme of activities which included publications, educational events and exhibitions and, in the post-Second World War period, expanded its interests to include research into the ideal measurements of furniture for the small home.

Two major twentieth-century exhibitions have served to communicate Swedish ideals to the rest of the world and to demonstrate the role of the Swedish Design Society in promoting these ideals. The first was the huge Stockholm Exhibition of 1930[23] which set out to reassert the importance of humanism in a world dominated by Functionalism and tubular steel. Gunnar Asplund (q. v.) was the exhibition's chief architect and he emphasized a social programme of planning and furnishing homes for overcrowded families. The elegance of the glass, ceramics and furniture at the exhibition earned Swedish design the title of 'Swedish Grace'.

The second major Swedish exhibition, Halsinborg '55,[24] simply served to reinforce the principles expounded in 1930. The consistency and practicality of the Swedish Design Society, which changed its name to Svensk Form in the 1970s, resulted in a highly successful programme of design promotion through this century. By the 1950s Swedish design had become synonymous, internationally, with high aesthetic and social standards and had become a model for many other countries. Also, because of the relatively homogeneous nature of Swedish society, the problem of a 'taste-clash' between the 'taste-makers' and the buying public was minimized.

Both Denmark and Finland, countries with similar craft traditions to Sweden, also made the transition from hand to machine production in an equally sophisticated way with the help of their respective design promotion organizations. In Denmark the silversmith and toymaker, Kay Bojesen [16], was the moving force behind the formation of a permanent exhibition which played a role in Denmark similar to that of

16 Kay Bojesen, Grand Prix cutlery, 1938.

Bojesen's cutlery set, available in sterling silver or stainless steel, was designed in 1938 and was awarded the Grand Prix at the Milan Triennale of 1951. It is a perfect example of the design style, or movement, which is referred to as Danish Modern which is essentially a functional style, in that it abhors extraneous decoration but, at the same time, respects design ideals that derive from tradition. These three pieces are, in fact, reworkings of designs executed by Georg Jensen in 1906. Each one has been made shorter and stronger in form. The knife, in particular, has had its point shortened radically on the assumption that it is really only the point of the knife that is used.

the Museum of Modern Art in New York. Den Permanente was opened in 1931 and has, since then, selected and sold on a commercial basis, the 'best' products available from a wide cross-section of Danish goods. Selection by Den Permanente in Denmark bestows on a product the same status as a Design Centre Award in Britain or the Compasso d'Oro prize in Italy.[25]

Finnish design entered the world picture after the Second World War when it made a huge impact on the world market, largely as a result of the promotion programme that accompanied its arrival. Finland was, and still is, very conscious of the role that design plays in the export of its manufactured goods, and it aims its high-quality furniture, textiles, glass and ceramics at the top end of the international market. The marketing of Finnish design depends upon a highly sophisticated promotion system which includes an active Design Society[26] which publishes glossy magazines at regular intervals, a lively professional designers' society, and much support from those manufacturers who depend upon design for their livelihoods [34]. The Finnish phenomenon is an example of design promotion at its most effective. The homogeneity of Finnish society, the sparseness of its population and the small scale of its craft-based industries have facilitated its work.

During the last thirty years it has become common practice, in those countries which depend upon design for the viability of many of their products on the world market, to develop an accompanying network of design promotional organizations and activities as a means of sustaining that role for design. Even Japan, one of the most recent but most powerful newcomers on the international design scene, already has its own promotion system well established. The Japanese Industrial Designers' Association (JIDA) was formed in 1954 and in March 1980 the Japan Design House was established. However, Italy – the country which sells much of its furniture and domestic objects in the name of design more seriously than anywhere else in the world – depends for its success more on the promotional work of manufacturers and a very lively and effective design press than on an organized promotional body, although the Triennale Exhibition and the annual furniture salons play a vital role in securing the role of design in Italy's international trading.

As design becomes a sales factor in goods aimed at an increasing wide spectrum of the market, its role in world trade continues to expand. In parallel, the promotional system which supports it performs an increasingly vital role in establishing national design characteristics and encouraging high standards. In the international evolution of that system in this century, the Werkbund in Germany was the model organization showing the way forward to other similar groups. It was aware, very early on, that design is essential to the national and international economy, and to the image a country presents to the rest of the world. The strategies outlined by the Werkbund for promoting design at home and abroad are still those employed most frequently today and its criteria for 'good design' are still at the roots of most definitions of the concept. Equally, the ideological function of these organizations has remained constant, and their role in encouraging higher standards of taste a constant one.

Notes: Chapter 4

1   Established in 1944 by the Board of Trade of the Coalition government, the British Council of Industrial Design was set up to improve the design standards of goods at home in order to increase British exports on the world market.

2   F. McCarthy, *A History of British Design 1830–1970* (London: Allen & Unwin, 1979), p. 13.

3   N. Pevsner outlines some of the advances in German art and design education in his introduction to *Pioneers of Modern Design* (Harmondsworth, Middx: Penguin, 1960).

4   Exhibition Catalogue, *Josef Hoffmann 1870–1956: Architect and Designer* (London: Fischer Fine Art Gallery, 1977), pp. 5–6.

5   J. Campbell, *The German Werkbund: The Politics of Reform in the Applied Arts* (Princeton, NJ: Princeton University Press, 1978), p. 10.

6   The term *typenmöbel* referred to the standardized unit furniture which the Deutsche Werkstätten produced in Germany and exhibited in 1910. The idea came from the USA where it had been used extensively in the design of bookcases in the Grand Rapids furniture industry.

7   The term 'International Style' was one of the names given to the aesthetic of the Modern Movement in architecture and design. In 1932 H. R. Hitchcock and Philip Johnson organized an exhibition with that title at the Museum of Modern Art in New York, thus establishing it as a term which passed into the critical and historical vocabulary of architecture and design.

8   Exhibition Catalogue, *Zwischen Kunst und Industrie: Der Deutscher Werkbund* (Munich: Die Neue Sammlung, 1975), p. 364.

9   N. Pevsner, 'History of the DIA', in *Studies in Art, Architecture and Design. Volume 2: Victorian and After* (London: Thames & Hudson, 1968), pp. 74, 75.

10 ibid., p. 76.

11   The magazines published by the Design and Industries Association were *Design in Industry* (launched in 1932), *Design for Today* (launched in 1933) and *Trend* (launched in 1936).

12   The term 'Efficiency Style' was used to describe the functionalist aesthetic which the DIA copied from the designed objects it had seen in Germany. The British version tended, however, to be less rigid in its interpretation and, in fact, owed much to contemporary Swedish design which, unlike its German equivalent, valued tradition and natural materials.

13   In the 1940s, the British Council of Industrial Design, in conjunction with Penguin Books, published a series of books on design called 'The Things We See' as part of its propaganda campaign.

14   Exhibition Catalogue, *Britain Can Make It* (London: Council of Industrial Design, 1946), p. 37.

15   G. Russell, *The Things We See: Furniture* (Harmondsworth, Middx: Penguin, 1947), p. 27.

16   The Museum of Modern Art began being interested in, and collecting, modern design in the 1930s. It held its Machine Art exhibition in 1934 and in 1938 an Alvar Aalto (q.v.) show, and from that year onwards it demonstrated a predilection for European design ideas. Eliot Noyes (q.v.) was the Curator of Design between 1940 and 1945 and was responsible for showing the work of Charles Eames (q.v.) to the American public while E. Kaufmann Jnr (q.v.) was preoccupied, between 1950 and 1955, with establishing the criteria for 'good design' and exhibiting it in the museum.

17   A. Drexler and G. Daniel, *Introduction to Twentieth Century Design from the Collection at the Museum of Modern Art, New York* (New York: Museum of Modern Art, 1959), p. 4.

18   ibid.

19   E. Kaufmann's thoughts on 'What is good design?' were part of a longer essay called 'What is modern design?' which, along with 'What is modern interior design?', were published as *Introductions to Modern Design* by the Museum of Modern Art, New York, in 1950, as part of its Introductory Series to the Modern Arts.

20   Established in the 1920s the Triennales were three-yearly exhibitions held in Milan, first of the decorative arts, and later of design. In the postwar period they acted as an international shop-window and forum for progressive design and all the countries which were keen to promote a new, national design identity were represented there. The Triennales of 1951, 1954 and 1957 were among the most exciting in that period. The 1968 show was disrupted by student action and the Triennale was not repeated until over a decade later by which time it had become a shadow of its former self.

21   A number of international annual design events were established in the 1950s, including the Aspen Conference – set up by the ex-member of the Bauhaus, Herbert Bayer (q.v.), and Walter Paepke, head of the Container Corporation of America – and the International Congress of the Societies of Industrial Design (ICSID), which holds conferences in different centres around the world.

22 P. Sparke, 'Swedish design: myth or reality', in N. Hamilton (ed.), *Svensk Form* (London: Design Council, 1981), p. 62.

23 The Stockholm 1930 Exhibition was organized by the Svenska Slöjd-foreningen to show the architectural and design achievements of the Swedish Modern Movement to the rest of the world.

24 In 1955, the Svenska Slöjdforeningen organized an exhibition of architecture and design at Hälsinborg to restate the values of the Stockholm 1930 event and to show that Swedish Modern was still a blend of functionalism and humanism.

25 The Compasso d'Oro was a design prize awarded by the Italian department store, La Rinascente, from 1959 onwards.

26 The Finnish Society of Crafts and Design was founded in 1875 to encourage the industrial arts and work of the artisan. It was taken under the wing of the Arts and Crafts School in Helsinki which was founded in 1871. Ornamo, the Finnish Association of Designers, was founded in 1912.

PART TWO

Modern Design, 1918–1945

5

Democracies and Dictatorships

During the inter-war years, the role of design in institutions of a governmental or near governmental nature becomes more marked, raising problems of the interpretation of design as autonomous process or as a reflection of the organisation of the state.[1]

From Nationalism to Internationalism

Industrial design forms an intrinsic part of the economic and political system of the country within which it functions, and is therefore necessarily affected both by its dominant ideology and by its more specific rules and regulations.

This has been the case since the second half of the nineteenth century when the European nation-states, as we now know them, were created. With the addition of Germany, unified under Bismarck by 1871, and Italy to the already powerful states of Britain and France, Europe became dominated at that time, both politically and economically, by the concept of nationalism. The late nineteenth century was also a time of rapid increases in the level of industrialization in all these countries and of a huge expansion in world trade. Between 1900 and 1913 the world trade in manufactured goods doubled and, in spite of increasing competition from the USA, Europe was still producing the bulk of what was sold on the world market. International relations were dominated, therefore, by the twin spirits of nationalism and international competition and this directly affected the design of the secondary goods involved in international trading in the years leading up to the First World War.

This was manifested most clearly in those newly industrialized countries which felt the strongest need to assert themselves on the world market. Germany, for example, exhorted its manufacturers to produce goods which manifested a clear German style, and in Scandinavia – still at that time a group of underdeveloped countries dependent upon a mixed economy – a movement, called National Romanticism,[2] emerged in its architecture and applied arts at the turn of the century.

As an umbrella style for architecture and the applied arts, Art Nouveau, or *Jugendstil* as it was called in northern Europe, displayed a growing internationalism, encouraged by the expansion of communication systems such as mass-circulation magazines and exhibitions. At the same time, however, it also served to reinforce nationalist tendencies shown by the variants of that decorative style which evolved simultaneously in a number of different countries: in Britain, for example, Celtic forms were integrated into its short-lived Art Nouveau Movement, particularly in the work of C. R. Mackintosh (q.v.) [10]; in Barcelona, Gaudi (q.v.) made references to Catalan traditions in his architectural work; and in the Scandinavian version of Art Nouveau, folk-inspired natural imagery asserted itself in the decorative work of Gunnar Wennerberg in Sweden, Thorvald Bindesbøll in Denmark and Gallen-Kallela in Finland (qq.v.).

The historian John Roberts has described nationalism as 'the need for men to feel linked to other men at a time when market society was increasingly making them isolated beings'.[3] Whatever the psychological motivation for this tendency, nationalistic sentiment and design innovation often went hand in hand in the years leading up to the First World War. These were years of confident expansion and, in Europe, a balance in world trade terms, between the importation of primary goods and the exportation of manufactured consumer products. It was also a time of a relatively relaxed attitude, on the part of the European states, towards the control of economic affairs. Britain's *laissez-faire* economic policy of the late nineteenth century had filtered through to the rest of the Continent and, as a result, relatively few restrictions were placed on the manufacturer and on the trading of manufactured goods. With the drastic changes in the European economic system after the war, however, this freedom was quickly removed.

Another characteristic of the pre-1914 period in Europe, in political terms, was the prevalence of the democratic system of state government. This was also due to change dramatically, however, when two distinct types of political systems emerged after the First World War: the first a development of the democratic ideal but the second radically different. Whether in the form of Bolshevism, as in the USSR, or fascism, as in Germany and Italy, a number of totalitarian regimes emerged in the interwar years, bringing with them a new breed of mass dictator who radically altered the political balance both in Europe and the rest of the world.

The economic position of Europe *vis-à-vis* the USA also changed after 1914. At that time, the expansion of US industry rapidly outpaced that of Europe due to its commitment to new industries, and the position of Britain as the exporter of capital to the USA was quickly reversed. The Wall Street Crash of 1929 put an end to the short period of the renewal of world trade which had begun in 1925, and the years up until 1935 were characterized by a worldwide economic depression. This was the backcloth against which the world powers attempted to stabilize themselves politically, economically and socially. Inevitably manufacturing and design played a crucial role in that search for stability. Unlike the earlier period, however, world trade was now increasingly affected by political intervention in the years up to 1939 and design was caught in the crossfire.

One reason for the drop in world trade at this time was that manufacturing countries were unable to sell their goods abroad because they were buying too little food and raw materials from primary producers in other countries. This imbalance, exacerbated by the fact that the fascist countries, Germany and Italy, were attempting to become as self-sufficient as possible, halted the flow of the international exchange of goods. Therefore, where the consumption of goods was concerned, the emphasis lay increasingly on the domestic market for most countries, and the international competitiveness of the prewar years was curbed. A more inward-looking attitude towards manufacture and design developed on the part of many governments – a phenomenon which contrasted sharply with the growing commitment to internationalism on the part of many avant-garde architects and designers of the period. The ways in which the various governments in the different regimes of these years coped with design and the ways in which designers responded to these initiatives form an important part of the history of design in this period.

Great Britain

By the 1930s Britain had attained a high level of governmental democracy and, in spite of the economic setbacks of this period, had set about establishing the basic structure of the future welfare state. Lloyd George's Coalition government was responsible for implementing the Housing Act of 1919 which provided the British public with ample homes in the period and, in 1920, the Unemployment Insurance Act was passed which also had far-reaching effects. The Labour movement gathered strength in the 1920s, gaining short bursts of power under Ramsay MacDonald, but the dominant state control lay in the hands of the Conservatives whose rule was, for the most part, isolationist and non-extremist. The dominant economic problem which beset the government, besides those of the slump and unemployment, was foreign trade and it devoted much time and energy to the question of protective legislation. Foreign tariffs made exports a problem for Britain and this, along with the dislocation of the traditional export industries, made the whole question of foreign trade a crucial one for the government. It failed, however, to recognize the full extent to which design was an intrinsic part of that question.

For the first time since the mid-nineteenth century the question of the appearance of manufactured products as a means of improving foreign travel was confronted once again in Britain. While no concrete decisions were made and no large sums of money were put aside to sponsor British design, the idea that improved design standards could lead to an amelioration in the economic situation was at least well aired, and was given tangible expression by the work of the British Institute of Industrial Art[4] which had been set up in 1914 to raise standards of design by various means. Through the 1920s it continued to fulfil its brief, largely through exhibitions intended to raise the level of public design consciousness, but it operated for most of this time on private funding and got little or no government support.

The early 1930s witnessed a short burst of governmental activity in the form of the establishment of the Committee on Art and Industry, headed by Lord Gorell in 1931, and in 1933 the formation, by the Board of Trade, of the Council for Art and Industry, which, although poorly funded by the government, was headed by Frank Pick (q.v.), who proved to be one of the most farsighted and effective of the British design reformers of the period. The government's efforts in the field of design were, on the whole, half-hearted and insular and had little effect on the mass of the British public, on the manufacturer who was too preoccupied with retaining his existing markets to bother with design, or on the international design scene which was emerging at the numerous international exhibitions held in that decade. A few manufacturers, mostly associated with the Design and Industries Association (DIA), paid lip-service, however, to the idea of bringing in an artist or designer. The Wedgwood Company, which had a long tradition of working with fine artists, turned once again to this area, asking Eric Ravilious, among others, to decorate some of their items [17]. Efforts like this were, however, on the whole fringe activities which had no influence on goods destined for the mass market.

While on a governmental level, politics and design failed to achieve a far-reaching relationship with each other in the interwar years, on a more Utopian level, a number of ideologically based experiments took place which allied themselves with the international Modern Movement in architecture and design. The socialist principles embraced by architects and designers like Wells Coates, Serge Chermayeff, Raymond McGrath, Berthold Lubetkin (qq.v.) and others, permeated their work for mass dwellings and public buildings, such as health centres and town halls. Lacking the necessary support of state socialism the effects of their efforts were minimal in the end, failing to influence the mass environment in a substantial way. While a few other individuals, including Jack Pritchard (q.v.) and his Isokon company which put Marcel Breuer's bent plywood chairs into production, Gordon Russell (q.v.) and his furniture company in the Cotswolds, and E. K. Cole and his radio manufacturing concern, also supported the Modernist ideal they were exceptions rather than the rule.

Sweden

Where Britain failed, Sweden succeeded, however. For here, the Modern Movement managed to ally itself, for a short time at least, with the Social Democratic government which held power in Sweden in the 1930s. Although still dependent on a mixed economy, Sweden had been developing rapidly since the nineteenth century and, as a result of its iron export trade, had established itself on the world market.

Like Holland and Switzerland, Sweden maintained its strength in the First World War through neutrality and emerged from it unscathed and

17 Eric Ravilious, Travel tea-set for Wedgwood, late 1930s.

The work of the illustrator, Ravilious, with the Wedgwood ceramics company between 1936 and 1941 is an example of the successful link between art and industry in Britain in the 1930s. He also worked in furniture and glass but for Wedgwood he designed a number of vignettes which were transfer-printed, in black, on to the surfaces of a number of tableware items, and often over-painted in enamel colours. The designs show the artist's debt to early English decorated ware and his sensitivity to the relationship of two- with three-dimensions. His best-known pieces include his Coronation mug of 1937 and his Boat Race bowl of 1939. This set illustrates a variety of forms of transport, thus allying it firmly with the modern age of machines. Although designed at the end of the 1930s, the set was not put into production until 1953.

ready to face the world slump ahead. By 1939 democratic governments had gained a strong hold in Scandinavia and the development of their social services and their ideas about social and economic equality were greatly admired by many other countries.

Although the Stockholm Exhibition of 1930 took place two years before the Social Democrats came to power in Sweden it anticipated many of the reforms that that government was soon to make. Architecturally, the exhibition was dominated by Functionalism, imported from Germany and France, but softened slightly for a Swedish audience. For Swedish architects, Functionalism meant more than an imported style; it incorporated an important social element as well. Inspired by the German experiments in Frankfurt and Berlin, the Swedes took a strong interest in the practical and economic implications of large social housing programmes and, although attempts to initiate state housing loans had been thwarted in the early 1920s, the Social Housing Committee was finally appointed in 1933 and the question of housing soon became firmly established in Sweden as a social issue linked to unemployment and the birth rate.

The exhibition in Stockholm was broad in content including in its display cars, buses, handicrafts, furniture, light fittings, glass, ceramics and textiles in addition to the housing which was exhibited in the form of a small town. The social emphasis permeated the industrial design as well as the architecture and the democratic principles outlined in 1919 by Gregor Paulsson (q.v.) took on a new lease of life. 'Beauty for All', in design terms, did not mean, however, as it did in architecture, allegiance to the austere Germanic machine aesthetic but to a more humanistic style which combined tradition with innovation, made extensive use of natural materials, and employed light decoration whenever appropriate. As displayed at the Stockholm Exhibition, Bruno Mathsson's and Alvar Aalto's (qq.v.) bent-wood furniture paralleled Marcel Breuer's (q.v.) and Mies van der Rohe's experiments with tubular steel [11] but maintained, with their more organic forms and commitment to natural materials, a human element that the Germans had sacrificed. Style was not all, however, and as Paulsson stressed in 1930 'sound staple products for the purchasing masses'[5] were to be emphasized at the exhibition. Economic reality, both in the contexts of production and consumption, was also to be considered the major component in his socially oriented approach to design.

After 1931 the exhibition architects, among them Gunnar Asplund, Sven Markelius, Uno Ahren, Eskil Sundahl (qq.v.) and others, had a significant impact on the Swedish environment, particularly in the new estates, shops and factories on which they were employed to work. The social gains achieved in architecture and planning in the 1930s were also paralleled in design, and the leading ceramics and glass companies, among them Gustavsberg, Rorstrand and Orrefors, began to mass produce the work of their leading artists and craftsmen, while, in furniture, designers like G. A. Berg and Josef Frank (qq.v.) developed a strongly humanistic style. Unlike Britain, during this period Sweden took a positive attitude towards the relationship between high design standards and world trade participating in all the major international exhibitions of the 1930s, including Paris in 1937[6] and New York in 1939,[7] thereby earning for itself a highly respected and highly envied reputation for what one critic described as 'Swedish Modern: a movement towards sanity in design'.[8]

The USA

Democracy and design were more closely linked, both practically and ideologically, in Sweden than in Britain but, in both cases, innovation was essentially limited to the fields of architecture and the applied arts. It was left to the USA to encourage similar developments in the products of the new, technically based industries. The US government took few initiatives, however, in the design area, preferring simply to encourage manufacturing and commerce and to leave them to deal with design when, and if, it arose. It had sent a delegation to the Paris Exhibition of Decorative Arts of 1925,[9] at which the USA had refused to exhibit because it lagged so far behind Europe. A report was written as a result which pointed this out, but no subsequent action was taken. In 1920 a study had been made of the state of the industrial arts and of industrial arts education in the USA, funded by the National Society for Vocational Education, but its scope had been limited to the field of the applied arts. Moreover, its effects were minimal and it failed to convince the federal government that it should support industrial arts education.[10] The US government limited its action to imposing large tariffs on trade and watching carefully over the balance of imports and exports. It remained committed to quantity rather than quality and to technological advance rather than aesthetic experimentation. The need for design, or 'styling', [20] was seen as a vital ingredient in the production and sale of goods in the competitive years of the 1930s, but

18 Dr Herman Gretsch, form 1382 for the Arzberg
Porcelain Works, 1931.
Gretsch, who trained initially as an engineer, produced this simple, elegant, white tea-set
for Arzberg. It subsequently became a 'classic' and remained in production for many
years, winning a gold medal at the sixth Triennale in 1936 and another at the Paris
Exhibition of the following year. This tea-set was a very early example of the idea of
'good form' which dominated German design thinking in the postwar period – although its
silhouette was softer than the severe rectilinear shapes which characterized so many
products from both the craft and the mechanical sector after 1945. Arzberg was, with
such companies as the Jenaer and Lausitzer Glassworks, among those firms which
continued to manufacture modern 'functional' products during the Hitler years in
Germany.

it was left to manufacturers to find creative individuals who could fulfil their requirements. This situation gave birth to the professional industrial designer, a product of expediency rather than idealism.

While a number of other democratic states supported design movements in the interwar years, their commitment being an important component of the effort to re-establish foreign trade, it was the totalitarian states of that period – whether fascist or Bolshevik – that exercised the greatest degree of state control over their economies and where design was totally dependent upon sponsorship from the state.

Germany

In fascist Germany of the 1920s and 1930s there was a certain degree of support for modern design. Without it Hitler would have been unable to develop his programme of rearmament as in Germany rational production and rational form were inextricably linked. The high concentration of German industry which had developed after the First World War was crucial to Nazi economic policy and the idea that Hitler was committed to the *Volk* community was only part of the total picture. He was also determined that Germany should become increasingly self-sufficient and to this end he encouraged the use of new materials in products as substitutes for the traditional, imported ones. This, in turn, implied a new rather than a folk-inspired aesthetic in manufactured products. Within the framework of the Third Reich, 'modern' designers like the Bauhaus-trained Wilhelm Wagenfeld and Herman Gretsch (qq.v.) continued to work producing, among other things, simple, white ceramic ware for the Arzberg company [18].

German government organizations, like the Standards Commission and the State Efficiency Board, strongly influenced by the scientific management movement in the USA, did much to encourage the rational, and therefore modern, approach to manufacture and design at this time, and wherever the defence programme was involved design, in terms of the rationalization of production, was given much attention. This, in turn, affected the civil sector in a number of instances, like the advances made in transport which grew directly out of Hitler's motorization programme which involved the construction of an efficient road system throughout Germany and the development of appropriate forms of transport for it. One such development was the state-

19 Ferdinand Porsche, Volkswagen Beetle, 1936–7.

The Beetle, so-called because of its resemblance to that insect, was designed by the streamlining expert, Porsche, as a 'people's car' which would fulfil Adolf Hitler's desire for a small, inexpensive vehicle, suitable for use on the German autobahns. Although it was prototyped in the 1930s it was not mass produced until after the war. The mass-production methods at the Wolfsburg plant were US in origin and the car was a simply assembled, highly standardized product. This picture shows a row of the very earliest models which had no rear window and a dramatic rear vent covering the engine. Britain, France and Italy all developed their equivalents of the small car in the 1930s – the Austin Seven, the Citroën deux chevaux and the Fiat Topolino – all of which were equally radical design solutions characterized by a commitment to 'function' rather than 'styling' where their aesthetic was concerned.

sponsored Volkswagen car which had been initiated by Ferdinand Porsche (q.v.) in the last years of the Weimer Republic but was encouraged subsequently by the Third Reich [19]. The Volkswagen's development was firmly integrated into National Socialist Party policy and it came to stand for the Nazi commitment to industrial modernity. Among the many design restrictions imposed on the Volkswagen was one taken from the *Rules Governing Application for a Volkswagen Savings Bank* of 1938 which stated that: 'The Volkswagen should be produced in a deep blue-grey finish'. [11]

Hitler did not differentiate the idea of design from the technical industrial and economic problems that beset him in his efforts to expand Germany's economy and defence systems and yet, by promoting these areas, he sponsored a programme of modern design, albeit by implication only.

Italy

Whereas Hitler had completely outlawed the Modern Movement in its architectural manifestations because of his belief that the style represented left-wing political tendencies, in Italy Mussolini was less dogmatic about its viability in a fascist regime. The Modern Movement, referred to in Italy as 'Rationalism', [12] was imported into Italy in 1926 and it was under its umbrella that many of the new experiments in architecture and design took place in the interwar years. Its early manifestations were limited to exhibitions, but from the beginning its supporters were conscious that they had to justify it to a fascist government if it was to survive and spread.

Italy was the first European fascist state to emerge in the interwar years. Mussolini first entered Italian politics in 1919 and by 1928 fascism had become the official state doctrine. Many critics and architects considered Rationalism to be the style best suited to a fascist regime and it is clear that they set out to attempt to persuade Mussolini that it was the right style for his government. He remained unconvinced, however, displaying a personal preference, like Hitler, for the Classical style which had more obviously appropriate authoritarian and imperial qualities. Many of the buildings constructed during his regime were, in fact, compromise solutions, incorporating both Rationalist and neo-Classical features, and classified as 'Novecento'.

A few Rationalist buildings were built directly under the auspices of

Mussolini, notably those designed by the architects Pagano and Terragni (qq.v.). The latter was responsible for the famous Casa del Fasci, constructed in Como in the early 1930s and containing pieces of tubular steel furniture, also designed by the architect. Other Rationalist architects, among them Mucchi and Levi-Montalcini (qq.v.), also worked on tubular-steel furniture during this period.

Mussolini's sponsorship of the industrial complexes which had developed in Italy during the 1920s under US influence also helped to support modern industrial design. Mussolini's insistence on self-reliance meant that he encouraged, and in fact subsidized, the importation of new production machinery from abroad. A few industrial projects, like Fiat's little Topolino (Mickey Mouse) car,[13] were given direct state support. Many of the 1930s experiments in modern industrial design in Italy, like Figini and Pollini's (q.v.) radiophonograph of 1933 – a radical innovative product with a transparent perspex body which showed its mechanical components – remained, however, in the prototype stage as industry was not generally interested in modern products in this period. It continued to take its cues from its existing market and conservatism generally won the day.

During the interwar period as a whole, however, governments had begun to show an interest in design, although the concept was understood in a number of different ways. Sometimes it was considered simply as a factor within general technical advancement, sometimes as an aesthetic factor in sales, sometimes as part of a programme of social improvement. The totalitarian states tended towards the former, more functional approach where all means were directed to a single end; socially oriented democracies saw it as a necessary factor in the quality of communal life, as well as a necessary aspect of trade; while democracies based on advanced capitalism, like the USA, considered it as predominantly commercial. These perspectives were inevitably mingled together in reality in varying proportions but, in all the industrial countries of the Western world, design was a subject for serious consideration at governmental level and, in some cases, for legislation.

Design also played a very particular role in the development of post-revolutionary Russia where the links between the state and the projects of designers like Tatlin, Rodchenko and El Lissitzky (qq.v.) were very strong. This was a rare and temporary instance of radicalism in design coinciding with political radicalism, and the work of these designers in graphics, constructions for propaganda purposes, workers' clothing, stage design, items for workers' housing and other material adjuncts of the Bolshevik Revolution, expressed both a new aesthetic and the new ideological base for Russian society. By the early 1930s, however, this commitment on the part of the Bolsheviks to artistic avant-gardism had been replaced by state-controlled Socialist Realism and the Russian modern design movement came to a sudden close.

There have been, throughout this century, a few instances when innovatory design has been used to radical political ends. For example, the commitment of the Italian Futurists[14] to fascism before the First World War and, in the case of graphic design, the work of the poster and propaganda artists in the Cuban Revolution and in the student uprisings in Paris in 1968 show how that medium can be used to support and promote a particular political ideology. In general, however, there has been relatively little direct interference by the state where three-dimensional design is concerned. In most cases, the policy has been one of sponsoring design education and of generally encouraging the design component within manufacturing and trade as part of the general economic well-being of a country. Few direct initiatives have been made, however, either to direct it or to specify its function. Equally, with the exception of a number of Modern Movement protagonists and the designers associated with the Russian Revolution, relatively few designers have defined their role as politically active and have tended to work within the context of the political and economic framework which sustains them.

Notes: Chapter 5

1 *Image and Process: Design History and Material Culture – Aspects of European Design between the Wars*, Working Papers, AAH Conference, London, March 1983, p. 2.
2 Scandinavian National Romanticism was a movement which manifested itself predominantly in Finland and Denmark and took the form of a kind of regional Art Nouveau which looked back to traditional forms and motifs for inspiration.
3 J. Roberts, *Europe 1880–1945* (London: Longman, 1967), p. 65.
4 The British Institute of Industrial Art (BIIA) was originally conceived by the Board of Trade in 1914 to organize British sections of British decorative arts exhibitions. It was created officially in 1920 with the brief to both raise the standards of British industrial design and the level of

public taste. In the early 1920s it acted mainly as an information centre but, due to a decrease in governmental financial support, became less important later.

5   E. Rudberg, 'Accepting', *Form*, vol. 2, no. 3 (Stockholm, 1980), p. 32.

6   The Paris Exhibition of 1937 was international in scope. Among the most impressive displays were those from the USA and Sweden, both of which presented a new image of modern design.

7   The New York World's Fair of 1939 was held in Flushing Meadow, in Queens. It was a homage to US consultant design and to the streamlined aesthetic. W. D. Teague (q.v.) masterminded much of it and Loewy, Dreyfuss and Bel Geddes (qq.v.) were all well represented. Foreign exhibits were also represented, including one from Sweden.

8   The term 'Swedish Modern', subtitled 'a movement towards sanity in design', was coined by a critic at the New York World's Fair in 1939 who was impressed by the simplicity of the Swedish exhibit compared with the US streamlined extravaganzas which dominated the exhibition.

9   The Exposition des Arts Decoratifs was held in Paris in 1925. This exhibition gave birth to the term 'Art Deco' and put that decorative French style on view to the rest of the world. There were also a number of exhibits from other countries, including Sweden and Britain, but the USA was not included, as the Americans felt that they were not advanced enough in the decorative arts area. Instead they sent a group to observe the exhibition and report back on what they saw there.

10 C. R. Richards was commissioned by the US government to look into the facilities provided in the USA for training in the applied arts. He published his findings in a book called *Art in Industry* (New York: Macmillan, 1922) which outlined the state of the applied arts at that time.

11 *Image and Process*, cit. at n.1, p. 36.

12 The term 'Rationalism' was used by Italian critics to describe Italy's version of the Modern Movement which it imported, in the mid-1920s, directly from Germany and France. As in those countries, it was essentially an architectural movement, but it also influenced furniture and interior design.

13 The little Fiat Topolino (Mickey Mouse) or Fiat Standard 500 was designed in the 1930s by Dante Giacosa. It was the first small Italian car and filled the same role for Italy as the little Citroën 2CV did for France and the VW Beetle for Germany in that decade. It was not until 1948 that Alec Issigonis (q.v.) designed his Morris Minor, the British equivalent of these small cars.

14 Italian Futurism was a movement in painting, poetry, music and architecture which, in the years 1914–17, provided images of a dynamic, machine-dominated environment. While the poet Marinetti was its chief spokesman, Boccioni, Carra and Balla were the best-known Futurist painters, and Sant' Elia the architect associated with the group. Later, in the 1930s, there was a second wind of Italian Futurism which this time focused its energies on interior design and ceramics, as well as on the fine arts.

6

The Industrial Designer

The modern industrial designer has both a technical and a cultural background and a sense of the public into the bargain and it is these three things which qualify him to perform his job of creating sales.[1]

This description of the modern industrial designer, written in 1936, focuses on his synthetic character, explaining that he is neither just an artist, nor simply an engineer, nor a market researcher but rather a combination of all three. It goes on to say that the world of commerce both created him and justifies his existence.

By the mid-1930s this definition of the designer for industry had become generally understood internationally. The debate about the relationship of the artist to industry, which had been raging since the mid-nineteenth century, was more or less resolved, primarily as a result of the situation in the USA where it was events rather than words that finally forced the professional industrial designer to emerge from his chrysalis. The intensity of competition during the Depression years had caused manufacturers to develop increasingly sophisticated sales tactics and, to this end, advertising was extended into 'styling'[2] as a means of selling the products of the new industries in an increasingly stagnant home market. Special skills were needed to provide this new service and these were located, by the manufacturers with the assistance of advertising agencies, in a set of individuals who, although visually trained, also had first-hand knowledge of the commercial world through early careers in areas such as advertising, stage design and shop-window display. The special economic circumstances of this alliance between art and industry were responsible for the creation, within a decade, of a fully fledged industrial design profession in a country which, hitherto, had paid relatively little attention to the question of design. Lengthy discussions on the same subject had already taken place during the previous century in many other countries, notably Britain and Germany, but neither country had succeeded in evolving an industrial design profession. Behren's (q.v.) work for AEG [13] certainly resembled that of the later consultant designer but his architectural background prevents him from being classified as an industrial designer in the professional sense. The same can be said about many of the British architects of the late nineteenth century who were associated with the Arts and Crafts Movement[3] and with Art Manufacturing.

In my book *Consultant Design: The History and Practice of the Designer in Industry* I wrote that 'Throughout the nineteenth-century, the term "designer" was surrounded by a mist of vagueness and ambiguity. As a simple job description it was applied to fine artists, architects, craftsmen, engineers, inventors, technicians, and lowly employees of companies'[4] and it is within this confusion – both semantic and actual – that the problem of the designer arises. Although by the end of the nineteenth century designing for industry had, as an activity, become widespread, as a job description for an individual or a group of individuals it was still not clearly defined. There were many reasons for this. The process of separating designing from manufacturing had been a gradual one and the remnants of craft activity still hung over production thus, although a manufacturing system of divided labour had been a reality for at least two centuries, specific job descriptions had not yet been fully defined. The dominance of the apprenticeship system had meant that until the advent of mechanization everybody involved in production possessed craft skills, and it was only with the abolition of the guild system that both unskilled workers and others with new skills began to emerge. Prior to mechanized mass production the job of designing, that is, of 'making designs or patterns for the manufacturer or constructor',[5] which is clearly distinguishable from that of 'making' a product, was therefore assigned to anybody in the production process, from the maker himself down to the humblest draughtsman. With the advent of machine-tools and mechanization, designing became a team activity, however, combining, say, the work of the draughtsmen, the tool-makers and the production engineers. In the textile industry, for instance, the 'putter-on',[6] who transferred the pattern on to the roller for printing, played an important part in that design process, while in the ceramics industry the 'modeller'[7] performed a parallel task.

The numerous reasons for the anonymity of the designer in the nineteenth century included the fear that a competitive company would steal a designer by offering him more money, copying, modifying designs from pattern-books, and using lowly employees as designers.

It was, however, with the growing realization on the part of the manufacturers of the saleability of 'art' in consumer goods aimed at the higher end of the market, that the idea of the artist in industry finally gelled. In Europe this phenomenon was limited, however, to those craft-based industries – ceramics, glass, textiles, furniture, metal-work, and so on – which had an 'applied art' tradition, and it was in this sector that the designer began to acquire an individual identity within the contexts both of production and sales. Where the latter was concerned this new individualism highlighted him as a provider of 'beauty', of implied social status, and hence of added desirability, to the product. The commercial idea of using named designers as a means of individualizing mass-produced consumer products has earned them what professional and social status they have and caused them to become, in a number of countries, increasingly less and less anonymous.

Art and Industry in the USA

When the USA created the industrial designer it was with an eye to sales rather than production, but the goods involved were no longer those referred to collectively as 'the applied or decorative arts'. In the years after the First World War, the USA's strength lay in the new industries – in the production of goods which depended upon advances in science and technology for their very existence. As a writer in *Fortune* magazine of 1934 explained: 'Now it was the turn of washing machines, furnaces, switchboards, and locomotives. Who was to design them?'[8]

Clearly designers, or 'form-makers', had existed in the new US industries back in the nineteenth century but little is known about them. Anonymity prevailed at that time and it was not until the late 1920s, when consultant designers began to set up their offices in New York, that named individuals began to emerge and the design profession began to mould itself. The growing need for increased product elaboration as a sales ploy led appliance manufacturers to seek out individuals who could, in the words of the designer Harold Van Doren (q.v.), 'make things irresistible'.[9] It was also Van Doren who described the designer's task at that time as being to 'enhance the product's desirability in the eyes of the purchaser through increased convenience, better adaptability of form to function; through a shrewd

20 W. D. Teague, National cash register, 1935.
Teague's streamlined design for the National Cash Register Company is pictured here surrounded by its predecessors. The plain steel surfaces of the former contrast sharply with the decorated body-shells of the earlier models which are either embossed with complex patterns or covered in wood grain. Typically Teague has transformed the cash register into a modern machine, abandoning in the process its earlier associations with the traditional applied arts. His design has a smooth, unified body-shell, the product of new metal-manufacturing processes, a metallic grey finish and a number of mechanical innovations, including the fact that the cash total popped up in windows on both sides of the machine. The inclusion of the name 'National' on the actual product emphasizes the links between industrial design and advertising in this period.

knowledge of consumer psychology and through the aesthetic appeal of form, colour and texture'.[10]

The emphasis on consumer psychology gives a clue to the roots from which US industrial design has grown, that is, advertising. Since the late eighteenth century, advertising had accompanied the development of mass production in the USA and in the 1860s advertising agencies, including J. Walter Thompson (q.v.), had been created to act as the middle men between the manufacturer and the advertiser. It was to these agencies that manufacturers went first in their search for designers and the individuals they found – among them Walter Dorwin Teague [20], Norman Bel Geddes, Raymond Loewy [21], Henry Dreyfuss [22], Donald Deskey, Russel Wright, John Vassos, Egmont Arens, Lurelle Guild, Joseph Sinel, George Sakier (qq.v.) and others – nearly all shared the same background experience of having worked in the commercial world, particularly within advertising. Teague, for example, like Bel Geddes and Loewy, had earned himself a reputation in advertising illustration before turning to industrial design, and Donald Deskey had headed an advertising agency at one point in his varied career. Most of them had received a visual training and had decided to apply their skills to the world of commerce. When Teague decided in 1926, for example, to specialize in industrial design all he had to do was to add the words 'industrial design' to his headed paper and continue to operate from the same office in Madison Avenue from which he had offered his services as an illustrator.[11]

That such people chose to work as 'consultants' rather than as 'in-house' designers[12] was a common decision and had several implications. It meant that the new industrial designers were generalists rather than specialists and that they could function as free agents, subcontracting work when necessary. They acted, for much of the time, as middlemen between the client and specialists like draughts-men, model-makers, market researchers, or engineers, and performed the function of businessmen in a new guise, spending most of their time at board meetings with clients, supervising design and development work, and collating market surveys. At the same time they also became public heroes, filling the pages of popular magazines which even described what they had for breakfast. They thus soon became symbols of the modern age, pointing to the future at a time when the economic situation was less than optimistic.

The work and career of Norman Bel Geddes typifies those of many other industrial designers in that period: his background in commercial

21 Raymond Loewy, fountain dispenser for the Coca Cola Company, 1947.
Loewy's fountain dispenser was part of a scheme his design team worked on for the Coca
Cola Company just after the Second World War (which did not include the logo). This
product characterizes Loewy's restrained and elegant form of streamlining which he
applied to a number of other objects in the period including the Studebaker automobile.
From a design point of view, its most interesting features include the way in which the
handle on the top is integrated into the line of the product by means of a small recess
below it – a detail which was also used in fridge and automobile handles – the lack of ugly
seams to break the flow of the body-shell surface, the simple and easily comprehensible
operating knob and the use of chrome to highlight the sculptural form of the object. As
part of a corporate scheme, this product was an integral part of the Coca Cola Company's
advertising programme as the logo on its side indicates.

22 Henry Dreyfuss, thermos pitcher with tray for American Thermos Bottle Company, 1935.
This little pitcher, which is 7¼ in. high, is one of Dreyfuss's most sculptural designs. It owes much to the curves of streamlining but also to the abstract forms of a sculptor like Archipenko. The pitcher is made of eminently modern materials, that is, enamelled metal and glass with chrome plating, and the tray is painted plastic. This design is mid-1930s Streamform at its best and shows the contribution that the new consultant designers made to the everyday US environment in those years.

art, his business-like approach to design, and his commitment to an expressive aesthetic that characterized US industrial design in the 1930s, were all elements in the formula. Bel Geddes started his career as a portrait painter, then moved to poster design followed by stage design – at which he had been highly successful in the 1920s working on sets on Broadway for, among others, *The Miracle* and Dante's *Inferno* – on to shop-window display and, finally, to industrial design. He justifies his final metamorphosis in his book *Horizons* of 1932 as follows: 'It is more important that I should be working at something that interests me, that is, of the present, such as the automobile, the airplane, the steamship, the railway car, architecture and furniture, than it is for me to keep working in the theater merely because I have spent 15 years doing so.'[13]

The real reason for the transition was, however, undoubtedly due to financial pressures, for industrial designers were, at that time, offered very high fees whereas income from stage design was unreliable. Henry Dreyfuss explained his own transition from stage to industrial design by the fact that he wanted to get married and have a family, and that only the latter profession could provide a secure enough financial background.

Bel Geddes set up his industrial design office in 1926 and, with a skeleton staff around him, started work on projects for, among others, the Toledo Scale Company, the Graham-Paige automobile company, J. Walter Thompson and the Simmons Bed Company, while working simultaneously on visionary projects for transport objects (cars, railways, ships and aeroplanes) for which there was no hope of realization. The Philco Radio Company was among his clients in the early years, and his report on that project revealed much about the way in which he approached a design brief. His work on it was presented as follows: 'The client's problem', which he described as being one of a lack of taste in questions of proportion and detail; 'Research', in which he reported his discovery from market research that 'despite the Depression, 1931 could be a record year in radio sales'; 'The client's restrictions', including the fact that the existing chassis had to be used and that the radio had to be acoustically resonant to frequencies of between 50 and 600 cycles; 'Design approach', in which he reported his decision to build the chassis, speaker and baffle into a unified whole and finish the exterior so that it would blend with the furnishings of any home of decent taste; and, finally, 'Result', where he described the four models he proposed, namely, the Highboy, the Lowboy, the Lazy-boy and the radio-phonograph combination. Bel Geddes recounts that when these models were first displayed before Philco distributors they brought forth a spontaneous cheer, and that by the end of 1932 Philco had captured 50 per cent of all US radio sales, undoubtedly in his eyes at least the result of successful design work.[14]

The detail in the report on the Philco project was typical of Bel Geddes's highly systematic approach to office management; everything was carefully filed and catalogued, and he believed that all he had to sell was 'time, ideas, advice and experience'.[15] This attitude was shared by most of his colleagues at the time. The majority of industrial designers enjoyed considerable material success in the 1930s and by the end of that decade their influence had been felt on a vast cross-section of products that filled US homes, particularly the kitchen. It was, however, at the New York World's Fair of 1939 that they were finally given free scope to express their imaginative powers to the full. Teague explained that 'At the fair the profession is coming into its own and emerging for the first time in its major, basic role as the interpreter of industry to the public',[16] and it was in the context of that 'fantasy' environment that they gave free rein to their visual creativity, expressed in huge temporary buildings and impressive displays for the motor companies.

A professional body for US designers was not formally established until 1944 and, by the end of that decade, their impact was in fact beginning to fade as their work was becoming too expensive for the average manufacturer. Although, in the USA, they began to be replaced in the postwar period by salaried, 'in-house' specialist designers, they nonetheless provided the inspiration for the rest of the industrial world to organize an industrial design profession along similar lines and to start looking seriously at the design of the new, technical products, as well as that of the traditional, applied arts.

Alternative definitions of the modern designer in industry also presented themselves in a number of other countries. In Scandinavia, for example, the craftsman-designer[17] permeated the ranks of the traditional art industries; and for a short time, in the 1950s, Britain tried to emulate this particular model as a means of making a smooth transition from craft to industrial production. Due to a total lack of training facilities for the industrial designer in Italy after the war it was left to the architect to venture into the fields of interior and industrial design. Lack of funds for architectural projects and the crying need on the part of manufacturers for designers produced that hybrid individual, the consultant architect-designer, who became a strong force in postwar Italian culture. In West Germany, the 'designer' had strong affiliations with the 'engineer' and tended to work more anonymously as a result. This was also the case in Japan where the team was much more important than the individual. Different approaches such as these made it difficult for the industrial designer to be identified with one single image in the post Second World War period. Instead, he took on a number of alternative identities, depending on the context within which he was generated.

The British Consultant Designer

While Italy did not set up its design professional body until 1956, Britain had been quick off the mark in that respect, having established the 'Society of Industrial Artists' in 1930. [18] The early line-up of the society consisted, however, almost entirely of designers from the graphic and exhibition fields, and it was not until the years following the Second World War that an indigenous consultant industrial design profession developed in Britain to parallel that of the USA. When the profession was finally established it modelled itself consciously on the US example. The Design Research Unit (DRU)[19] was formed in 1942 as part of the general reaction to Britain's urgent need to increase its exports and to the recognition that design was an important aspect of sales where manufactured consumer goods were concerned [23]. The DRU defined itself as a co-operative and its constitution consisted of a central panel of architects, designers and engineers working in permanent consultation under the chairmanship of Herbert Read (q.v.). Unlike its US counterparts, however, the DRU emphasized packaging and exhibitions and ignored the area of industrial design proper, that is, the design of appliances and technical products. This was still, at this time, the territory of the engineer and 'styling', as it called the work of the US industrial designer, was frowned upon by the British design establishment because of its 'vulgar' aesthetic and commercial implications. Raymond Loewy (q.v.) had, in fact, established a London office in the mid-1930s and a number of Britain's future industrial designers did their apprenticeships there, but it was not until the 1940s that British designers, like Richard Lonsdale-Hands (q.v.), set up their own consultant offices. The bulk of the freelance British designers' energies were, however, dedicated to graphic design and its related

23 Design Research Unit, 'Birth of an Egg-Cup: What Shall the Egg-Cup Look Like?', Britain Can Make It Exhibition, 1946.

This display, designed by Misha Black and Milner Gray of the DRU, was designed to explain the role of the industrial designer. By showing a wide range of different egg-cups – from a ceramic Humpty-Dumpty children's cup, to a simple, streamlined plastic example – it showed how varied design solutions could be even though they all derived from the same brief, which was to hold an egg, the size of which was determined only by the hen that laid it. The Surreal nature of the display and the didactic tone of the message were common in postwar Britain and derived from the work that many designers, including the DRU members, had undertaken for the Ministry of Information during the war.

fields. This was perpetrated in the work of the British design consultancies founded in the 1950s, 1960s and 1970s, and which established an international reputation for themselves in those decades, among them Pentagram and Wolff Olins (qq.v.).

Thus while they embraced industrial design at their periphery they concentrated most of their energies on corporate identity programmes and other graphics-related projects. For the most part, Britain's industrial designers remained anonymous employees of mass-manufacturing industry and received little of the glory that had been bestowed on their US counterparts in the previous decade.

With the increasing emphasis on design as part both of production and, more significantly as time went on, of sales, the status of designers rose noticeably, both within the hierarchy of industry and in the eyes of society as a whole. They are, however, still very young professionals and their skills and functions are still being defined. There are many grey areas still to be clarified in, for example, the education of designers, their job descriptions and their codes of professional practice. While it is clear that industry and society need the specialist skills of, for example, automotive designers, product designers, furniture designers, textile designers, fashion designers, graphic designers, and so on, there are still many areas of overlap among these specializations and a need for generalists who can operate in several of these fields simultaneously. Thus, there is as great a need for the consultant as for staff designers, and as much emphasis on anonymity as upon individualism.

It may emerge that the word 'designer' is in fact too general a term to be very useful in the future. Its current application, in advertising, to any commodity that is in need of 'added desirability'[20] has stretched its semantic limits even further, and the international application of the word is increasing rapidly, carrying with it connotations of 'high style', 'high fashionability' and 'high quality'. However, the gap between the appropriation of the term by product promotions and its original meaning as a job description is enormous. Many companies have created design managers, but there are still numerous problems of communication between the visually trained designer and the management which has usually had a technical or business education. Another traditional gap in communication is that between the designer and the engineer who tend to speak in very different languages.

As industrial society develops and changes, so the nature and function of designers will change with it, but their final contribution will lie in their ability to adapt and modify their function accordingly. With the advent of new technologies, for instance, their traditional skills will become less and less relevant. Drawing and modelling, for example, the traditional communicative and expressive means of the industrial designer, will be largely superseded by computer-aided design and designers will find themselves involved increasingly with the development of software. In the words of Raymond Loewy: 'The designer is a nimble creature and a dependable one. Flexibility is his most valuable asset.'[21]

Notes: Chapter 6

1 P. McConnell, 'SID – American hallmark of design integrity,' *Art and Industry*, vol. 47 (1949), no. 4, p. 84.

2 The term 'styling' came to be used, from the 1930s onwards, as an alternative to 'industrial design' in products where the design work was involved with the surface or body-shell only. It came to imply superficiality and strong links with manufacturing industry and, as such, was used by European critics of the US industrial design movement to condemn what they saw as its shallowness and overt commercialism.

3 The term 'Arts and Crafts Movement' describes the work and ideas of the group of individuals who, working in Britain in the latter half of the nineteenth century, were inspired by William Morris (q.v.). Exponents of Arts and Crafts ideals include C. R. Ashbee (q.v.), C. F. A. Voysey, Mackmurdo, Walter Crane, and others. The movement had widespread international influence and became the basis, ironically, for most European ideas about industrial design in the first half of this century. It also gave birth to the more craft-oriented tendency which had existed in parallel in many countries during this century.

4 P. Sparke, *Consultant Design: The History and Practice of the Designer in Industry* (London: Pembridge Press), p. 7.

5 The *Oxford Shorter Dictionary* defines the designer in this way and claims that, in this sense, the word entered the English language in 1662.

6 Sparke, *Consultant Design*, p. 8.

7 ibid.

8 'Both fish and fowl', *Fortune*, no. 2 (February 1934), p. 40.

9 H. Van Doren, *Industrial Design: A Practical Guide* (New York: McGraw-Hill, 1940), p. 22.

10 ibid., p. 37.

11 A biographical article about W. D. Teague (q.v.) called 'The industrial classicist' appeared in the *New Yorker*, December 1934.

12 'Consultant designer' is the term used to describe the independent, freelance designer who gives his services to a number of different manufacturing industries simultaneously. 'In-house design' describes the work of a designer who is in the regular employment of a single

manufacturer and who works on company premises. He is also called a 'staff designer'.

13 B. Geddes, *Horizons* (New York: republished by Dover, 1977), p. 5.
14 The information on this project by Bel Geddes (q.v.) came from the file (199) on the Philco Company which is lodged in the Bel Geddes archives in the Humanities Index in the University of Texas at Austin.
15 ibid., File 940 on Office Procedure.
16 W. D. Teague, 'Building the world of tomorrow. The New York World's Fair', *Art and Industry*, no. 4 (April 1939), p. 127.
17 The concept of the 'craftsman-designer' is best exemplified by the Swedish examples, that is, those men who applied their craft backgrounds to the problem of industrial production and worked on both one-off and mass-produced projects, in studios within the factories who employed them. This approach resulted in a design aesthetic which respected craft traditions but also implied an image of modernity at the same time.
18 The Society of Industrial Artists was founded in Britain in 1930 as a professional society for designers. Through the 1930s it emphasized the work of graphic and exhibition design but turned later to industrial design. In 1965 it was renamed the Society of Industrial Artists and Designers.
19 The Design Research Unit was the first British consultant design team. Set up in 1942 by Herbert Read (q.v.), Milner Gray and Misha Black it quickly made links with manufacturers and has produced corporate identity schemes for, among others, Dunlop, BOAC and British Rail.
20 L. Wolf, *Idéologie et production: le design* (Paris: Editions Anthropos, 1972), p. 10.
21 R. Loewy, 'Selling through design', in J. Gloag (ed.), *Industrial Art Explained* (London: Allen & Unwin, 1946), p. 74.

7

From Mass Taste to Mass Style

The eccentricities of the intellectual in one generation have a way of becoming the accepted standard for the discriminating in the next . . .[1]

In his statement of 1953 Paul Reilly (q.v.), soon to become the director of the British Design Council, was expressing a heartfelt belief that taste values move automatically downwards through society. This view was, however, quickly becoming an outdated one. It stemmed from the period before mass production and mass consumption when taste had been controlled by a landed and intellectual aristocracy whose values, in that socially stable context, had provided the model for the rest of society to emulate. In modern society it has become increasingly difficult to isolate such a simple pattern of social behaviour and, as a result, the question of taste and its dissemination have become both highly problematic and increasingly central to discussions about culture and design.

Today, two fundamental approaches towards taste are in common currency. While the Victorian concept of 'taste' as a synonym for 'good taste' has moved into this century and is frequently expressed, it is also understood simply as a component of the complex interaction between society and the material world.[2] This latter model is the preserve of the sociologist who discusses taste in terms of social class and available options without value judgements. Whichever stance is adopted, there is little doubt that taste needs to be approached from numerous perspectives and that social, economic, psychological *and* aesthetic data are all needed to explain its complex manifestations.

Taste is created by numerous means in today's society, both on a large scale, by the mass media, design propaganda, exhibitions, etc., and on a more local scale by what is available in shops and the influence of individuals within the same social, or peer, group. In analysing the role of taste values within the design of consumer goods, it is the visual style of the object that provides a starting-point as that is how taste is identified and discussed. Through style, objects and society communicate with each other; and through the manipulation of style, the designer plays an essential role in satisfying the tastes of his markets. While the socio-economic framework of production and consumption actually determines mass taste, style is its visible manifestation.

The emergence of a recognizable mass taste can be dated to the moment when mass consumption became a reality in the early nineteenth century in Britain. This was not precipitated by a sudden break with the past but rather by the changes of scale which occurred when industrialization made more things available to a larger sector of society. More people bought things instead of inheriting them, making them, or doing without them, and the nature of the market altered dramatically as a result.

It was not until the early twentieth century, however, that both in Europe and the USA the mass manufacturers took over the business not merely of meeting new demands but of creating them on a large scale and, to this end, the 'taste-makers' took to working through the mass-communications media. This phenomenon, which had its roots in the last century, is perhaps the most significant development in the creation of twentieth-century mass taste and marks the point when the first truly popular, mass-produced modern styles began to have an international impact.

With the increasing technical possibilities of mass production and the expansion of mass consumption to include consumers who had not had the same possibilities open to them before and who had, therefore, few traditions or precedents to rely upon, it became increasingly important that the objects destined for the new markets contained a high level of instantaneously perceived overt symbolism which served to reassure them of the 'correctness' of their taste values and their new social status. The mass-produced modern objects had to compete in the market-place with goods that reproduced period styles, or second-hand items, which already had a high degree of symbolism built into them.

As a result, the modern mass styles of this century have tended to manifest more obviously expressive qualities than their more exclusive, avant-garde counterparts. In the 1930s, for example, while the Modern Movement with its austere forms and abhorrence of decoration, remained the preserve of an exclusive intellectual minority, objects which were described as 'Modernistic'[3] – a design style which combined decorative features from Art Deco and Streamlining with a Modern base – became much more popular and had considerably more far-reaching effects on the mass environment. It is also a characteristic of twentieth-century design that while minority styles have been heavily theorized, mass movements have emerged in a much more spontaneous way and have received, as a result, less historical and critical attention.

Surveying Mass Taste

If the question of deciding how taste values are formed and acquired is highly problematic, so is the task of assessing them once they are embedded within society. A few attempts have been made to gauge the taste or tastes of the day and to assess their origins and manifestations. Most have adopted the guise of sociological surveys, collecting sample opinions about consumption choices and preferences, and generalizing from them.

The work of the Mass Observation project, which was established in Britain in the 1930s by Tom Harrisson, is one example of a non-commercially oriented taste survey. It set out to discover in a quasi-anthropological manner how people live in contemporary society and, to this end, undertook, among other projects, a survey of the Council of Industrial Design's exhibition at the Victoria and Albert Museum in 1946, Britain Can Make It.[4] The conclusion eventually arrived at was that the mass of the British public wanted more excitement, decoration and fun than they were being offered by that particular exhibition. The exercise seved to highlight the gap that existed between the essentially paternalistic, middle-class attitudes of the British design establishment of the time and the desires and aspirations of the general public, a gap which was to become all too evident in the following two decades.

Similar surveys of mass taste included a 'Questionnaire on industrial art' undertaken by Nikolaus Pevsner (q.v.) in the 1930s and an exhibition organized by the Design and Industries Association (DIA) in the 1950s called Register Your Choice, held at Charing Cross Station. Pevsner conducted his survey at a Midland Industrial Art exhibition in Birmingham in the summer of 1934. After working out his questionnaire carefully, he approached ninety-three people who represented, in his opinion, a cross-section of society in terms of gender, age and occupation, although he was conscious of a bias towards teachers, students and artists, and a lack of contributions from the professional and the working classes. Pevsner's findings indicated a number of general conclusions, among them the fact that the public was, at that time, generally unaware that 'electrical appliances and hardware should have an aesthetic just as much as furniture or an elaborate dinner set',[5] and that, in the end, the market will accept what it is offered, whether or not it is 'well designed'. The value judgements were Pevsner's, of course, and dictated the bias of the analysis, but the results of the survey showed clearly, none the less, that supply can, and usually does, determine demand and that most of the British public's taste decisions at that time were characterized by caution and moderation. In true Modern Movement fashion, Pevsner despaired of the jewellery preferred by the group – 'a group of enamel things in an unquestionably vulgar and cheap taste'[6] – but blamed it on the recalcitrance of the British jewellery trade. His final conclusion was that the survey had been a useful exercise in gauging public taste and one which manufacturers should emulate.

In Britain during the 1930s the question of public taste was one of great importance as it was considered the main stumbling block in the attempt to raise the standards of design in mass-produced goods. Without mass acceptance, 'good modern design' was seen to be an impossibility. Numerous attempts were made to raise the level of public taste and that of the manufacturer and the retailer who were considered to pander too often to the uneducated tastes of the masses in their rush to make a profit. The DIA was convinced that the answer to the problem lay in 'the capacity of the public itself to encourage good design largely through the exercise of the selective faculty in purchasing'.[7] In spite of that organization's reforming zeal the most popular styles of the day had little in common with what it promoted.

The relationship between taste and style is a very direct one. Style is the particular inflection of the visual language of the object, or set of objects, that communicates the taste values of its consumer; taste, in turn, is more than a simple question of aesthetic discrimination on the part of consumers as it also depends on a complex interplay of social, economic and anthropological factors which are outside their immediate control.

One body of theory exists which maintains that the most significant consumption decisions operate less on the basis of the choice of a certain object – a chair, for example – than on the choice of the visual characteristics of a particular object, that is, its style.[8] Stylistic choice is of vital importance to the consumer as it implies not simply the selection of particular objects but of a complete way of life, and therefore of a social position which if not achieved can at least be aspired to. The role of the mass media in communicating the stylistic alternatives is clearly vital as it provides the information on the basis of which the consumer makes his choice. Not all social classes have, however, the same access to the means by which such information is disseminated and therefore different styles are consumed simultaneously by different sectors of society.

Art Deco

Heralded as 'the last of the total styles',[9] Art Deco was certainly one of the first mass-produced styles to find an audience of mass consumers. Although it originated in the highly exclusive hand-made French decorative arts of the 1920s,[10] it was quickly exploited through the cheap mass production of new materials – metals, plastics and glass – and found its way into cheap, ephemeral, mass-produced decorative items such as cigarette cases, perfume bottles, household ceramics and glass, fashion textiles and accessories, and cocktail shakers. As a decorative style it could be applied to the forms and surfaces of any number of objects, thereby endowing them all with the same quality of instant modernity and fashionability.

Like many of this century's popular styles, Art Deco had its roots in high culture, in this case Cubism,[11] the Russian Ballet,[12] American Indian Art and European Purism,[13] but its appeal lay in its decorative eclecticism rather than in the significance of any one of its sources. A combination of factors led to its popularity in the 1930s: the relative low price of the goods it accompanied – a direct result of cheap mass production and the use of new materials – was clearly a *sine qua non*, but this in itself was not enough. A further condition was its symbolic appropriateness. This is often explained by the fact that it made overt references to luxury and extravagance during a period of economic depression thus providing a form of escapism for the public. The way in which the style was disseminated also encouraged its availability and, hence, its popularity. Art Deco was, for example, the style that

24   Travel and Transport Building, Century of Progress Exhibition, Chicago 1933.

The Paris 1925 Exposition des Arts Decoratifs had a very strong influence on the Chicago Fair of 1933. Joseph Urban, the architect responsible for the fair, had come from Austria and worked in a predominantly European style. This building, for example, had the stepped forms and sun-ray motif, so typical of the 1925 Art Deco style, which were to appear on numerous US buildings, in many US interiors and on many US products in the first half of the 1930s. Technological innovation was, however, also the order of the day in the USA. The roof of this particular building consists of metal plates which are suspended by steel cables from twelve steel towers. It was the first application of the suspension bridge principle to architecture and the roof spanned 200 ft. without a single arch.

Hollywood chose to use in many popular films of the period and it reached masses of people through that medium. In addition to its use in packaging and advertising, which made a significant impact on the mass environment, Art Deco also penetrated the architectural environment, embellishing the façades of new commercial and entertainment premises such as shops, cinemas, factories and even the new luxury liners, as well as being used as the major architectural style in large exhibitions, like the Century of Progress Exhibition in Chicago in 1933 [24]. It came to symbolize efficient, modern living and to convey a new, exciting life-style which was highly attractive to the mass consumers of the interwar years for whom fashionability was becoming an increasingly important means of expressing their social aspirations and status.

Where consumer goods were concerned, the mass consumption of Art Deco was, however, a piecemeal activity. It remained, in its pure forms, a middle-class style and only filtered down market in its very cheapest forms or as part of a stylistic mish-mash. In Britain a number of carpet manufacturers, who aimed their goods at the lower end of the market, realized the new style's commercial potential. However, they were also aware of the essential conservatism of a sector of their audience and as a compromise they often included small, abstract patterns on the same carpets which depicted such traditional images as sprays of leaves executed in old-fashioned, murky colours. These were sold alongside other ranges which were either totally modern or completely traditional in design. [14] The inhabitants of the new, semi-detached houses built in the 1920s and 1930s in a choice of Tudor, Arts and Crafts or Modern styles could, therefore, be as radical or conservative as they wished, and choose from a range of alternative carpets designed to suit their varied tastes. By the mid-1930s, modified Art Deco could be found in countless suburban homes, 'from the sunray motifs on garden gates and the fronts of the wireless sets to the stepped fireplaces in the Aztec temple style and the geometric shapes of armchairs and sofas'. [15]

Streamform

In the USA where style and commerce were most closely intertwined in the interwar years, the popularity of European Art Deco, or what the Americans called the Modernistic or Jazz Modern style, [16] was quickly superseded by the emergence of a more indigenous US modern style. Deriving, simultaneously, from aerodynamic experiments in transport and Futurist painting, Streamform, like Art Deco, rapidly became a highly fashionable and symbolically potent part of the modern environment. Its strength lay in its depiction of power, speed, mechanization and the future, and its application to objects of transport, like the Chrysler Airflow, designed in 1933 [25], was soon extended to those static mechanical and electrical products – the refrigerator, the washing-machine, the iron, and so on – which had been overlooked by Art Deco and which were so important to the new hygienic and efficient US life-style. Its popularity derived, like that of Art Deco, from its wide availability and low price, due once again to the introduction of new production techniques, in this case steel stamping and die-casting. The curved radii and bulbous forms of its objects were justified by propagandists at the time by the need for reducing material costs and hand labour but equally, if not more important, was the fact, as Harold Van Doren admitted, that 'the public likes the smooth, easily cleaned, nearly jointless surface'.[17]

By the late 1930s Streamform had, like Art Deco before it, entered the popular vocabulary of international design and taste and had been absorbed into the mass environment, along with a number of other foreign-based styles – such as Swedish Modern in its popular form – which were received enthusiastically by the new US mass market. By the end of the decade rapid stylistic redundancy had become increasingly the norm, as had the mingling together of styles on the part of the manufacturers in their attempts to meet the needs of different markets. Aided by market research, mass production, advertising and the mass media, a number of alternative design styles became more widely available than ever before and their consumption permeated all levels of US society for the first time.

Contemporary

After the Second World War, the pressure of mass taste began to assert itself upon the British design establishment such that, on the one hand, the power of the latter was drastically minimized and, on the other, design theorists, designers and manufacturers began to look to mass values as a means of redefining the parameters of 'good design' and to rethink the relevance of that phenomenon to a mass-consumer society.

25 Chrysler Airflow, 1934.
This radical car design was the first 'streamlined' car in production. It was based on a discovery by a Chrysler researcher, Harold Hicks, that by welding a steel tube frame on to the chassis frame of a car the speed could be raised, and designed by Carl Breer who discovered, through wind tunnel tests, that cars were more efficient going backwards. He therefore gave his design a 'back-to-front' look. It was shown at the Chicago Fair in 1933 and went into manufacture in 1934, but its smooth, curved silhouette and its integrated body-shell proved too advanced for the public and, as a result, the model was dropped in 1937.

The Contemporary design style of the 1950s highlighted the gap that existed between the taste values held by the Council of Industrial Design and the British public. The Council was very keen at that time to promote a new, postwar design style which would satisfy the growing public demand for novelty and fun while, at the same time, maintaining the old, prewar values inherited from the DIA which were so close to its heart. The moralizing tone that the Council adopted in its propagandizing was at serious odds, however, with the voice of the public, which was continually expressing its need for a new style to symbolize the new values of the new age. The visual qualities of the Contemporary style which emerged in furniture included features like tapered legs, light woods and winged backs, and there was a new emphasis on colour and pattern. It was a style which was particularly at home in the domestic living room [26], but it meant two different things to the council and the general public. While the former – faithful to its Arts and Crafts heritage – was insistent that the objects should reflect 'sound construction, modest proportions, simple lines, careful choice of timbers or fabrics, attention to finish and detailing and generally a decent, well-bred elegance'[18], the latter was much more interested in the symbolic content of the new furniture and its relevance to the new postwar life-style and values. Commenting on the Contemporary room at the Charing Cross Station DIA Exhibition of 1953, one member of the public explained: 'In the left room I could settle down with a pipe and a drink with the radio going, but in the one on the right I'd have to have a cocktail by my side all the time.'[19] In sharp contrast, Ernest Race (q.v.), one of the designers heartily approved of by the council, commented regretfully and somewhat patronizingly in 1952 that 'they [the public] see the "contemporary style" merely as a fashion'.[20]

The difference of interpretation revealed the social and ideological chasm between the educated, middle-class values of the design propagandists of the period and the untrained responses of the average mass consumer. By the 1950s a much larger proportion of society constituted the bulk of the market and it became increasingly difficult for the Council of Industrial Design to impose taste values and theories of design on to the general public.

Pop – from Theory to Practice

In the early postwar period a number of theorists, among them the members of the Independent Group[21] based at the Institute of

26 Robin Day, British exhibit at the Tenth Triennale, Milan 1954.
Day's exhibit for Milan is Contemporary design at its best. The splayed, steel rod legs
and lightness of the furniture, the use of abstract patterns on the curtain fabric, the
sculptural form of the lamp, and the inclusion of small 'human' decorative items, such as
plants and pieces of ceramic, are all part of the interior aesthetic which Day and others
developed in Britain in the early 1950s and which was imitated by many designers later in
that decade, often with less restrained results. The influences of Scandinavia and of
Charles Eames are both present in this setting which contains Day's timber-framed
Chevron chair of 1954. The chair was manufactured by Hille, the company who financed
Day's display at Milan, where he was awarded a silver medal.

Contemporary Arts in London, began to work on analyses of mass culture which focused on the symbolic content, rather than the formal and aesthetic qualities, of consumer goods. They based their studies on an acceptance of object expendability and styling – ideas which the public accepted without question but which had been stumbling blocks for the design propagandists – and rejected what they considered to be outmoded concepts like 'good' and 'bad' design, focusing instead on a concept of design judged by the degree of its appropriate popular symbolism.

For the Independent Group, consumer products formed part of the same cultural cluster as advertising, pulp novels, and sci-fi films and could be analysed with the same intellectual tools. Their definition of culture was akin to the 'whole way of life' approach of the anthropologist and they were among the first to apply this model to the design of mass-produced artefacts. In their search for products with a high symbol content they turned their eyes on the USA, and the US automobile of the 1950s, with its overt references to sex and power, provided them with a perfect example of object symbolism.

While the Independent Group worked on ways of analysing popular taste and design in the mid-1950s, a few British manufacturers and designers began, at the beginning of the 1960s, to respond directly to the needs of the public, and produced a number of consumer goods which incorporated the new mass values. They took their lead from pop music, fashion and the youth revolution that patronized these new cultural phenomena, and set out to exploit the qualities of expendability, symbolism and fun in designed objects. Fired by their enthusiasm, the graphic designer Michael Wolff expressed his hopes for the future when he wrote in the journal of the Society of Industrial Artists in 1965 that: 'It will be a great day when furniture and cutlery design, to name but two, swing like the Supremes.'[22]

By the mid-1960s a number of designers – such as Peter Murdoch (q.v.) with his paper chair and Paul Clark (q.v.) with his Union Jack and target mugs, trays and clocks in Britain [27], and Scolari, D'Urbino, Lomazzi and De Pas (qq.v.) with their inflatable chair for Zanotta in Italy – set out to overthrow the vestiges of Functionalism and to develop a new set of design criteria which took consumption rather than production as their symbolic starting-point. Central to this new attitude was the belief that image, style and fashion were more important to the product than any rational or moral justifications put up in its defence. The revenge of mass taste had finally taken place and in

119

27   Paul Clark, Pop designs, 1964.

Paul Clark's Pop ephemera from the mid-1960s – clocks, mugs, tea-cosies, dish-cloths and souvenirs – were marketed by Perspective Designs and many of them were included in the Design Centre Index. They epitomized the 1960s' interest in surface motifs, in this case, flags and bulls-eyes, which were applied to a whole range of objects, regardless of their function. Thus the Modern Movement theory of 'form follows function' was ignored and replaced by a new emphasis on fun and expendability. These objects quickly became the symbols of Swinging London in the mid-1960s and were retailed through shops like Gear of Carnaby Street. These alternative design values have remained common ones in objects which form part of the so-called gift trade where expression and symbolism are of paramount importance.

1967 even Paul Reilly (q.v.), by now the director of the Council of Industrial Design, admitted that things had changed and that he and his colleagues would have to start learning to enjoy colours that they would have previously dismissed as vulgar.[23]

As it took its lead from the world of commerce, Pop design was inevitably absorbed into that context and eventually became indistinguishable from it. It served, none the less, as a symbolic liberation, opening up the possibility that the values that the public required from designed products would become the ones that motivated designers as well. Thus, from the late 1960s onwards, the mass domestic design styles that followed rapidly on each other's heels – from stripped pine, to High-Tech, to period revivals, to Post-Modernism – all defined themselves in terms of symbolism and life-style rather than function, rational production, or morality. Today, mass taste increasingly influences designers as, in the post-functionalist era, they find that they must confront the problems of stylistic and symbolic appropriateness in addition to the other, more traditional concerns of function, cost and materials.

The question of varied markets is also of vital importance in this context as in contemporary society the relationships between social and economic groups are becoming increasingly complex. Although 'upward emulation' still occurs on a wide scale dictating many consumption patterns this is not the only direction in which stylistic influence works. The increasing importance of fashion to design means that all new trends, whether they emerge at street level or in the designer's studio, are open to commercial manipulation. While many subcultural groups now create their own styles, they are almost always appropriated by commerce and mass production and are thus rendered fashionable. In a parallel way, the furniture of the Italian avant-garde group Memphis[24] [47], for example, which took its initial inspiration from the mass design styles of the 1950s and 1960s, has found itself back where it started, albeit in a watered-down form. All new styles, wherever they originate, are now potentially fashionable mass styles, transformed by the joint mechanisms of mass production and mass consumption, and fulfilling the recurrent desire for 'novelty' that both the economy and the consumer require. Central to this picture is the concept of mass taste: whether manipulated or 'real' it is the concept upon which the whole economic structure of production and consumption hinges and one which neither the manufacturer nor the designer can afford to ignore.

Notes: Chapter 7

1 P. Reilly, in *Idea*, no.5 (1953), p. 12.
2 The Victorians used the word 'taste' in the absolute, aristocratic sense of 'good taste', and this meaning has also influenced contemporary ideas about 'good design'. The other definition of the term is sociological and anthropological in origin and implies a relative concept dependent on social and cultural determinants and with no absolute form. Taste, in this latter context, simply means the aesthetic preferences of a certain social group in a certain cultural situation and is therefore relevant to the discussion of any and every mass-produced consumer artefact.
3 The term 'Modernistic' is used to describe the popular appropriation of the more purist Modern style of the 1920s and 1930s. Although still inspired by geometric abstraction, Modernistic was a more showy style incorporating decoration and expressive motifs. It was more geared to psychological fulfilment than to philosophical ideals, and was at its most extreme in countries like the USA where there was a large mass market.
4 The Mass Observation Archive, now lodged in the library at the University of Sussex, is a record of British public opinion in the late 1930s and 1940s. Set up by Tom Harrisson in 1937 it aimed to be an 'anthropological survey'. The report on audience reaction at the Britain Can Make It Exhibition of 1946 shows clearly the gap between mass and establishment values in that year.
5 N. Pevsner, 'Questionnaire on industrial art,' *Design for Today*, no.4 (April 1935), p. 146.
6 ibid.
7 The DIA Register Your Choice Exhbition in *DIA Yearbook* (1953), p. 12.
8 This thesis implies that style is the most seductive element in the 'desirability' of a consumer product. Thus the consumer is, in many cases, buying a life-style rather than an object he or she needs for its utilitarian function when a purchase is made.
9 B. Hillier, *Art Deco* (London: Studio Vista, 1968), p. 9.
10 The term 'Art Deco' derives from the name of the Exposition des Arts Decoratifs which was held in Paris in 1925.
11 The movement in painting, called Cubism, which occurred in the years around 1907 to 1914 was led by Pablo Picasso and Georges Braque and concentrated on depicting the geometric structure which lies beneath 3D reality. It had two phases, analytic and synthetic, the latter developing a particular visual language of abstract form which became one of the major influences on the Art Deco style in the 1920s.
12 The colours and forms of the costumes and sets of the Russian Ballet led by Diaghilev in the years before the First World War were among the many influences on that eclectic style, Art Deco.
13 Purism was the name of the movement in painting which, led by Jeanneret (alias Le Corbusier, q.v.) and Amédée Ozenfant in France in the 1920s developed an interest in the minimal depiction of industrial, standardized forms like bottles and jugs. Le Corbusier's architecture has, by extension, also been labelled 'purist'.

14 Suzette Worden's 'Furniture for the living room: an investigation of the interaction between society, industry and design in Britain 1919–1939' (PhD thesis, Brighton Polytechnic, 1980) deals at length with the idea of popular design in Britain in the 1930s.

15 A. Prochaska, *London in the Thirties* (London: London Museum, 1973), p. 8

16 The term 'Jazz Modern' – an alternative term to 'Art Deco' – was used in the USA in the 1930s to describe the popular, decorative style which evolved, in that country, as an extension of European Modernism.

17 H. Van Doren, 'Streamlining: fad or function?', in *Design*, no. 10 (October 1949), p. 3.

18 P. Reilly, 'Look before you buy', *Daily Mail Ideal Home Yearbook* (1955), p. 62.

19 Mass Observation Report on 1953, DIA Register Your Choice Exhibition at Charing Cross Station, in *DIA Yearbook* (1953), p. 16.

20 Ernest Race, 'Design in modern furniture', *Daily Mail Ideal Home Yearbook* (1952/3), p. 62.

21 Set up in 1952 at the ICA in Dover Street, the Independent Group – made up of Eduardo Paolozzi, Richard Hamilton, John McCale, Alison and Peter Smithson, Reyner Banham (q.v.), Lawrence Alloway and others – was concerned, first, to examine the effects of technology on the arts and, later, the whole question of mass culture. They took US mass culture as a starting-point and looked at Hollywood movies, pulp novels, advertising and industrial design in their attempts to evolve a critical framework which would cover the spectrum from popular to high art. In 1956 the group organized the exhibition entitled This Is Tomorrow at the Whitechapel Gallery which, in many ways, represented the peak of their achievement. The British Pop Art Movement grew out of the spirit that the Independent Group engendered and the ideas they developed.

22 M. Wolff quoted in the *Sun*, 27 January 1965.

23 P. Reilly, 'The challenge of Pop', *Architectural Review*, vol. 52 (October 1967) pp. 255–7.

24 The Memphis Group showed its first range of bizarre furniture, inspired by forms and patterns in mass culture, in Milan in 1981. The group was master-minded by Ettore Sottsass (q.v.), the leader of Italian Radical Design since the early 1960s. Ironically, as is the case with all avant-garde experiments, the work of the group became associated with the same exclusiveness which it had set out to debunk. The shocked reaction to Memphis's 'disrespectful' approach was manifested in establishment design circles around the globe.

8

New Materials, New Forms

Base metals were transformed into marvels of beauty, expressive of our own age.[1]

Throughout this century the discovery of new materials and innovations in production technology have provided constant challenges to designers. Since the early days of industrialization, manufacturers of consumer goods, always keen to create new markets and expand existing ones, have increasingly sought cheaper means of mass production and have constantly substituted new materials for the more expensive, traditional ones. The two developments have moved hand in hand resulting in an expansion of possibilities for the designer who has had to respond by inventing ever new and appropriate product forms.

Iron and Steel

In the nineteenth century, while countless new machine-tools were developed – among them the screw-cutting lathe, the block-making machine, the wood-turning lathe, the planing machine, the band-saw and the grinding machine[2] – advances in materials were mostly limited to the field of metals. Iron, in its cast or wrought state, and later in the form of steel, was the material of the day. The decorative balconies, staircases and metro stations, characteristic of the Art Nouveau style, for example, owed their very existence to the potential of wrought-iron and, in the hands of architects like the Frenchman Hector Guimard and the Belgian Victor Horta (qq.v.), came to represent a new style for a new century.

On a less decorative front, the USA was the first country to develop the all-steel car body, an innovation which was only made possible by the use of the new steel-stamping machinery. Britain was also quick to

28 W. D. Teague, Gas range for Floyd Wells Company, 1935.
Teague's gas range, made from stamped steel sheet with a white enamelled finish, was
an early example of what later came to be referred to as 'white goods', superceding
previous models which were usually made out of black cast-iron or marbleized sheet
metal. It was put together, like an automobile, on an assembly line from standardized
parts, the steel panels being simply hooked on to a tubular steel frame. Teague's design
also eliminated the tall legs of previous models and included metal panels which folded
down over the burners for easy maintenance and a more 'streamlined' appearance.

realize the potential of this development, and Morris Motors persuaded the US company which had patented the new process, Edward G. Budd of Philadelphia, to join them in setting up a steel-pressing plant in Cowley.[3]

Traditional craft-manufactured products, like furniture, were also influenced by the new metals, and cast-iron chairs made out of pipes, flat bars and rods became quite commonplace, usually intended for the garden but occasionally for the domestic interior as well.[4] Steel-stamping was also employed in the manufacture of body-shells for the new domestic machines like refrigeraters, washing-machines and cookers [28]. The USA was more adventurous in this area, producing from the 1840s onwards a vast array of innovative furniture in cast-iron and distributing it widely, often through catalogues, with the help of mail order. While most were exercises in stylistic revivalism, a few anticipated the more functional forms of the following century.

Where the manufacturer is concerned, the principal motivating factors behind the search for a new or substitute material are always the need to decrease costs and to increase efficiency. Bent-steel, which followed closely on the heels of cast-iron, was strong and durable as well as elastic and, as a result, remained in production until well into the twentieth century. Nineteenth-century designs for furniture using this material tended to imitate traditional styles and few attempts were made to use the new material as an excuse for visual innovation. In the USA, cost and efficiency provided the only justifications for the rejection of a traditional material like wood, and it was not until the advent of tubular steel, bent plywood and plastics in this century that furniture designers really began to respond aesthetically to the potential of new materials, inventing new forms for them which were appropriate to the modern age.

Aluminium

The metal which had the strongest impact on the manufacture and design of products in the interwar years was aluminium. Obtained from bauxite and made available on a commercial scale by the arrival of cheap electricity, aluminium provided the answer to a search that had gone on since the nineteenth century for a new metal which would combine the strength of iron with the conductivity of copper. It was not until the turn of the century that it became possible to isolate and purify aluminium and to manufacture it in sufficient quantities and at a low-enough price to make it commercially viable. In Britain the modern aluminium industry can be said to date from 1894, the year of the formation of the British Aluminium Company.

The practical qualities of aluminium – its lightness, its resistance to corrosion, its high thermal and electrical conductivity, and its formal flexibility – made it ideally suitable for a number of different functions. Thus, a writer in 1937 explained how useful it was in designing and manufacturing products at that time, particularly the motor-car, because 'the combination of ductility and low weight makes aluminium quite suitable for the whole range, from the streamlined body of the racing car to the specially shaped body of the trade van'.[5] The material's versatility made it a popular choice in the 1930s. At the Chicago Century of Progress Exhibition [24] of 1933, for example, an all-aluminium Pullman coach was on display: every part of it, apart from the axles and springs, was made of aluminium alloy and the whole thing weighed only a little more than half the Standard all-steel Pullman of equivalent capacity.

In many ways the Chicago Exhibition represented a shrine to the new materials which were beginning to filter on to the marketplace. The temporary buildings themselves were made of plywood, light steel, asbestos and gypsum board and the Homes and Industrial Arts section of the exhibition consisted of eight model houses, each one made of a different material, including steel, Masonite, brick, glass and wood. The central theme of the exhibition was described as the 'dramatization of the achievements of mankind, made possible through the application of science to industry'[6], and the emphasis throughout was upon scientific efficiency and the role that new materials could play in the new, clean environment. Epitomizing this near-obsession with cleanliness and hygiene, the kitchen was described as a scientist's laboratory which could be cleaned simply by the housewife turning on a hose.

In the USA the use of aluminium in consumer products was widespread throughout the 1930s, spanning a range of goods from ovenware to furniture. Notable among these was Frederick Kiesler's (q.v.) nest of aluminium coffee tables of 1936 which combined abstract sculptural form with physical lightness, while Russel Wright's (q.v.) spun aluminium stove-to-table ware of 1933 exploited the material's heat resistance, as did Lurelle Guild's (q.v.) line of aluminium utensils for the Ware-Ever Company of the following year.

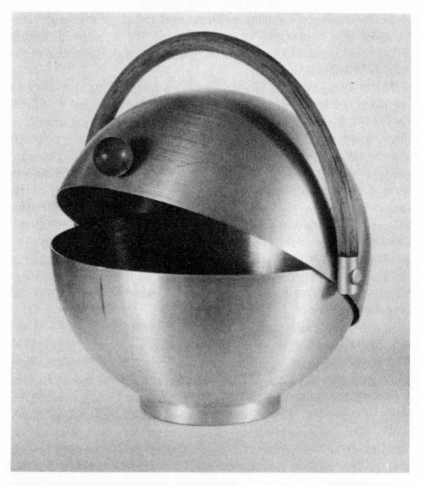

29   Russel Wright, bun warmer, 1929–35.
Manufactured by Wright Accessories, Raymor, New York, Wright's bun warmer is 8 in.
high and made of spun aluminium. Wright used this material as a pewter substitute and
treated it with an emery cloth to produce a comparable look. He designed a whole range
of products in this material, including cheese servers, ice-buckets, sandwich humidifiers,
beer-mugs, pitchers and spaghetti sets. The shapes were, for the most part, determined
by the spinning process and therefore rounded forms tended to characterize many of
Wright's designs.

Russel Wright, one of the USA's most innovative designers where this new material was concerned, used spun aluminium extensively as a substitute for pewter and chromium-plated steel [29]. He rubbed the surface with emery cloth to make it resemble pewter and enjoyed the new material for its 'workability and its permanent integral colouring'.[7] The rounded, exaggerated forms Wright developed were a direct result of the spinning process and this new aesthetic proved to be a huge commercial success, in spite of the fact that the aluminium was often fashioned with sharp edges and bent with alarming ease. Mary McCarthy, the novelist, underlined the highly fashionable quality of his work in her book about Vassar graduates, *The Group*: 'Look at Russel Wright, whom everybody thought quite the thing now; he was using industrial materials, like the wonderful new spun aluminium, to make all sorts of useful objects like cheese trays and water carafes.'[8]

The enthusiasm and optimism associated with the advent of new materials in the USA was unequalled elsewhere. The demand for ever cheaper consumer goods in the years of the Depression encouraged extensive research into the application of new materials and production techniques and their arrival was heralded with applause. The question of which came first, however, the new streamlined style or the new materials, is a chicken and egg problem. Without doubt, the production technology developed to work the new materials, as well as the structural requirements of the materials themselves, had a tremendous influence on the objects' finished forms. Aluminium, for example, could be cast, pressed, or spun and every product made from it showed signs of its particular method of manufacture, whether in its general outline, the radii of its curves, or the expanse of the metal employed. Features like ribbing were also usually structural necessities rather than decorative afterthoughts.

While aluminium was much used in streamlined objects, it also played a decorative role in interiors of the period as it could be dyed various colours and polished. The US industrial designer and interior decorator, Donald Deskey (q.v.), employed the material in many of his multi-media decorative interiors, including those for Radio City Music Hall of the early 1930s. The canning industry also used aluminium widely as its combination of lightness and strength made it the perfect material for the canning of certain foodstuffs and for the manufacture of collapsible tubes to contain toothpaste and similar products. Although more costly than tinplate cans, this was largely offset by the ease with which it could be stamped, which saved labels, and by its lightness, which reduced freight costs.

Wherever aluminium came to be used as a substitute material in the mid-1930s, whether in railway rolling stock or in the construction and furnishing of ships, it justified its existence through the reduction of weight, its increase in fire resistance and its decorative potential. It became, in fact, one of the chief industrial metals of the interwar years. British consumption of aluminium, for example, increased 120 per cent between 1924 and 1929, a result both of well-directed propaganda and of the reduction in price. Because it was new, the aluminium industry was not hampered by tradition and, like the electrical industry, it was born into an age of large-scale, internationally oriented production which facilitated its development.

The problem of appearance for the products made from new materials was, inevitably, an enormous one and required the close co-operation of the engineer and the designer in order that new, viable solutions could be found. The US designer Donald Dohner, who came from an engineering background and was employed by the Westinghouse Company, was adamant that the forms of the new products should not echo those of traditional ones: 'Imitating other materials may be an interesting technical stunt for some engineer but it robs the new material of its birthright, destroys its identity and natural beauty, thereby degrading it.'[9] This kind of commitment to new forms for new materials underpinned most US design activity at that time and helped to revolutionize twentieth-century attitudes towards product design. Dohner's own designs, like his Micarta table-top with an abstract decorative pattern on the surface made of dyed inlaid aluminium and, on a more technical level, his portable schering bridge which had red Micarta panel dial plates and black-eyed aluminium inlaid into the panel, were essentially experiments with new materials.

Designers in other countries were also to exploit the design potential of aluminium. The Swiss, Hans Coray's (q.v.) famous Landi chair was planned as a stacking chair for the Swiss National Exhibition in Zurich of 1938. Its construction exploited new developments in aluminium technology, in terms of both alloys and hardening treatment, and the chair expertly combined the material's flexible qualities with lightness and strength. The Dutch De Stijl designer, Gerrit Rietveld (q.v.), also worked on an aluminium chair in 1942 while the Englishman, Ernest Race's (q.v.) aluminium chair was shown at the Britain Can Make It Exhibition in London in 1946. This exhibition was very keen to show

how advances made in the technology of aluminium and other materials, including plywood and plastics, during the Second World War were going to affect developments in postwar civilian manufacturing. In one of its sections 'New aluminium saucepans were displayed indicating that a refractory process invented during the war to extend the life of the exhaust stub of the Spitfire could be of domestic use',[10] while some aluminium alloy toys were also shown next to a Lancaster bomber fuel-valve component, both of them manufactured with the same hands and machines.

Following the Second World War, however, aluminium was virtually replaced by plastics as far as consumer goods were concerned. It has continued to be used in the industrial and capital goods sector, particularly in components production, but has had less impact on the exterior design of products. Wherever and whenever the ratio of weight to strength is important, aluminium still has a part to play but, on the whole, it has faded into the background as a material with a modern image, although since the oil crisis of the early 1970s there are signs that it might be re-emerging.

Plastics

In sharp contrast, plastics came into their own in the second half of this century and have succeeded in evolving an aesthetic which has changed the way we think about many of the products in today's mass environment.

Like aluminium, plastic items first became available to a wide market during the Depression, at a time when manufacturers of consumer goods began to think both about new methods of production and the appearance of their products. The main reason for the invasion of plastics into manufacturing industry was as an aid to reducing costs through the replacement of hand-engraved moulds by machine-cut forms. Production costs were thus reduced and could be undertaken on a mass scale and, at the end of the day, the product could be sold at a cheaper price than its traditionally produced competitors. The possibility of new forms emerging from the new production methods acted as a challenge to designers, encouraging them to innovate.

The origins of the synthetic materials which are grouped together under the umbrella term 'plastics' date from the mid-nineteenth century when the huge population increase of those years put a strain upon the supplies of natural materials such as silk, rubber and ivory. Early examples of polymer materials included Celluloid,[11] patented in the USA in 1869; Casein,[12] patented in Germany in 1897, and Parkesine,[13] patented by Alexander Parkes, a Birmingham inventor, in 1864. In 1909 Dr Leo Baekeland first introduced Bakelite,[14] a brown material which was first used in electrical fittings but was soon extended to telephones, wireless cabinets and ashtrays: it not only offered desirable electrical properties, but could be moulded into intricate shapes as well.

Progress was made in the development of plastics during the First World War as a result, once again, of a reduction in the availability of natural materials and, by the interwar period, they had become a part of the manufacturing process of a vast range of goods. The chief justification for their use was economics and it soon became clear that plastics were becoming a prominent feature of the everyday environment, and that they had the potential of making necessary products appear more luxurious.

One of plastic's major functions was to make more goods available to more people and the vast numbers of small goods manufactured from plastics, such as buckles, cheap jewellery, hairbrushes, buttons and cigarette cases, which appeared on the market bore witness to its role in helping to democratize consumption.

While for many of these small ephemeral goods plastics were really only a cheap substitute material and tended, as a result, to ape the appearance of their predecessors – whether horn, wood or ivory – in the field of the new machines, they had a more radical role to play in providing the body-shells for products which lacked both a traditional function and form. In Britain the radical radio cabinets designed by Serge Chermayeff and Wells Coates (qq.v.) for the Ekco Radio Company in the 1930s were splendid examples of plastic bodies performing the dual function of concealing the complex workings of the product and of providing a new visual image appropriate to the modern age of mass communications. Similar advances in body-shell design were made in the USA, which also exploited the qualities of plastics. Raymond Loewy's (q.v.) famous reworking of the Gestetner duplicating machine of 1929 was another early exercise in plastics casing[15], as was the design of many mass-produced consumer machines like the Fada Baby radio of 1934 [30].

A similar metamorphosis occurred to many other mechanical and electrical products in the interwar years and plastics played a major role

30   Fada Baby Radio, 1934.
This little radio was made of yellow cast phenolic, a material which was characterized by an opaque appearance and was available in a wide colour range. It was used widely in such products as clocks, jewellery, cutlery, handles and hairbrushes, as well as in aircraft machine-tools. The radio's dimensions are 6¼ in. by 19½ in. by 5½ in. It was mass produced in the USA in the mid-1930s and became a highly popular object there. It took full aesthetic advantage of the technological possibilities of plastics manufacture and its appearance was essentially 'streamlined'. with its one rounded end and the parallel lines which formed the speaker grill. The disposition of its features, all of which were there for a functional purpose, was highly harmonious. The knobs had little flutings on them for easy handling and the dial was designed to be very clear. The radio was one of the first mass-produced electrical consumer objects to develop a modern visual identity for itself with the help of plastics.

in that transformation. Numerous products such as sewing machines, pieces of office machinery and vacuum cleaners were all transformed into simple, desirable, hygienic products with the simple addition of a plastics housing.

The process was a two-way one, however. Just as advances in materials technology were looking for new products to which to apply themselves, so manufacturers looked to the new materials both as a means of reducing production costs and of restyling their goods. The Plaskon Company in the USA, a large producer of urea moulding components, was created, for example, as a direct result of the Toledo Scale Company's desire to improve its products. The latter company had been trying for several years to find structural materials suitable for a scale housing and in 1928 it founded a fellowship at the Mellor Institute of Industrial Research in order to continue its search. The result was the development of Plaskon. The development of the manufacturing technique required for the large mouldings needed by the Toledo Scale Company was undertaken by the Plastics Department of General Electric which produced the first scale housing moulded from pure white urea-formaldehyde.[16] This kind of research and co-operation was commonplace in these years and resulted in the USA making huge leaps forward in the technology of plastics production.

The methods employed in manufacturing plastics items or casings inevitably limit the aesthetic possibilities open to the designer. The primary means of turning plastics into a product is through the moulding method and much progress has been made in developing the alternative forms of moulding plastics through this century. The very word 'plastics' means, in fact, 'capable of being shaped or moulded'. When the industry was seeking a generic name for the group or industry as a whole, the name 'plastics' was selected because the ease of moulding these new materials appeared to be their most outstanding characteristic, although other techniques – casting, machining, laminating and rolling – are also commonly employed. Of the moulded products, two general classes are used – thermosetting and thermoplastic – and the different moulding processes include compression moulding, transfer moulding and injection moulding, the last being the one most commonly employed by thermoplastics.[17]

The technique employed for injection moulding is very simple: the material is heated, forced into the mould cavity and then cooled by water or air. The die is then opened and the moulded part is pushed out by the ejector pins. It is a process very widely used in product manufacturing. The designer performs a vitally important role in this process but it is essential that he co-operates closely with a plastics engineer. The aesthetic limitations imposed by the production methods are particular to this particular process. An emphasis on curves, the compositional role of the 'parting line', colour and size are crucial visual components of plastics design, the technical limitations of which the designer has to discuss carefully with the engineer before design can begin. In the 1930s generous radii were preferred because sharp corners caused production problems and crowned surfaces were used to avoid an impression of the product's surface sinking. Flutes which doubled as structural reinforcements were widely integrated and large, plain surfaces were usually broken up by ribbing to avoid plainness. Perhaps more than any other single material it is plastics which have encouraged designers and manufacturers to move towards aesthetic simplicity in the mass-produced artefact. Inevitably ideas emanating from the architectural Modern Movement were used to reinforce and justify this move towards simplicity, and complex machines became subject to the same minimal, aesthetic language that had inspired the craft objects of the Bauhaus. By the 1960s plastics production technology had improved to the extent that radii could be made much sharper and surfaces firmer, and a number of companies, like Braun in Germany, had perfected a minimal, geometric aesthetic for its plastics electrical equipment.

In the 1930s and 1940s the transition from metals to plastics had facilitated the emergence of a more streamlined, unified shape with fewer joins and dust-collecting details. A dual emphasis on simplification and hygiene came to epitomize products from that period and these features were eagerly picked up as promotion points by manufacturers and advertisers alike.

After the Second World War, the ever-increasing range of available plastics products brought with it the problem of aesthetic degradation as, increasingly, these 'cheap' substitute goods began, in the eyes of many, to be associated with shoddiness. In their defence some writers, like the industrial designer Misha Black, were more forward-looking in their approach and to his own question 'Can plastics ever possess the attributes which allow aesthetic contemplation and empathy?' he replied that 'the plastics designer . . . in the intricate elaboration of his miniature engineering has sometimes created minor formal masterpieces'.[18]

Apart from isolated instances of progressive plastics design, like the work of Gaby Schreiber (q.v.) for Runcolite (a company which was headed by a manufacturer who believed that plastics products could be better if professionally designed), of David Harman Powell (q.v.) for British Industrial Plastics, and that of Martyn Rowlands for Ekco Plastics [31], few advances were made in this field in Britain and it was left to Italy and Germany to exploit plastics' full aesthetic potential. In Italy, with the help of designers like Roberto Menghi, Marco Zanuso and Vico Magistretti, companies like Kartell, Brionvega and Artemide reached a level of visual sophistication in the design of plastics household equipment, electrical equipment and furniture that has still not been superseded. [19] The late but rapid expansion of Italian manufacturing after the war meant that it could invest in the most advanced production machinery and its work in plastics in that period was, in line with products in other materials designed in that country at that time, utterly innovatory, drawing on, among other sources, forms of contemporary organic sculpture for inspiration. Today, there are signs that the popularity of plastics is waning due both to the increasing cost of their production after the oil crisis of the early 1970s, and the ecological problem they present. Manufacturers are increasingly seeking out new materials, often returning to metals as the only viable solution.

Although developments in metals and plastics have dominated the advances in materials technology for manufacturing industry in this century there have been a few other innovations which have also had far-reaching effects. Among those which came into their own in the interwar period were rayon and new forms of glass. In the latter area, materials with such evocative names as Aklo, Tuf-flex, Vitrolux, Thermolux, and Vitrolite[20] hit the market hard on each other's heels. A company called Triplex, for example, had been producing safety glass since 1924 but it was not until 1927 that Henry Ford decided to use it in automobiles as a result of an accident in which he was injured by broken glass. On hearing of his injury the company had sent him a telegram which read 'Fit Triplex and be safe',[21] which he promptly did. The arrival of rayon had an enormous impact upon both the production and consumption of clothing in the second half of this century. By the 1920s there was an almost insatiable demand for clothing in Britain and with the arrival of artificial silk, or rayon, a greater quantity of cheaper clothes was made available and consumed by a larger market than ever before.

While the immediate effects of these new materials were on the

31 Martyn Rowlands, baby bath for Ekco Plastics, 1957.
As head of industrial design at Ekco Plastics in the 1950s Rowlands was responsible for using the technical possibilities of plastics manufacture to achieve a 'contemporary' look for plastic products. This polythene baby bath which was moulded in one piece has an organic, sculptural form which was in keeping with the aesthetic favoured for many other products at that time. It sits on a wooden base whose splayed, tapered legs had much in common with 'contemporary' furniture also. Rowlands was one of the very few British designers trying to create a modern image for plastic objects in the 1950s, and this object received a Design Centre award.

levels of economics and aesthetics, they had another level of significance which concerns the symbolic relationship of man to his material
environment, namely, that a commitment to new materials implies a
commitment to the present and to the future and the discovery of new
materials throughout this century has generally been accompanied by a
mood of optimism and excitement. Latterly, however, with the demise
of this commitment to 'the shock of the new' and the reassertion in
many quarters of an interest in nostalgia, revivalism, traditional skills
and vernacular styles, the value of new materials has also been thrown
into question. In this century the age of new materials belongs,
therefore, to the period between the two world wars when, in spite of
sustained economic pessimism, the optimism engendered by a belief in
the future was fuelled by the new materials, and the modern aesthetic
that designers created for them.

Notes: Chapter 8

1 P. Frankl, *New Dimensions* (New York: Payson & Clarke, 1928), p. 23.
2 All these new machine-tools emerged in Britain in the period between
   1790 and 1850. The screw-cutting lathe was the first to appear and
   Maudsley (1771–1831) was the central figure in its development. The
   engineers Whitworth and Nasmyth emerged from their workshops to
   work on other machine-tools. All their discoveries were dependent on the
   development of the accurate screw thread which emerged at the end of
   the eighteenth century. The block-making machine was first used in
   Portsmouth Dockyard.
3 For more details about the development of the steel industry read D. L.
   Burn, *The Economic History of Steel-Making 1867–1939* (Cambridge:
   Cambridge University Press, 1940).
4 For more information about cast-iron furniture consult D. Hanks, *Innovative Furniture in America from 1800 to the Present* (New York: Horizon,
   1981).
5 A. Plummer, *New British Industries in the Twentieth Century* (London: Sir
   Isaac Pitman & Sons, 1937), p. 196.
6 *Official book of the Fair: The Century of Progress Exhibition* (Chicago,
   1933), p. 7.
7 W. J. Hennessey, *Russel Wright: American Designer* (Cambridge, Mass.:
   MIT, 1983), p. 21.
8 M. McCarthy, *The Group* (Harmondsworth, Middx: Penguin, 1963),
   p. 14.
9 D. Dohner, 'Modern technique of designing', *Modern Plastics*, 14 March
   1937, p. 71.
10 'Spitfires to saucepans', in a note in the Exhibition Catalogue, *Britain Can
   Make It* (London: Council of Industrial Design, 1946), p. 4.

11 Celluloid was first patented in the USA in 1869.

12 Casein was first patented in Germany in 1897.

13 Parkesine was named after its inventor, Alexander Parkes, and was first introduced at the British Exhibition of 1862. It was a forerunner of modern plastics and was used to insulate telegraph wires.

14 Bakelite was invented in 1909 by Dr Leo Baekeland. First used exclusively for electrical fittings, it soon became the main material used for products such as telephones and radio cabinets.

15 Raymond Loewy (q.v.) restyled Sigmund Gestetner's photocopying machine in 1929 by adding a neat, Bakelite body-shell to the original, exposed Victorian machine.

16 Urea-formaldehyde resin is a thermo-settting resin manufactured by condensing urea with commercial formalin. It is a thermo-plastic which was first developed in the late 1930s.

17 The manufacture of most plastic products occurs through a moulding process, by pressure or injection, or die-casting, which have very specific visual implications for the product.

18 M. Black, 'In praise of plastics', lecture at the Royal College of Art, 1972.

19 The main companies to develop plastic products in Italy after the war were the Kartell Company, set up in the early 1950s and which employed Gino Colombini to design small household products like buckets and containers; Brionvega which employed Marco Zanuso and Richard Sapper to work on the plastic body-shells of its electronic equipment; and the furniture company, Artemide, which was the first of many to produce an all-plastic dining chair named Selene, designed by Vico Magistretti (q.v.) in the early 1960s.

20 In the 1930s a great number of glass variants were produced, many of which are listed in M. Grief, *Depression Modern – The Thirties Style in America* (New York: Universe Books, 1975), p. 37.

21 G. Turner, *The Car Makers* (Harmondsworth, Middx: Penguin, 1964), p. 23.

PART THREE

Modern Design, from 1945 to the Present

9

The Admass Society

The conditions were present for the arrival in Britain of that complex and pervasive phenomenon to which J. B. Priestley, returning in 1954 from a visit to the United States, affixed, by a happy stroke, the name of 'Admass'.[1]

In the decade which followed the Second World War, industrial society became characterized increasingly by the role that the mass media played in determining the nature of its institutions, its organizations, its consumption patterns and the life-styles of its populations. More than ever before, the effects of the press, the radio, television and the cinema entered the lives of practically every individual in the industrialized world, providing new sources of information, creating new expectations and suggesting new values. Inevitably, within this changing cultural climate, design took on new guises and performed new roles.

These new forms of communication had already, in the years before the Second World War, begun to intensify their impact. The oldest of them, the press, had existed in some form or another ever since the early days of printing in the sixteenth century but, with the advent of steam printing in the early nineteenth century and, in 1853, the abolition of the tax on advertisements, it expanded rapidly throughout the end of the last century and into our own, paralleling as it did so the expansion of adult literacy. The first wireless was patented in 1896 but it was not until the 1920s that the full effects of that medium were felt and, while TV had been introduced first into Britain in the 1930s, it failed to become a truly popular medium until after the war. Critical opinions about these developments varied enormously. While the American social commentator, Marshall McLuhan, was convinced that the impact of radio and television was, along with that of the other products of the electronic age – the telephone and the computer – an extremely radical one and that their role in the transformation of the world into what he called a 'global village'[2] was irrevocable, in Britain

Raymond Williams, the cultural historian, was critical about the impact on the content of TV, which he considered to be part of the highly undesirable upsurge of the masses against 'high' culture: 'Isn't the real threat of "mass culture" – of things like television rather than things like football, or the circus – that it reduces us to an endlessly mixed, undiscriminating, fundamentally bored reaction.'[3] The notion of discrimination, of making choices, underpinned all the cultural debates of the postwar period; debates which, inevitably, touched the question of design, albeit only at their periphery.

During the early postwar period, which was one of economic, social and cultural reconstruction in the industrialized world, design played a crucial, although usually silent, role. It became an important factor within two areas of postwar life; the first as part of the need to create a national identity for products on the international market and the second in the formation of mass culture – both of them highly significant aspects of the world history of the post-1945 period.

Postwar Reconstruction

The question of international trade was one to which all the countries emerging from the Second World War, whether victorious or defeated, were eager to address themselves. Their first requirement was to turn their economies back to full production for peacetime needs and, where a number of countries were concerned, US financial aid was necessary if this was to happen. As a direct result of the loan scheme that was initiated, a number of countries, including Britain, France, Italy, Japan and West Germany, were soon busy re-establishing their peacetime industrial manufacturing. The trade tariffs which had been imposed by the USA before the war were gradually being abolished and the way was soon open for the resumption of free, international trading. Recovery was slow at first but once begun, it accelerated rapidly thus initiating a period of unusually fast economic growth which, in North America, Western Europe and Japan, was sustained for two decades.

Within this economic rebirth the manufacture and trade of goods played a major role. Between 1945 and 1958 world manufactures increased by 60 per cent, while between 1958 and 1968 the figure rose to 100 per cent. These rises were paralleled by a growth in export figures over the same period and by 1957 the world trade in manufactured goods exceeded that in primary produce for the first time ever.

The reasons for this resurgence were complex but the strongest stimulus, in addition to the numerous social and economic changes that occurred in these years, was the rapid development of technology. Many advances had been made during the Second World War, including the development of radar and work in aircraft production which, in Britain, was sustained into the 1950s. Perhaps the most significant development of the late 1940s, however, was that of the transistor which made possible the miniaturization of electronic equipment, including computers, which in turn were to play such a central role in the postwar period, both in the automation of production and in information retrieval.

As a result of the numerous social, economic and technological changes that took place in these years, manufacturing expanded rapidly and provided industrial designers with their major challenge. In several of the countries participating in international trade, design became the means by which goods were distinguished from those of competitive countries and made more desirable for the purchaser, both at home and abroad. The lesson presented by the prewar USA example that 'design sells' was learnt and digested and became one of the major strategies in most countries' programmes of industrial reconstruction and within international trading in the postwar period.

Postwar Italy

This was particularly true of Italy which involved designers in its assault on the world market very early on in the postwar years. Italy industrialized relatively late and many of its manufacturing companies in the areas of furniture, electrical equipment and household goods did not emerge until the 1950s. The companies Artemide, Arflex, Azucena, Flos, Kartell, Brionvega and Tecno[4] were among the many which were born in the two decades following the end of the war, the period during which manufacturing formed a central part of Italy's programme of reconstruction. This rebirth was not limited to the economic sphere, however, but embraced culture as well. As Ernesto N. Rogers, the editor of *Domus* magazine at that time, wrote: 'It is a question of forming a taste, a technique, a morality, all terms of the same function. It is a question of building a society.'[5]

With this high-minded idealism to the fore, many of the new manufacturers sought out architects to design, or 'style', their archi-

32 PininFarina Cisitalia, 1946.

The Cisitalia coupé, designed by Carrozzeria PininFarina in Turin, was the first of the great postwar Italian car designs. Its form was based on aerodynamic principles and consisted of a smooth, rounded metal skin over a compact tubular frame. The beauty of this car lies in the attention to compositional detail of the necessary features like the windows, doors and wheels and in the avoidance of any unnecessary extras. There are no square forms in the whole design and the low hood combined slipstream stability with maximum visibility and a visual emphasis on its length which was also emphasized by the fender shape over the rear wheel. The Cisitalia's sculptural qualities made it a natural choice for the permanent design collection at the Museum of Modern Art in New York.

tectural accessories for them, along the lines of their prewar US counterparts. The primary motivation behind the numerous marriages that ensued was one of creating a visual impact on the world market that was specifically Italian in character, and it was not long before a number of observers, like the designer F. H. K. Henrion (q.v.), were remarking on the emergence of a 'family likeness'[6] among Italy's consumer goods. The products he isolated for comment, as early as 1949, included Gio Ponti's (q.v.) coffee machine for La Pavoni of 1948;[7] the Vespa motor-scooter of 1946; and PininFarina's Cisitalia car [32], all of which manifested the same elegant, streamlined curves which were as expressive as, but much more restrained than, their transatlantic equivalents.

Postwar Italy demonstrated two distinct advantages in its position in world trade, both of them brought about by its late arrival. First, by the 1950s the concept of the designer had become a known, international quantity and, secondly, by that time new machinery to work the new materials, among them plywood, aluminium and plastics, had become commercially available. Also, because most Italian manufacturing companies were craft-based, and therefore relatively small, they remained highly flexible and were able to make rapid modifications to their production, following the changing demands of the market.

Design in postwar Italy was quick to develop into a highly sophisticated marketing exercise. Because its products were aimed from the beginning at a small, wealthy, international market, Italy was able to focus on quality and aesthetic innovation as the two defining characteristics of its consumer goods. This inevitably placed a strong emphasis on the role of the designers, giving them the sole responsibility of finding the right visual formula for the product. For the most part, disillusioned with prewar Rationalism because of its associations with fascism, they took their cue from contemporary fine art incorporating into many of their designs sensuous curves directly inspired by the abstract, organic sculpture of artists like Henry Moore, Hans Arp, Alexander Calder and Max Bill (qq.v.). The Turinese furniture designer, Carlo Mollino (q.v.), took this expressive aesthetic to an extreme in what he called his 'streamline surreal' tables and chairs [33]. As a result of this pioneering work Italy, in particular Milan, soon became a centre for debate and discussion about progressive attitudes towards design, and the postwar Triennales,[8] three-yearly exhibitions of design which had been initiated in the 1920s and which were

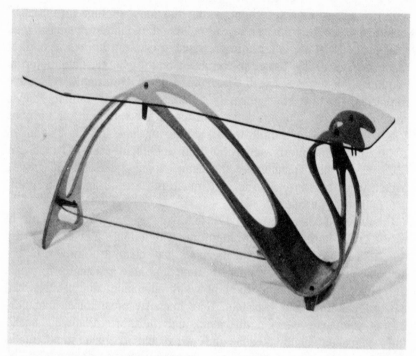

33   Carlo Mollino, tea-table, 1950.
Mollino was the most idiosyncratic of the Italian postwar furniture designers. Based in Turin rather than Milan where most furniture designing went on, he developed a personal style which he described as Streamlined Surreal and which derived, he claimed, from natural phenomena like branches of trees and antlers' horns and from the curved paths of downhill skiers, a sport at which he was adept. This little table, which is made out of organically shaped laminated plywood and glass joined to each other by small wooden pegs, is typical of Mollino's forms and represents Italian postwar sculptural design at its most extreme.

resumed in 1947 [26], turned into a necessary pilgrimage for enthusiastic young designers all over the world.

Finland

Finland was among the other countries which presented a unified and exciting image of postwar design at the Triennales of 1951 and of 1954. Although late in starting its onslaught on the world market, and in spite of being well behind its Scandinavian partners which by 1939 had established both Swedish Modern and Danish Modern[9] as significant mid-century design styles, Finland's impact, when it came, was both more dramatic and more immediately effective. Like Italy, Finland focused on exclusive products aimed at the top end of the market and evolved a highly expressive style which had little in common with Sweden's and Denmark's socially democratic approach to design. Instead, Finland's postwar programme was a sophisticated, well-executed exercise in public relations and marketing which earned that country a unique position in world trade.[10] The names of Finnish designers, in particular those of Tapio Wirkkala (q.v.) [34] and Timo Sarpaneva (q.v.), were associated closely with their products. These were among the first of the European 'superstar' designers who were marketed along with their products and whose very names were enough to render a product more desirable than its anonymous competitors.

West Germany

Another country to make an impact at the Triennales of the mid-1950s was West Germany which was by then making a rapid recovery from the setbacks it had received during the war. West Germany created its particular postwar image for the product on the basis of a superrational aesthetic [38] which was manifested most clearly in the design of its electrical and electronic consumer goods. This represented a deliberate return to the pre-Nazi, 'ideologically acceptable' days of the Bauhaus and, by the 1960s, West Germany had re-established itself as a leader in world trade, largely on the basis of this rigorous approach to design and its commitment to technological research.

34 Tapio Wirkkala, Kantarelli vase for Iittala, 1947.
Finland's experiments in glass design in the early postwar period laid the seeds of a new
Finnish design wave. It was characterized by elegant, expressive, organically shaped
forms which implied luxury and exclusiveness. Trained initially as a sculptor, Wirkkala
was one of the main exponents of this new glass style and this vase was among his first
projects for the Iittala Glass Company. It won him a prize in an Iittala competition held in
1947 and another at the Milan Triennale of 1951 and helped pave the way for much of the
Finnish design produced in the postwar period.

35 Honda, Super-Cub motor-cycle, 1958.
Like so many of the early postwar designs to come out of Japan, the appearance of this product was dictated by its functions rather than by any abstract notion of styling. Shigeru Honda's little motorized bicycle, which began life with a 50 c.c. engine but later acquired a 100 c.c. one, was a step-through model designed to go across rice-field trails and through the narrow alleys in Japanese cities. Honda needed a low-priced, light, manoeuvrable bike with a small but powerful engine which he situated under the bicycle-style seat so that it could be cooled by the breeze. A platform was put on the back for the delivery boy. Through clever promotion, Honda succeeded in capturing a large US market for his design.

Postwar Japan

Although it was not yet obvious at the Triennales of the 1950s, Japan was also beginning to recognize the benefits of a positive design policy. Like Italy and Finland, Japan had industrialized late and very rapidly but unlike these countries commitment to craft-based industries concentrated its energies on products of a more technical nature such as cameras, hi-fi equipment and motor-cycles [35]. In the early stages of Japan's onslaught on the world market the combination of advanced technology and low price was sufficient to secure a ready place for these goods, but as the wealth of the industrialized world increased, and Japan sought to expand its markets, it began to think about the importance of design, not simply as a necessary element within production, but also as an aid to sales. Like so many countries before it, Japan turned, first, to the US model for inspiration, emulating that example as a means of encouraging its own indigenous design profession. With its traditional cultural emphasis on the team rather than the individual, however, Japan was keener to emphasize the name of the company than that of the designer who became, as a result, an anonymous but none the less essential element within the manufacture and sales of Japanese consumer products.

The postwar emphasis on design as a means of promoting a national identity within international trade meant a significant shift of definition for the concept. It became in fact a kind of product signature in a world where mass communication made it possible for, and indeed inevitable that, goods produced in one country were very quickly available and desirable in another. Many products were, in fact, made only for export and were never seen by the home market. This resulted in the emergence of a select group of exclusive 'designed' objects which attained an international status and seal of approval. This was encouraged by the professional magazines, exhibitions, competitions, museum collections and other forms of mass communication and propaganda which specialized in design and which served to form an international consensus on the subject. The design collection at the Museum of Modern Art in New York, for example, consisted of the same products – most of them from Scandinavia, Germany and Italy – which filled the pages of the Italian magazine *Domus* and the British magazine *Design* in the postwar period. In the late 1950s an international concept of 'good design' emerged and the objects which earned this label achieved the status of super-products. Even in Japan the 'G' mark was evolved as an award granted by the Japanese body concerned with exports – JIDPO – to those international products which merited the description of 'good design'. Among the goods they selected were machines manufactured by Braun and Olivetti.

Design and Mass Culture

While one facet of design in the post-Second World War context was characterized by this exclusive, international, establishment-promoted 'high cultural' phenomenon which played a significant role within world trade, its other major manifestation in the period, which was equally dependent upon the role of mass communications media for its dissemination, was within the context of mass culture.

As a result of its early realization of the alliance between design and the popular imagination, the USA were well in advance of Europe in its acceptance of design as part of mass culture. By the 1940s and 1950s, in the streets outside the exclusive objects housed in the Museum of Modern Art, the USA were pioneering an approach to design in which object symbolism, obsolescence and overt consumerism played a fundamental role [12]. The products involved were aimed at a different sector of society from the one which consumed 'international, good design' and, visually, they had very little in common with it.

The US economic presence in Europe during the early postwar years encouraged a process of 'cocacolanization'[11] which, in turn, began to influence the nature of European production and consumption. This did not go without opposition, however, and there was strong resistance from some representatives of the old 'minority' culture. In Britain a number of people condemned the new culture which was beginning to invade Britain, including Raymond Williams who wrote in 1962 that: 'In Britain, we have to notice that much of this bad work is American in origin. At certain levels, we are culturally an American colony. But of course it is not the best American culture that we are getting',[12] and by the early 1950s articles about the evils of stream-lining had already begun to fill the pages of *Design* magazine.[13]

In spite of such misgivings, mass culture on the US model did infiltrate Western Europe during this period, encouraged by the mass media, particularly advertising and popular magazines, and by the mass consumption of products whose design was aimed at instant gratification. During the 1950s Europe was flooded with the sudden abundance of the same consumer goods that the USA had experienced in the 1920s and, as a result, the commercial emphasis moved firmly into the sphere of electric and electronic goods rather than any other consumer durables. By 1957, for example, 'One in every three middle-class and one in every five working-class homes in Britain had an electric washing machine'.[14]

One reason for the sudden availability of the new products was technological, as automation had brought with it expanded possibilities for manufacturing. Socially, the growth of mass consumption was, in Britain for example, encouraged by an increase in general wealth in the period up to the late 1960s. This, in turn, was a direct result of government policies of full employment and healthier balance of payments figures. New phenomena, like the extension of hire purchase and other credit facilities, and the increasing wealth of most young people also helped to expand the market enormously, as did the growing number of working wives. Much of the advertising for consumer products was in fact aimed at women who had both more money to spend than ever before and a large say in what went into the home. In Britain this was reflected in the introduction of the concept of design into popular women's magazines like *Woman* and *Woman's Own* which, in addition to general articles about 'how to furnish your sitting room' and indications as to where to buy which items, also included references to 'contemporary' design in their short stories, hinting at the instant social status that accompanied the purchase of such items. The do-it-yourself movement was also imported from the USA in these years and illustrations on the covers of *Do-It-Yourself* magazine in the 1950s showed married couples busy at work building cupboards and stripping walls together.

The availability of so many new consumer goods in Britain in the 1950s acted as an agent of social change along with other manifestations of the mass media. These changes were as visible in the office and the street as they were in the home. The new postwar youth cults, for example, were becoming highly consumer-oriented and the consumption of certain items – among them the Vespa motor-scooter, the fast motorbike, the record-player, the 'transistorized' pocket radio and the tape-recorder – became necessary entry requirements into certain subcultural groups.

The Vespa motor-scooter serves as a prime example of the way in which products' meanings can change as they become appropriated by different cultural groups. It is also an interesting instance of the way in which consumption and use can modify, if not dramatically alter, the symbolic and iconographic intentions of both the manufacturer and the designer.[15] The Vespa was developed in Italy by the Piaggio engineering works after the Second World War as a result of prewar experiments, wartime technological discoveries, and as a means of utilizing production machinery which would have otherwise remained unused. From the start it was intended to meet the needs of the female motor-cyclist. When it appeared in 1946 the Vespa represented a radical design breakthrough inasmuch as it provided a completely new image for a piece of transport machinery. It became one of the visual symbols of Italy's economic and cultural reconstruction after the war and it developed quickly into a familiar 'wasp-like' appendage of the urban environment, used both by men and women as a practical urban tool for short-distance rides. For many it functioned also as a political symbol for the new democracy and the break with prewar fascism. With its introduction into Britain in the 1950s, along with the espresso coffee bars and Italian suits, it soon developed, however, into a cult object, used almost exclusively by young male members of the subcultural avant-garde.

By the early 1960s this subcultural group had become more specific and regimented and its members were known collectively as Mods who stood, ideologically, in opposition to the Rockers for whom the motorbike, rather than the motor-scooter, was a sacrosanct object. The Mods adorned their Vespas with aerials, hung with furry tails and flags, and covered the fronts with mascots and badges – decorative and symbolic additions which D'Ascanio, the Vespa's engineer back in 1946, could never have envisaged. This variability of significance is typical of products which become absorbed into mass culture through mass consumption and turn into the ritualized appendages of the life-style of different social and cultural groupings and subgroupings.

In his book *Future Shock*, the American Alvin Toffler has pointed out that whereas in the first stages of mass production, standardization of parts and products was both the norm and the ideal, with the advent of automation and differentiated markets within mass consumption it has been superseded by 'endless variations'[16]. This allows consumers to purchase, in the case of a car for example, a basic design and then to add, or simply pay for, as many extra, personalized spare parts as they wish. It also encourages the production of small batches of varied models rather than large runs of undifferentiated designs.

With the expanded market of the postwar period, eclecticism became increasingly inevitable and mass culture succeeded in exerting not just one new set of values but several. As Susan Sontag has pointed out: 'The new sensibility is defiantly pluralistic; it is dedicated both to an excruciating seriousness and to fun and wit and nostalgia.'[17] Although the USA continued to influence Europe where mass culture was concerned throughout the 1950s, the early 1960s witnessed a reassertion of Europe over the USA in terms of cultural hegemony. The Pop revolution of those years was predominantly a British phenomenon but its influence was worldwide and, by the middle of the decade, the products of Swinging London were reaching an international audience [27]. The mood changed dramatically, however, in the early 1970s when the curve of economic expansion began to drop significantly downwards for the first time in twenty years and inflation became a worldwide reality.

Pluralism and complexity have remained the norm, however, where design is concerned. With the ever increasing growth of the mass communications media, and its accompanying democratization of information, products are visible in popular magazines almost as soon as they are picked up by the specialist press and while the avant-garde is busily borrowing images from mass culture, the commercial world is also quick to take ideas from subcultures and to mass produce them. By the end of the 1970s, along with advertising and TV, the 'admass' society had appropriated design as one of its major communicative forces.

Notes: Chapter 9

1 H. Hopkins, *The New Look: A Social History of the Forties and Fifties* (London: Secker & Warburg, 1964), p. 231.
2 Marshall McLuhan wrote a number of books in the 1950s and 1960s including *The Mechanical Bride: Folklore of Industrial Man* (New York: Vanguard, 1951), *The Gutenberg Galaxy: The Making of Typographic Man* (Toronto: University of Toronto Press, 1962), *Understanding Media: The Extensions of Man* (New York: McGraw Hill, 1964) and *War and Peace in the Global Village* (New York: Bantam, 1968) in which he examined the multiple ways in which the mass media had affected contemporary social and cultural life.
3 R. Williams, *Communications* (Harmondsworth, Middx: Penguin, 1968), p. 99.
4 Many Italian manufacturing companies were created, after the Second

World War, in the areas of furniture, small domestic items and consumer electronic equipment. Artemide, Arflex, Azucena, Tecno and Flos were among the new furniture and lighting firms which, from the outset, employed consultant designers and even, in the cases of Arflex and Azucena, had designers on their boards, while Kartell was established, in the early 1980s, to work on small plastic products and Brionvega was set up at the same time to manufacture TVs and hi-fi equipment.

5　E. Rogers, 'Editorial', *Domus*, no.60 (January 1946), p. 3.

6　F. H. K. Henrion, 'Italian journey', *Design*, no.1 (January 1949), pp. 7–10.

7　Gio Ponti's (q.v.) design of 1949 for the La Pavoni coffee machine epitomized the new streamlined, industrial style that Italian manufacturers and designers developed as a symbol of their bid for a new, democratic society.

8　The first postwar Triennale took place in 1947 and took, as its central theme, postwar reconstruction and the need for furnishings for the new homes. In the 1950s the exhibitions reflected a growing aesthetic emphasis on Italian design and also acted as a show place for other international developments.

9　Danish Modern was a design style which reached its peak in the years just following the Second World War. It was most closely associated with the work of the furniture craftsmen-designers – Hans Wegner, Borge Morgensen and Finn Juhl – but the metalwork of George Jensen, Kay Bojesen and Henning Koppel also played a vital role in the international image of Danish design.

10　In the postwar period Finland made an effort to integrate design into its manufacture. The efforts of the glass company, Iittala, in employing, in the late 1940s, both Wirkkala and Sarpaneva (qq.v.) were amongst the first positive moves in this direction and a strong Finnish design movement emerged, manifested predominantly in glass, ceramics, textiles and furniture. It was a movement which exhibited a bold, highly expressive aesthetic and bore little relation to its Swedish and Danish counterparts.

11　The term 'Cocacolanization' implies the way in which, along with its financial aid, the USA imported US culture into Europe in the early 1950s. This was most evident in the Hollywood films, pulp novels, popular music, TV programmes, consumer products and advertising campaigns that flooded the European mass market at that time.

12　Williams, *Communications*, p. 102.

13　A number of articles emerged in *Design* magazine in the early 1950s condemning the vulgarity and 'dishonesty' of US streamlining. They are documented in Dick Hebdige's article 'Towards a cartography of taste 1935–1962', *Block*, no.4 (Middlesex Polytechnic, 1981), pp. 62–9.

14　Hopkins, *The New Look*, p. 309.

15　D. Hebdige, 'Object as image: the Italian scooter-cycle', *Block*, no.5 (1981), pp. 44–64.

16　A. Toffler, *Future Shock* (London: Pan, 1971), p. 247.

17　G. E. Stearn (ed.), *McLuhan Hot and Cool* (Harmondsworth, Middx: Penguin, 1968), p. 295.

10

Educating Designers

The question of what constitutes an adequate training for designers, destined for careers in industry and mass production, has resurfaced repeatedly throughout this century. The demands made on designers for industry are very different from those made, on the one hand, on the fine artist and craftsman – both of whom are expected to explore the limits of their own creative individualism – and, on the other, on the engineer who is trained primarily in technical expertise. While designers require some of the training offered to these two groups neither of them is sufficient, and the question of how their needs might be formulated into an educational programme has preoccupied many minds through this and the last centuries.

Nineteenth-Century Experiments in Design Education

Before the idea of providing a specialist education for designers emerged in the middle of the nineteenth century they had been trained by the parallel structures of academic art education and the apprenticeship system. Many of the British manufacturers who were using the new production machinery, and catering for the new mass market, were in desperate need of individuals who could combine artistic with technical skills, and they began to campaign for a workforce which had been trained in an appropriate way. The government of the day was, however, more preoccupied with the problem of raising the general level of taste than simply with providing the manufacturers with employees, and it was with the former end in sight that it set about establishing the design schools in the middle years of the century. The first example, the reorganized Normal School in South Kensington, was rapidly followed by similar schools established in all the major industrial centres, including Manchester, Paisley, Birmingham and

158

Leicester. Their primary aim was to instil the principes of fine art into a new breed of designers for industry, thereby raising the aesthetic standards of the country's mass-produced goods. The manufacturers were disappointed in the results of this experiment, however, as it soon became evident that the fine art basis of the new so-called design schools failed to provide students with the necessary technical and specialist skills demanded of a designer for mass-production industry.

As with so many British developments in the nineteenth century the main impact of the design schools was felt most strongly abroad as, in the years around the turn of the century, a number of other countries repeated the British experiment, often with more success. The work of Lethaby (q.v.) at the Central School in London and that of John Sparkes at the Lambeth School were especially noticed and emulated for their particular approaches towards the training of craftsmen for industry.

In the USA numerous efforts were made to establish an education for designers at that time. One such experiment was a school which opened in Cincinatti in the 1880s as an attempt to sustain the marriage between the arts and industry that had been consummated for the first time at the Centennial Exhibition in Philadelphia of the previous decade. Among the subjects on the school's syllabus were decorative designing, metalwork and industrial art. This was also the period of the establishment of the Art Institute in Chicago and of a number of other art schools in a number of other major US centres. As in Britain, however, the emphasis moved, on the whole, towards fine art and away from vocational design training and, once again, many objections were voiced about the inadequacies of this approach. In Massáchusetts, for example, the governor attempted to abolish the State Normal Art School because the students were modelling human figures in clay.

It was in Germany that some of the most advanced thinking on art and design education occurred around the turn of the century, thanks largely to the contribution of the art historian, Alfred Lichtwark (q.v.), who was particularly influential within the context of elementary and secondary education. In Weimar, the Belgian Henri Van de Velde (q.v.) took over the directorship of the School of Applied Arts in the early twentieth century, remaining there until 1914, and progressive educational principles were also evident in a number of other centres in Germany where many new and influential teachers were busily being appointed, among them the architects Peter Behrens in Düsseldorf, Hans Poelzig in Breslau and Bruno Paul (qq.v.) in Berlin.

The Bauhaus

It was within this same mood of educational optimism and reform that the architect, Walter Gropius (q.v.), was called to Weimar in 1919 to head a new school which combined the Academy of Fine Art with Van de Velde's old School of Applied Arts. The Bauhaus was the result of this amalgamation. Here, for the first time, a thoroughgoing attempt was made to rationalize the theoretical and practical implications of the transition from hand to machine production and to develop a curriculum for training designers for industry on that basis.

In pedagogical terms, Gropius sought to educate the individual in the visual language of mass production. Like Muthesius (q.v.) before him, he based his philosophy of design upon the craft process and saw his work as an extension of the theories of William Morris (q.v.). In the Bauhaus Manifesto of 1919, for example, Gropius was clear about this commitment, and about what he saw as the necessary links between aesthetic and social ideals: 'Architects, sculptors, painters, we must all turn to the crafts. Art is not a "profession". There is no essential difference between the artist and the craftsman.'[1]

The mood of the first years at the Bauhaus was one of artistic individualism and Gropius surrounded himself with some of the leading Expressionist painters of the day – among them Lionel Feininger, Wassily Kandinsky, Paul Klee, Oscar Schlemmer and Gerhard Marcks (qq.v.), who introduced students to basic drawing skills and to the language of abstract form. By 1923, however, Gropius had moved towards a more objective concept of form and he is recorded as saying in that year: 'The teaching of craft is meant to prepare for designing for mass production'.[2]

The change of emphasis was reflected in the alterations in teaching personnel at that time. The Vorkurs, that is, the preliminary course, was, at first, in the hands of Johannes Itten (q.v.), a member of the mystical cult of Mazdaznan[3], who brought to the Bauhaus a highly individualistic version of the pedagogical principle of 'learning by doing'. With the dismissal of Itten by Gropius in 1923 the Bauhaus course took on a whole new direction.

Klee and Kandinsky concerned themselves with what the latter described as the 'objective basic existence of form and colour elements'.[4] While Klee was involved with the constructional elements of composition – points, lines and planes – Kandinsky concentrated on colour, using the colour circle as an analytical tool. Of the two, Klee was the more empirical in his teaching and philosophical pursuits, while Kandinsky was more spiritually oriented.

Following the Vorkurs, students went into craft workshops and became journeymen, in the medieval sense, perfecting their skills in the areas of carpentry, metal, pottery, stained glass, stage design, weaving, or typography. In the workshops craftsmen and artists taught alongside each other. Gerhard Marcks, for example, co-operated with the potter Otto Lindig (q.v.), while Klee worked with tapestry and Kandinsky with stained glass. After 1925, and the move from Weimar to new, purpose-built premises in Dessau [36], a few Bauhaus graduates, among them Marcel Breuer and Josef Albers (qq.v.), went on to teach at the school. They were able to synthesize the work of the fine artists and the craftsmen for the first time and to move more positively in the direction of mass production and a more objective kind of instruction. Laszlo Moholy-Nagy (q.v.), who replaced Itten at the Bauhaus, brought with him his Eastern European Constructivist ideas and skills and helped move the course further away from expressive individualism in the direction of reductive collectivism, thus helping to encourage a more objective approach towards the construction of three-dimensional form.

In 1928 Walter Gropius, disappointed with his failure to push the Bauhaus syllabus through into architecture, which he considered the 'mother of the arts', left the Bauhaus and his successor, Hannes Meyer (q.v.), changed the mood there drastically. Meyer encouraged a highly systematic approach towards design, denying the role of aesthetics and emphasizing, instead, engineering and technology. By the time of the arrival of Mies van der Rohe (q.v.), the school's third and final director who remained in office until the closure of the Bauhaus by the Nazis in 1933, Gropius's vision had become completely transformed.

Throughout its career the Bauhaus was characterized by diversity in its ranks and it is difficult, as a result, to summarize its achievements which, in terms of its subsequent influence, were both numerous and substantial. Although, during its lifetime, it seldom moved beyond the production of prototypes for mass production and made few attempts to work on products from any other than the traditional art industries, the teaching at the Bauhaus sowed the seeds none the less for modern

36 Walter Gropius, the Bauhaus building in Dessau, 1926.
The new building in Dessau, to which the Bauhaus staff and students moved in 1926, was a purpose-built construction which housed teaching and workshop areas, a theatre, a canteen, a gymnasium and twenty-eight studio-flats for students. The building was progressive from an architectural point of view for a number of reasons, which included its skeleton of reinforced concrete, its flat roof which employed a new water-proofing material, and its floors of hollow tiles which rested on beams. It took just over a year to build it. On the left of this picture, is the vast glass curtain wall which ran along one side of the workshops, known as the aquarium. The interiors were all designed by the Bauhaus workshops.

industrial design education. It eagerly embraced the aesthetic, social and cultural principles of mass production and attempted to instil into students a vision of the new technological society and its constraints. Although the Bauhaus vision was highly abstract it encapsulated, nevertheless, the spirit of the age and an emotional commitment to objective, standardized, democratic form for the mass-produced object. When, in 1954, Mies van der Rohe looked back at the Bauhaus he came to the conclusion that: 'The Bauhaus was not an institution with a clear programme – it was an idea.'[5] It was an idea which combined the objective values of standardization and technology with the humanism of craft production and thereby confronted, even if it did not resolve, the major issue in the education of the designer in this century.

The New Bauhaus and the Institute of Design

The impact of the Bauhaus upon US art and design education was considerable as a direct result of the fact that, in the years of the Nazi regime in Germany, many of the Bauhaus protagonists moved across the Atlantic and continued their pioneering work on American soil. While Walter Gropius (q.v.) took up a Chair in Architecture at Harvard, Mies van der Rohe (q.v.) went to the Massachusetts Institute of Technology, Josef and Anni Albers (qq.v.) became teachers at Black Mountain College, and Moholy-Nagy (q.v.) opened the New Bauhaus in Chicago. Another US educational institution founded on European principles was the Cranbrook Academy of Art in Michigan, but the Cranbrook experiment was less German in spirit than Finnish. Eliel Saarinen (q.v.) was the founder of the school and the architect of its buildings and he lived with his family in a house, also built to his own design [37], on the Cranbrook complex. The idea of an artistic community was central to the educational philosophy behind Cranbrook, and the school's most famous graduates – among them Ray and Charles Eames, Harry Bertoia [41], Jack Lenor Larsen and Florence Knoll (qq.v.) – remained committed to the alliance between fine art and design in their professional careers. There was a move, in the 1940s, to introduce some industrial design teaching into Cranbrook but it proved short-lived and the school remains best known for its success in the field of the applied arts, in particular furniture, textiles and ceramics.

37 Eliel Saarinen, dining-room, Saarinen House, Cranbrook Academy, 1928–30.

Among the other buildings on the Cranbrook campus Saarinen also built a house for himself and his family and, in the spirit of the Arts and Crafts concept of 'total design', also designed its dramatic interiors. The dining-room which is illustrated here, has a strong Art Deco feel about it. It was an octagonal room with a stepped, domed ceiling, the walls were covered in rectangular fir panels, and the interiors of the corner niches were painted Chinese red. Saarinen also designed the Art Deco dining-suite, the side chairs being later manufactured by the Company of Master Craftsmen. They were also made of fir, covered in black and ochre paint and upholstered in red.

The New Bauhaus in Chicago was, however, more effective in transferring specifically German educational ideas to the USA, finally consolidating many of the ideas that had existed, in embryo, in the 'old world'. Moholy-Nagy arrived in the USA in 1937, via Britain, as a political refugee and was asked, on the recommendation of Gropius, to go to Chicago to head a new school. Sponsored by the Association of Arts and Industries, which was eager to improve the quality of US manufactured products through an educational programme, the school was first named by Moholy, the New Bauhaus, with the added subtitle, American School of Design.

The syllabus resembled that of the German Bauhaus with a preliminary year dedicated to the 'rudiments' of art followed by specialized study in workshops. An old Bauhaus student, Hin Bredendieck (q.v.), led the preliminary course and other members of staff included an old co-patriot of Moholy's, Gyorgy Kepes (q.v.), who was in charge of the light workshop and photography, Alexander Archipenko (q.v.) who ran the sculpture workshop, and David Dushkin who was in charge of the music element. Work on the preliminary course included paper-cutting exercises and experiments with prisms and mirrors. A major modification to the earlier Bauhaus syllabus was the inclusion of non-artistic subjects, including philosophy, physics and biology. Moholy was deeply conscious of the new chronological and geographical context of the Chicago experiment and felt that, with the expansion of technology that had occurred since the German days, there was an increased need to bridge the gap between the arts and the sciences. In spite of the enthusiasm which surrounded the new venture it lasted no more than a year as the Association of Arts and Industries disapproved of Moholy's ideas and withdrew its support. As a result, the school was forced to close in 1938 even though new staff, among them Herbert Bayer and Jean Helion (qq.v.), had been employed for the following year.

Moholy remained undefeated, however, and instantly began planning a new school of his own which he opened in 1939 and called, at first, the School of Design, later the School of Design in Chicago, and finally, in 1944, it became known officially as the Institute of Design in Chicago. Sibyl Moholy-Nagy has described the efforts that went into cleaning out the abandoned bakers that they used as the school's premises and into finding ways of financing the operation: 'Moholy had to hock his wristwatch with the head waiter of the Kungsholm Restaurant in order to pay for a smorgasbord dinner to which he had invited his staff the night before the opening.'[6]

From 1939 to 1946 the school operated with relatively few problems and Moholy was able to develop his educational ideas to the full. The preliminary course followed the model established by the New Bauhaus and, through the idea of direct contact with materials, Moholy gradually evolved his own theory of form, central to which was the concept of 'organic' design. Moholy was also conscious of the need for a social context for design and he evolved a somewhat obscure theory of what he called 'socio-biological' design which he outlined in his book *Vision in Motion.*[7]

Linked to these ideas was an emphasis on the emotional or 'sensorial' nature of design which Moholy saw as a vital addition to Rationalism and in his writings he referred constantly to the 'whole man' in which reason and emotion were balanced. Moholy felt that emotion had been eliminated from creativity by an overemphasis on the ethic of industrialization and he sought to reinstate its function in design. Other premisses of his pedagogical principles included the legacy of Freudian psychoanalysis, yet another recurrent theme in *Vision in Motion,* and the teaching methods of Montessori in which play and exploration of the emotions play a fundamental role.

After their first year, the students at Chicago went on to specialize by choosing a workshop. Three main areas – architecture, product design and the light workshop – were available to them, with subchapters of weaving, photography, motion pictures, painting and sculpture. The workshops provided the focus for teaching as Moholy laid firm emphasis on the individual within the group and on the teacher/student relationship. He was less concerned with knowledge in itself than with the attitude that encourages learning, and workshop study was supplemented by related studies such as sciences, contemporary arts, form and civilization, the philosophy of progressive education, economics and foreign languages. Architecture was taught to all students at some stage as, like Gropius before him, Moholy saw that discipline as the art to which all the others aspired. Although, to a limited extent, the industrial design workshop encompassed areas like transport design in its scope of inquiry, the emphasis at the school was much more clearly upon the production of craft-based objects, particularly furniture.

Like the Bauhaus before it, the high-minded idealism which inspired the Institute of Design removed it from the context of the professional designer and the commercial world of industrial design. No links were made, for example, with the US consultant industrial designers who had emerged during the Depression to service the manufacturers of the new mechanical and electrical consumer goods, as Moholy disapproved strongly of body-styling. As Herbert Read wrote of him: 'No-one participated more fully than he in the spirit of the age. It was the age that failed this visionary pioneer.'[8] A few Institute of Design students did, however, become successful designers, albeit within craft-based industries. Charles Niedringhaus, for example, designed some furniture for Knoll (q.v.) in the late 1940s and Margaret de Patta (q.v.) became a leading jeweller in the 1950s and 1960s.

Moholy was succeeded at the Institute by Serge Chermayeff (q.v.), another political refugee from Europe soaked in Modern Movement principles, but his successor, Jay Doblin (q.v.), emerged, in contrast, from Raymond Loewy's (q.v.) highly commercial design consultancy. The employment of Doblin suggests that, by the 1950s, there was a general recognition in the USA of the need to inject marketing and knowledge about the consumer into the education of the industrial designer. In 1949 the Institute of Design was fused with the Illinois Institute of Technology, where it remains a department today. This final move triggered off certain changes in the institute's training programme for the designer, notably the introduction of a tougher intellectual and academic element and a stronger emphasis on product design and its commercial context. As Doblin explained: 'We don't see the designer in the old way as half artist and half engineer. He has got to make room for at least one third sociology.'[9]

The Hochschule für Gestaltung
at Ulm

The idea that the designer needs a rigorous training rather than simply being left to fulfil his individual creative potential was a common feature of a number of design educational experiments that took place in the post-Second World War period. Notable among them was the work of the Hochschule für Gestaltung, set up in Ulm in West Germany, where the emphasis moved away from creativity and simple problem-solving towards a vision of design as a much broader, cultural phenomenon and of designers as the transmitters of that culture.

Created in 1951 by Inge Aicher-School as a tribute to members of her family who were killed by the Nazis, the Hochschule defined itself, in its early stages under the directorship of the sculptor Max Bill (q.v.), as a natural extension of the prewar Bauhaus, but with all the modifications necessary in a new age. It was with the resignation of Bill in 1956 that the emphasis changed, however, to the broader, more culturally based approach to design education with which Ulm is most commonly associated.

From the mid-1950s onwards, the school emphasized, in the industrial design and building departments, the design of industrial products and, in the visual communication and information departments, the design of visual and verbal means of communication. In addition to workshop practice the foundation course, established by the Argentinian, Tomas Maldonado (q.v.), laid a strong emphasis on mathematics, sociology and cultural history, and all the four studio departments also stressed the role of socio-cultural history within their syllabuses.

The philosophical premises of the teaching at Ulm, as outlined by Maldonado, were founded on a view of design as both a systematic process, following the laws of what he described as 'scientific operationalism'[10] and as a form defined as the communication of symbolic meanings. The role of aesthetics was played down and formalism, in the Bauhaus sense, totally rejected. The method of form instruction at Ulm was highly mathematical in nature and this led Ulm designers to evolve a highly geometric, neo-Functionalist aesthetic for their products, a neo-Rationalist style which characterized in fact much German design in this period [38]. Maldonado and his colleagues were strong supporters of Functionalism but were adamant that it should not be seen as a style, but as a theory of design, which equates needs with production and which thus bypasses the neo-kitsch[11] which they saw as an inevitable part of postwar capitalism.

The social and economic context of design was also of central importance to Hochschule educational theory: in the first year roughly 27 per cent of the students' time was devoted to sociology, economics, political economy, psychology and ergonomics. This encouraged a critical approach towards the role of design in modern society and it was this which determined both the successes achieved at Ulm and, eventually, the demise of the school. The heads of the, by then, three departments – Maldonado, Giu Bonsiepe and Claude Schnaidt (qq.v.) – were all themselves highly critical of the role that design played within the capitalist economy which stressed demands rather than needs, and their attitude inevitably pervaded the whole institution and the activities that went on in it.

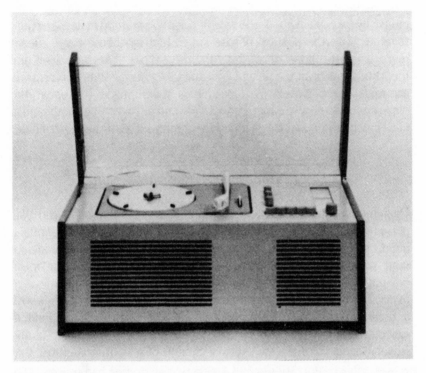

38 Dieter Rams, Phonosuper SK4 for Braun, 1956.
Rams's record-player from the mid-1950s typifies the German preoccupation at that time with rectilinear forms in product design. The Braun company, with the help of Rams and students from the Hochschule at Ulm, led the field with their severely geometric designs for domestic electric and electronic equipment. The Phonosuper SK4 was the first record-player with a transparent plastic lid and it was nicknamed 'Snow White's Coffin'. The harmonious disposition of the speaker grilles and the neat arrangement of the knobs are enhanced by the way it has been photographed straight on.

By 1968, the year in which it was closed down, the school was split internally by conflict about the role of scientific method in design. This, together with the political debate which had reached a head, meant there was little hope of a future for the school. The radicalism and theoretical rigour of the design educational experiment at Ulm remains unsurpassed, however. Attempts have been made to repeat the experiment on new ground, in Germany and in Italy, [12] but nothing has yet emerged to equal the strength of commitment of the Hochschule.

Design Education in Postwar Britain

Design education in Britain in the immediate post-Second World War period manifested no real changes from the situation in that country a hundred years earlier. As Britain was still preoccupied with the idea of craft training and an emphasis on the individual, few of the ideas developed in Germany had any significant impact. Some moves were made, however, in the 1930s to establish industrial design courses with a technical and a professional base at the Central School and in Leicester, and in the late 1940s there were some rumblings at the Royal College of Art (the Normal School of a century before) that changes were afoot. By the mid-1950s that institution had reorganized itself along new lines under the dynamic leadership of its new rector, Robin Darwin (q.v.). Realizing the anachronistic qualities of the Royal College of Art, Darwin wrote in 1950 that: 'The technical complexity of production methods has increased so greatly and will go on increasing with the introduction of new materials, that a greater degree of specialisation has become essential.'[13] His changes were of a practical rather than an intellectual nature: six separate, materials-based design schools were established, the administration of the college was reorganized accordingly, and the qualification of DesRCA, which at that time was only awarded after students had spent nine months in industry, was instituted. A generation of British designers for industry, including Robert Welch, Robert Heritage and David Mellor (qq.v.) [39], emerged as a result of these developments. The nature of Darwin's changes demonstrated the essentially vocationally biased nature of British design education which is still dominant today in spite of the decision made in the 1960s to award first degree design students Bachelor of Arts degrees.

In recent years design education in Britain has received few

39 David Mellor, polystyrene cutlery for Cross Paperware, 1969.
David Mellor was one of the first graduates from the newly reorganized Royal College of Art in the 1950s. He started out as a silversmith but moved into the field of industrial design, although the design of cutlery has remained his primary concern. This simple, elegant, modern-looking set of plastic cutlery was designed a decade after his graduation. It shows how well he can handle a non-traditional material even though many of his best-known designs for cutlery, including Pride and Chinese Ivory, are essentially steel-pieces. Mellor has set up his own small manufacturing plant in Sheffield.

injections of vitality. The ambiguity between vocational training and education remains and no thoroughgoing revision of the craft-based approach to industrial design teaching has been made. While some institutions in industrial centres, like Leicester and Manchester, have made links with manufacturers this has largely taken place on an *ad hoc* basis. Additional instruction in subjects such as management, ergonomics and in technical skills have been injected into a number of British design courses, but nothing like the Ulm experiment with its fiercely theoretical underpinning has yet been attempted. Design education in Britain remains based on an idealism which derives from an historical moment which has little contemporary relevance and it fails, for the most part, to confront the whole question of design for industry and to reformulate its ideals in the light of economic and social changes. In underdeveloped countries like India, ironically, where need is more apparent than demand, more radical design educational experiments are taking place and, even more ironically, in places like Italy, where design seems to have had the greatest cultural impact, there is very little design education to speak of.

The gap between design education and the general efficacy of design within industry is particularly strong in Britain which educates more designers than any other country, but which gives a much lower profile to design in its manufacturing industry and its commercial life. These are the kind of realistic problems that confront design education today and which, in fact, threaten its very existence. There is a sense also in which the most far-reaching design educational experiments, like those undertaken at the Bauhaus and at Ulm, seemed to stand, ideologically, in opposition to the economic status quo and thus to represent a threat to the very structure which, in modern capitalist society, supports the industrial designer. Throughout this century, design education has tended to swing between the two poles of utopianism and vocationalism, unsure, ultimately, of its aims. It is a dichotomy which is still in evidence today and there are few signs of a solution to the dilemma that it presents to the design educationalist.

Notes: Chapter 10

1   G. Naylor, *The Bauhaus* (London: Studio Vista, 1968), p. 50.
2   R. Banham, *Theory and Design in the First Machine Age* (London: Architectural Press, 1960), p. 281.
3   According to Frank Whitford, 'Mazdaznan was a faith which was derived

from ancient Zoroastrianism, was distantly related to the beliefs of the Indian Parsees and was the creation of a German-American typographer who had given himself the name Dr OZ (for Zarathustia) A Ha'njsh, and that it is no more than a veil obscuring a higher and more authentic existence' (*The Bauhaus*, London: Thames & Hudson, 1984, p. 53).

4   This was Gropius's expression quoted in *50 Years Bauhaus* (London: Royal Academy of Art, 1968), p. 27.

5   H. Wingler, *Bauhaus – Weimar Dessau Berlin Chicago* (Cambridge, Mass.: MIT 1969), p. 17.

6   R. Kostelanetz (ed.), *Moholy-Nagy* (New York: Praeger, 1969), p. 42.

7   L. Moholy-Nagy, *Vision in Motion* (Chicago: Paul Theobald, 1947).

8   Kostelanetz (ed.), *Moholy-Nagy*, p. 203.

9   'Illinois Tech opens new building and new era for Institute of Design', *Industrial Design*, no. 274 (October 1956), p. 108.

10 Tomas Maldonado's (q.v.) theory of 'scientific operationalism' was founded on the idea that design was a process which could be systematized and he promoted it as a means of avoiding the cul-de-sac of formalism in design.

11 The term 'neo-kitsch' is used in this context to describe the proliferation of 'bad taste' in the environment which in the postwar period resulted from design's becoming increasingly consumer- rather than production-led. This was seen, by many critics, to be a decadent state of affairs which could only be halted by allying manufacture (and design) with 'real' needs rather than the 'fake' needs created and encouraged by industrial capitalism.

12 When the Hochschule für Gestaltung was closed in 1968 some of the individuals involved, including Tomas Maldonado (q.v.), came to Italy where they continued their teaching, particularly in Milan and Venice. Others remained in Germany, where they attempted to integrate their 'Ulm' ideas into other educational curricula. The School at Offenbach, for example, took a radical approach to design education in the 1970s.

13 R. Darwin, 'The Royal College of Art today', *Design*, no. 17 (September 1950), p. 9.

11

Design and the Company

Industry used to treat designers as cosmeticians. We would be presented with a pen which a company had developed and our contribution would be limited to saying 'make it black with a red line around it'. (A designer for Porsche)[1]

The nature of the relationship of design, and of the designer, to manufacturing industry has been the main influence on the way design has evolved and on the way it has affected modern culture. Since the nineteenth century the rapport between design and industry has undergone several shifts of emphasis, and today there are a number of different ways in which a designer can co-operate with a manufacturing company. The major alternatives open to the manufacturer, where his commitment to design is concerned, are of employing a full-time, or in-house, designer (or design team depending on the size of the company); paying for the services of an independent consultant designer; operating both systems simultaneously; or working without a designer at all. There are many reasons why one policy may be preferable to another. The small company, for example, may not be able to support a full-time designer on the pay roll; the advantage of employing a consultant designer lies in the fact that he has an overview and knowledge about competing companies that a full-time, in-house designer cannot obtain; the in-house designer can develop specialist technical skills which are useful to the manufacturer; while companies which have a stable market and a cheap, functional product may have little need of help from a professional designer.

Whatever the particular nature of the arrangements between companies and designers, in recent decades design has become an increasingly important and recognized aspect of mass manufacturing and mass sales across a broad spectrum of the market. While some companies may play down this function in their promotions, choosing to sell their products through other factors such as economy, safety, ergonomic qualities, efficiency, or technical sophistication, many others emphasize the role that design, and in many instances even the designer, have played in the creation of the product. In turn, the link between design and sales guarantees a role for designers within production, as they are responsible for giving the product its image, its aesthetic appeal and its status symbolism – all the qualities which help in transferring it from production into consumption and use.

This commercial aspect of designers' roles is not, of course, their only function within industry. They are also employed to improve the utilitarian aspects of the product, to resolve the technical with the aesthetic requirements, to consider its ergonomic and safety properties, and to reduce, wherever possible, the costs of manufacture. The designer as stylist[2] or packager – whose name may be used in the promotion of a product – stands at one end of a spectrum, the other end being occupied by the more work-a-day, anonymous industrial designer who operates much more like an engineer than an ad-man. Both are essential elements in the production of technical, consumer products. They work together as team members, co-operating at the same time with the research and production engineers and with the marketing department, and resolving any conflicts that may arise between these two areas.

If the function of designers within manufacturing companies is both varied and complex, their position and status within the industrial hierarchy are no less so. There is a world of difference in terms of status between a craft-trained company designer working anonymously in, say, a small High Wycombe furniture company which produces downmarket products consumed largely for their competitive prices and, at the other, a highly paid consultant designer brought in as a guarantor of taste by, for example, a large automobile company or a multinational firm producing electronic equipment. This variation of function and status makes it very difficult to talk about 'designers' as a generally understood concept, a fact which, in turn, has made public appreciation of their role minimal.

Art and Manufacture in the Nineteenth Century

The idea of a company evolving a design policy goes back to the pioneering work of Josiah Wedgwood (q.v.) [17] whose early, marketing-based decision to employ fine artists on one range of his ceramic production, while dealing solely with anonymous utility ware for the other end of the market, set a precedent which, by the end of the nineteenth century, had been emulated by a number of other manufacturers within the applied arts sector of British industry.

The ceramics company of Doulton, for example, which began life in 1815 as a small riverside pottery in Lambeth producing a range of utilitarian salt-glazed stoneware had, by the end of the century, involved 'art' in its manufacturing. This was a direct result of Henry Doulton's decision to employ a few graduates from the Lambeth School of Art and to open up an art studio.

The decision to provide an artistic range of unique pieces which would exist alongside the company's mass-produced sanitary-ware was part of a clear decision policy and by the 1880s the studio had over two hundred artists working in it. The fashion soon caught on and a number of other manufacturers quickly imitated the Doulton experiment, opening art studios either in their factories, or on separate premises, keen to exploit the growing interest in consumer products with a highly explicit art content. From the beginning, the work produced by Doulton's Lambeth Studio was accompanied by the names of the artists, among them George Tinworth, Arthur Barlow and Frank Butler. In the 1890s and early 1900s Doulton also engaged artists to work on a series of mass-produced art wares and, in this case, it was the art director, Charles J. Noke, who was identified personally, along with some of the artists who worked with him.

By the turn of the century, Doulton had a highly developed design policy which formed an intrinsic part of his approach both to manufacturing and sales. For the top end of the market he manufactured his art-inspired, sophisticated goods created by named artists; whereas for the bottom end of the market he concentrated on more sentimental and naïve imagery using anonymous, and presumably cheaper, artists to design the prototypes. In the area of sanitary production there was, however, no question whatsoever of a designer being either mentioned or recorded and these goods were marketed solely on the basis of their function and price with no references in their sales literature either to taste or artistic content.

This sophisticated, multilevel policy of dividing the market into sectors and of producing diversified products with a different design content for each one was an early instance of design being closely linked to marketing and is a typical tactic of a manufacturer who aims to reach a broad range of the consuming public. Within each area of the production the designers inevitably performed a different function. While in the more exclusive sector they were given a free hand, in the mass sector their decisions were more strongly market-led, and for the sanitary-ware their brief was strongly determined by technological and economic constraints.

The Doulton example was emulated widely and many other firms began to divide up their market and to diversify their production and their designs accordingly. Herbert Minton (q.v.), the director of the Minton Ceramics Company from 1836 onwards, manufactured floor tiles as well as porcelain, and employed freelance artists such as Pugin and the sculptor John Bell on special products while his in-house art director, Leon Arnoux, was responsible from 1849 onwards for the employment of designers for the bulk of the company's production.

These design policies were the brainchilden of a particular breed of nineteenth-century entrepreneurs – Wedgwood, Doulton and Minton among them – whose farsightedness enabled them both to attract the right people to work with them and to have an instinctive feel of what the market, or markets, both needed or wanted.

Industry and the Designer in the Twentieth Century

One aid to the manufacturer in the formulation of a design policy in the twentieth century has been the growth of market research and the expansion of marketing departments within industry. In the USA in the 1930s the new consultant designers saw market research as an integral part of the service that they offered to industry, in addition to advising on the reduction in costs of production factors like retooling. It was also in the USA that the manufacturers of the new technological products first felt the need to evolve some kind of design policy, and employing freelance designers was often the only means of selling products in the glutted market of the Depression years. The equation of the costs of production, marketing and styling was carefully considered and the consultant designers were brought in by the often desperate manufacturer as the only way out of bankruptcy. They were frequently paid vast sums for their services and, in many cases, succeeded in enabling a company to keep its head just above water until the financial situation eased.

This US model was adopted widely in many other countries and

40   Arne Jacobsen, Ant chairs for Fritz Hansen, 1951.
This interior contains Jacobsen's chairs and another Fritz Hansen product, the 'super-elliptical' table designed by the Dane, Piet Hein, with the Swede, Bruno Mathsson. The mood of the setting with its lightness, its use of wood and the flowers on the table is that of the Danish Modern style which was much emulated in the 1950s. Jacobsen's Ant chair, which is still in production today, is made of nine layers of thin plywood finished in a choice of teak, oak, beech, or colour and has chromed steel rod legs. It was the first chair to be manufactured by a mass-production industrial process in Denmark and the back and seat are pressed in one piece.

during the economically depressed years of the 1930s more and more manufacturing companies, across a whole spectrum of goods from decorative ceramics to electrical equipment, became design-conscious, and styled their products in an attempt to remain part of national and international trade. While the smaller craft-based companies, which already knew and largely satisfied their markets, often continued to use craftsmen or individuals on the shop floor to provide them with their designs, many others, particularly the new companies, turned to the consultant designer in an attempt either to create new markets or to expand existing ones.

After 1945 many manufacturers, particularly those aiming their goods at the top end of the market, decided that it was design itself with which they were trading and intensified their efforts accordingly. In Britain the furniture companies, Race and Hille (qq.v.); in Sweden the ceramics company, Gustavsberg, and the glass firm, Orrefors; in Denmark the furniture company Fritz Hansen (q.v.) [40] and the manufacturers of audio equipment, Bang & Olufsen; in Finland the textile manufacturers, Marimekko and Vuokko (qq.v.); in Germany the ceramics companies of Arzberg and Rosenthal (q.v.) and the electronics company, Braun; and in the USA the furniture companies Herman Miller and Knoll (qq.v.) [41], and the electronic equipment firm, IBM; and in Japan, Sony and Honda (qq.v.) were all among the countless manufacturing companies who flew the banner of good, modern design in their promotional campaigns through the 1950s and 1960s.

Since the nineteenth century, however, manufacturers of products with a strong mass-market appeal have traditionally not stressed the individualistic qualities of their goods and have therefore been slower in isolating the artist or stylist responsible for the product's appearance. Thus although the automobile, for example, has sold on the basis of its styling since the early days, rarely have individual names been associated with their designs. Also, because of the need for secrecy in such a competitive world as that of automobile styling, manufacturers in this field have tended to employ resident rather than freelance designers. In 1927 Harley Earl joined the art and colour section of General Motors and turned it into the prototypical, in-house automobile styling section evolving the principle of the 'closed door' and producing designs which stressed consumer symbolism, often at the expense of ergonomic and safety factors. The principles of the 'annual model change' and 'built-in obsolescence' were inevitable results of

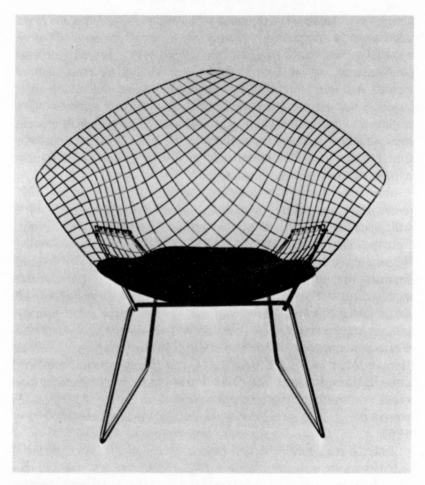

41 Harry Bertoia, wire chair for Knoll, 1952.
This is often referred to as the 'chicken wire' chair because of the fineness of the steel rod
used by Bertoia. It was one of a series of designs, which also includes a dining-chair and a
child's chair, evolved by the sculptor Harry Bertoia from a brief provided by Hans and
Florence Knoll. It is very much a sculptural exercise, as light passes right through the
wire grid creating a sense of spatial openness, and it is available with a painted, chrome,
or coloured plastic finish. Bertoia also designed the jigs used in its manufacture which still
function today.

Earl's policy at General Motors and they rapidly became the norm for all automobile manufacturers.

With only a few exceptions, like Alec Issigonis (q.v.) and his Austin Mini, produced in the early 1960s, automobile design remained an anonymous profession until the 1970s. When the Italian designer Giorgio Giugiaro (q.v.) became the celebrated creator of such models as the Volkswagen Golf, the Lancia Delta and the Fiat Panda, the cult of the personality designer had finally penetrated the world of the popular car.

The Italian Manufacturers and Design: Olivetti and Cassina

Since the Second World War, design and individualism have gone hand in hand in Italy whose highly styled goods are aimed, unequivocally, at the top end of the market and direct their appeal at a highly design-conscious public. The strongest force behind the Italian design phenomenon, which since the 1950s has dominated the international concept of design, is the manufacturer who during the years of the Italian industrial expansion of the early postwar period embraced design wholeheartedly in his search for a new product image. The Italian furniture and light manufacturers – among them Arflex, Artemide, Zanotta, Cassina, Flos, Tecno and Arteluce – the producers of electrical equipment, notably Olivetti and Brionvega, and of small plastic household goods like Kartell, all saw design as a fundamental quality of their consumer goods. Their support alone made the publication of so many design magazines[3] possible in Italy and it is they who invested vast sums of money in promoting Italian design in the rest of the world.

Among the first Italian manufacturers to evolve a positive attitude towards progressive, modern design was the Olivetti Company. Created in 1908 by Camillo Olivetti (q.v.), who had just come back from the USA where he had observed US production techniques at first hand, the company was responsible for the production of the first Italian typewriter. From the beginning Camillo Olivetti was less concerned with the invention than the appearance of this new product and wrote at that time: 'A typewriter should not be ornate or in questionable taste. It should have an appearance that should be serious and elegant at the same time.'[4] An engineer by training, he designed the typewriter himself and showed it at the Turin World's Fair of 1911.

This early commitment to modern design was consolidated and expanded by Camillo's son, Adriano, who became the president of the company when his father retired in 1938. Like his father, Adriano Olivetti (q.v.) was both an engineer and a humanist and it was he who was responsible for turning the company into one of the leading patrons of modern design. He had studied engineering at the Polytechnic of Turin and visited the USA to study its production and organization techniques. His subsequent modifications to the Olivetti Company production line – which he altered from a piecework system to one which was organized on more modern analytic lines – accelerated its output at a remarkable rate, allowing the company to expand rather than retract its efforts during the Depression.

It was during the 1930s that ideas about modern architecture and design began to filter into Italy and Adriano Olivetti was quick to put to commercial use the Bauhaus-inspired ideas that were being picked up at that time by the Italian Rationalists. He turned his attentions to the company's graphic design policy and took on a number of individuals with an avant-garde reputation – among them the Bauhaus graduate Alexander Schawinsky (q.v.), the Italian designer Giovanni Pintori (q.v.), the sculptor Constantino Nivola, and the engineer and poet Leonardo Sinisgalli – in order to transform the company's advertising graphics. His new team rapidly rationalized the aesthetic impact of Olivetti's brochures and posters utilizing photography and typography inspired by the new Functionalist style.

In the wake of this revolution in graphic design, Adriano Olivetti went on to transform the company's product design policy and, to this end, hired the services of Marcello Nizzoli (q.v.). Nizzoli had already made his name as a graphic and exhibition designer in Italy and was best known for his work, executed in collaboration with Eduardo Persico (q.v.), on one of the exhibits in the 1934 Italian Aeronautical Exhibition. In 1936 Nizzoli took over, on a consultancy basis, the design of all Olivetti's products. He also helped with advertisements and assisted on some of the company's architectural projects including its workers' housing developments in Ivrea and its headquarters in Milan. His major successes were, however, his designs for typewriters and office machines, in particular the Summa 40 adding machine of 1940, the Lexicon 80 typewriter of 1949 [42] and the portable Lettera 22 typewriter of 1950. Unlike his counterpart consultant designers in the

42 Marcello Nizzoli, Lexicon 80 typewriter for Olivetti, 1949.
Nizzoli's first typewriter was one of the 'family of objects' which emerged in Italy in the late 1940s. Its form was largely determined by the state of metal casting technology of the day, but its main appeal lies in Nizzoli's attention to visual detail in, for instance, the positioning of the seam line linking the two main parts of the body housing, the balance of the curves with each other and the careful placing of the graphics. The machine was available in French grey, thought to be a neutral, inoffensive colour popular in office design at that time. Nizzoli worked closely with the Olivetti engineer, Guiseppe Beccio, in developing this forward-looking design.

USA, Nizzoli was not involved with production efficiency, market research, or sales, but was employed simply as a sculptor to style the typewriter's body-shell.

The fact that at Olivetti the top management has been continually involved in design policy decisions has enabled the company to adopt a clearcut and progressive attitude towards modern design. This is in addition to the farsightedness of the Olivetti family, particularly Adriano, who has been recorded as saying that: 'If the top executive does not understand, we are lost.'[5] Olivetti expects its top management to understand artistic as well as scientific principles and to influence, rather than simply reflect, the progress of culture. From the early days the company assumed that industry should play a strong, active role in the creation of a nation's cultural life and should not simply be a passive mirror of public taste. The fact that it has succeeded in this mission reflects the fact, however, that the market, or its selected sector of the market, was ready for good design and did not need too much persuading.

Marcello Nizzoli was succeeded in 1956 by Ettore Sottsass (q.v.) who evolved a highly personal philosophy about the design of electronic equipment. Like Nizzoli, Sottsass worked, and still works, for Olivetti on a consultancy basis and thus retains enough freedom to work simultaneously on private, experimental projects and to head his own product design office. This relationship, which has since been repeated with Mario Bellini (q.v.), the designer of Olivetti's typewriters since the early 1970s, means the greatest possible commitment for Olivetti from its consultants combined with the maximum freedom for the designer.

In 1958 Sottsass designed Olivetti's first electronic computer, the ELEA 9003, in which he assessed many of the physical and aesthetic problems of early computer design, an area which had never before been confronted by a designer. Among the particular solutions that Sottsass offered was a decision to bring all the elements together into an architectural unity and to rationalize the compositional qualities of the components. These aesthetic considerations were coupled with a strong commitment to the ergonomic factors of the design and much of Sottsass's time is still spent on analysing the ways in which people relate to office furniture and equipment. This dual interest, in both innovative form and human factors, is reflected in the Olivetti Company's commitment both to design and to the welfare of its labour force for which it has provided, since the 1930s, sophisticated health, school and habitation facilities in Ivrea.

43 Gio Ponti, 699 Superleggera chair for Cassina, 1957.
Ponti's elegant little chair made of ash was modelled on a traditional chair made in Chiavari near Genoa in the nineteenth century. Designed in the early 1950s and remodelled towards the end of that decade, it represented one of the first attempts by the Cassina company to break into the international furniture market with a product designed by an Italian architect. It also demonstrates Ponti's concern that traditional craft techniques and values should underpin the modern Italian design renaissance.

While Olivetti has succeeded in integrating a strong design policy into its basic company policy, and in promoting its office equipment and furniture on the basis of their sculptural refinement, the Cassina furniture company has been involved since the war in promoting Italian design as part of the domestic environment.

Producers of furniture from the early 1920s, the Cassina brothers, Umberto and Cesare, did not become conscious of the marketing possibilities of modern design until the years following the Second World War. In the 1930s the design of their products had been largely an *ad hoc* affair, involving picking up 'what was around' in an eclectic manner and all aesthetic decisions were, at that stage, made according to the requirements of their clientele who varied greatly in wealth and taste. After the war, however, encounters with leading architects, namely Franco Albini and Gio Ponti (qq.v.), and a commission to supply furniture for ships, caused the Cassina company to rethink its policies. It decided to move away from its custom furnishing craft-base and to mass produce a limited range of architect-designed furniture pieces. Around this new policy, the company soon began to evolve a particular self-image for itself and in 1957 Ponti designed the Superleggera chair for Cassina [43] which rapidly became an Italian design classic and which is still being made and sold today by the same company.

From the collaboration with Ponti, others with leading designers – among them Carlo de Carli, Vico Magistretti, Tobia Scarpa, Mario Bellini and Gaetano Pesce (qq.v.) – were initiated during the following decades. From this point onwards the company limited its production to designs by important designers and ceased to manufacture furniture according to the whims of its clientele. In addition, in 1965 Cassina decided to initiate a project called the 'Masters',[6] which involved reproducing 'classic' designs from the late nineteenth and early twentieth centuries, thereby exploiting the commercial advantages of the growing interest in stylistic revivalism.

Inevitably, Cassina has expanded over the years and now employs a large team of design managers and public relations people who continue the work of the brothers in promoting the company's well-established relationship with 'classic, modern design'. Cleverly, the company is creating its own place in history, for by including the 'Masters' series in its production alongside contemporary 'classics' it is, by implication, producing the 'Masters' of the future and securing, in the process, its own future success. Its definite and aggressive design policy characterizes the approach of many other Italian furniture companies in the years after the Second World War.

Japanese Industry and the Designer

While postwar Italian manufacturers have depended upon individualism, exclusive markets and the named, consultant architect-designer as a means of marketing their consumer goods, their Japanese counterparts have preferred to retain the designer within their companies as an anonymous, shadowy figure.

The use of the in-house designer or design team by Japanese manufacturing companies developed as an intrinsic part of Japan's rapid industrialization in the years after 1945. Since the end of the previous century Japan had succeeded in finding ways of importing technology and capital from abroad and had been involved in a process called 'leap-frogging', that is, of emulating foreign models and then improving upon them. From its early commitment to heavy industries, such as shipbuilding and steel production, in the years after the Second World War the country moved into the manufacture of smaller, technological consumer goods, such as cars, motor-cycles, cameras and video- and audio-equipment. A few companies, like Honda, Toyota and Sharp (qq.v.), had grown out of smaller prewar organizations. Toyota, for example, had originally been involved with the production of automatic looms, while Sharp derived its name from the Ever-Sharp propelling pencil which its owner invented in 1915. Others, like Sony, were established after 1945.

The postwar expansion of Japanese industry was largely dependent upon US aid, both technological and financial, as well as direct sponsorship from the Japanese government. The main incentive behind it was the need for self-sufficiency and the manufacturers' desire that Japanese goods should compete on the world market. Shigeru Honda wrote, for example: 'I resolved to discourage imports and promote exports by enhancing technology and developing engines that were the highest in performance in the world'[7], and it was with these aims in mind that he developed his little Super-Cub step-through motor-cycle in the 1950s [35] and succeeded in penetrating the US market with it on an unprecedented scale.

The dual commitments to advanced technology and high quality have meant that Japanese industry has depended greatly both on research and development as well as on design. While the former tends to call the tune, design is none the less, albeit in a quiet way, a crucial aspect of its manufacturing, serving both as a means of 'humanizing' the technology and of meeting the ergonomic and product-image requirements needed to sell the goods and beat their competitors.

Made up of a group of professionally trained, anonymous company-men, the design team within a Japanese manufacuring company is responsible for the firm's image, in addition to the product's packaging and the sales brochures. It is characterized by its total integration into the company structure and by the rigorous organization of its work. At Canon, for example, the designers responsible for the company's photo-copying machines and cameras are divided into teams of seven and given a project for which they have to provide a solution within a limited time period. The rapid obsolescence of Japanese products – a Sharp calculator, for example, has a life-span of about six months – means that there is constant pressure on the designers to meet deadlines.

Each Japanese company has a specific design policy or slogan – while Toyota talks of 'harmonizing human needs with mechanical requirements', Sharp is committed to 'priority on easy operation' and Canon, in turn, to 'products with few defects'. Few design team-leaders are, however, important enough to be part of company management and they tend to be represented, instead, at board level by the head of the marketing division.

Japan is at the forefront in using computer-aided design to assist in its product development and has gone further than anywhere else, except perhaps West Germany and the USA, in rationalizing the work of the designer within industry. During the last forty years the same ground has been covered in design within Japanese industry as in Europe over the last hundred years. In Japan design has increasingly adopted dual affiliations with both production and sales, and more and more Japanese goods are finding their markets through design rather than, as before, simply through their low price, technical competence and reliability.

The Japanese company which exploits most fully the commercial advantages of a modern design aesthetic, in terms of its reputation on the world market, is the electronic equipment firm, Sony (q.v.). While most other Japanese companies have evolved a design style which indicates technical sophistication, often at the expense of visual clarity, Sony has evolved a more sophisticated design policy which involves emulating the careful attention to aesthetic detail of the European companies with which it is in direct competition. This policy forms an intrinsic part of the company's aggressive marketing tactics. Sony has also evolved a unique place for its design section within its company structure which allows it to overlap with every other major department in the company rather than being relegated to the marketing division alone. Thus within Sony, design innovation can be initiated by the design department as well as by research and development and this occasionally occurs, as in the instance of their famous Walkman product. The image of a Sony product is the visual reflection of the company's commitment to technological innovation and therefore the image of the company itself.[8]

The evolution of the concept of design in this century has been largely determined by the developing size and structure of manufacturing companies and their changing and varied policies. The numerous efforts made since the early 1960s to rationalize and systematize the design process have grown out of management's increasing desire to integrate design into top-level decision-making. As the economic context of manufacturing develops and changes, so design will evolve alongside it and manufacturers will determine its progress either, like Adriano Olivetti and Akio Morita of Sony, by considering it to be amongst the most important aspects of production and sales and therefore the responsibility of the man at the top, or by relegating it to a minor role within production and marketing and therefore of little interest to the management team. In the industrialized world, the future of design, not simply as a process within production but as a cultural phenomenon is largely in the hands of the manufacturers for they are the most important patrons of modern design.

Notes: Chapter 11

1 M. Hill, 'A compunction to function', *Sunday Telegraph Magazine*, 18 March 1979, p. 85.
2 The definition of the designer as a 'stylist' who was only concerned with the superficial appearance of a product emerged in the USA in the 1930s with the work of the early consultant designer for the new electrical industries. It became associated, also, with the design of automobiles where the engineer worked on the engine while the 'designer' was exclusively concerned with the body. By the 1950s 'styling' had become a derogatory term in many professional design circles because of its explicitly commercial implications.

3 Italy is remarkable for the number of design magazines that it publishes. Milan alone is said to have over forty, the best known of which include *Domus, Casabella, Casa Vogue, Gran Bazar, Gap Casa, Modo* and *Abitare*.

4 M. Hartland Thomas, 'Design policy begins at the top', *Design*, no.14 (February 1950), p. 9.

5 ibid., p. 8.

6 Cassina launched the 'Masters' series of reproduction modern furniture in the mid-1960s with the Le Corbusier (q.v.) armchair. Since then it has reproduced pieces by G. Rietveld, C. R. Mackintosh and Gunnar Asplund (qq.v.).

7 S. Sanders, *Honda: The Man and His Machine* (Toyko: Charles E. Tuttle, 1975), p. 70.

8 The best account of the history and work of the Japanese company Sony is available in S. Bayley (ed.), *Sony: Design* (London: Conran Foundation, 1982).

12

Anti-Design

The missionary who set out to improve the quality of life is not in danger of becoming the ogre who systematically is setting about destroying it.[1]

In addition to European misgivings about the influence of US mass cultural values on its 'traditional culture', there were also worldwide signs in the 1950s of a feeling of disillusion with the social and cultural implications of the marriage between design and manufacturing industry. These were expressed in a bout of publications which examined the consequences of design as the handmaiden of capitalist production and sales, and which suggested possible alternative ways in which design might be realigned directly with society and culture.

This crisis of values was not limited to the world of design but formed part of a more general malaise within Western society as a whole. When at the end of the 1960s the international economy became increasingly unstable, the general sense of disillusion with materialism, and with the abuse of technology and other resources to political and economic ends, resulted in a wave of revisionist tendencies, many of them involving design in some form or other. These manifestations tended at first to be polarized into two distinct camps, pro- and anti-technology, but gradually a middle path began to emerge and the concept of intermediate technology looked like a viable alternative. Although the dilemma arose within Western, industrialized society, some attention also moved at this time to countries which had not yet experienced the same economic and industrial expansion, and the question of design in underdeveloped countries became a focus for a number of related issues.

The End of the American Dream

On a pro-technology front, in the 1930s the pioneering visionary, Richard Buckminster Fuller (q.v.), had examined a number of ways in

44 Richard Buckminster Fuller, Dymaxion car no. 3, 1934.
Fuller's experimental Dymaxion car was part of a series of objects he designed according
to his principles of resource consciousness and total design in the 1930s, which included
his Dymaxion house and his Dymaxion bathroom. The former was a revolutionary design
which employed the 'tear-drop' shape inspired by the aerodynamic experiments which
Norman Bel Geddes had also incorporated in his visionary transport designs of the late
1920s and early 1930s. Fuller's car was never mass produced and had a number of major
faults, such as its complete lack of rear visibility. It was invented in 1927 and was built in
an old plant of the Locomotive Company at Bridgeport in Connecticut. Designed with the
help of the naval architect, Starling Burgess, the first prototype was fairly heavy while
the second and third (illustrated here at the Chicago World Fair) versions were much
lighter.

which technology could be used to serve the needs of man rather than those of industry, and in which the designer could reject the status quo which forced him to 'design ways to make money first, with which hopefully to buy living means afterwards, rather than making better living itself through directly applied design competence and unpatronised design initiative'.[2]

In the mid-1930s Fuller designed his series of Dymaxion cars [44] which made use of innovatory engineering as well as body styling, and began to expound his theories about a worldwide network of resources which would act as a design-base, ignoring national boundaries and the political and economic limitations that nationalism implied. He also evolved at that time his concept of the design-scientist who was a generalist, less concerned with the product alone than with the whole concept of production and its social implications.

Fuller was adamant in his dismissal of the Bauhaus and its influence which he saw as involving itself only superficially with the question of design. The Bauhaus had failed, he felt, to examine the economic structures behind production and had limited its attention to the surfaces of end-products. His ideas were truly radical as they questioned not only all the assumptions behind design but also the foundations of the economic, social and political framework that sustained it. Many of the themes Fuller introduced in these early years were to form the basis of a number of critical writings about design and society which emerged after the Second World War.

In the mid to late 1950s many design students, disillusioned with the big-business approach to design and its appendage, the designer star system, were desperately seeking for alternative strategies and looked to Fuller as a source of new ideas. At the same time, a spate of 'alarmist' literature which examined the nature of advanced capitalist society, and the dangers of mass consumption and technology linked to the sole interests of commerce, began to emerge. It found a ready audience in the same student population which had begun to lose faith in the culture that had produced the chrome-trimmed, bulbous, streamlined automobile.

Among the doom-laden, finger-pointing books of this period was Richard Neutra's *Survival through Design* of 1954 which extended Fuller's principle of 'general and integrated design on a world wide scale' as well as Neutra's belief that 'acceptance of design must turn from a commercial into a psychological issue'.[3] The writings of the journalist Vance Packard also had far-reaching influence at that time.

Packard's treatises about the evils of object obsolescence and consumer manipulations were well-timed exposés of the dangers of US
capitalism gone mad and, by implication, of the role of design within
capitalist society. In both *The Hidden Persuaders* of 1956[4] and *The
Waste-Makers* of 1961,[5] he attempted to analyse the subtle workings of
capitalist economics and to inform the public about the double-headed
character of mass consumption which, he claimed, brought with it both
increased wealth and manipulation. Consumption led inevitably,
according to Packard, to overproduction, to the need for built-in
obsolescence in what are called, ironically, consumer-durables, and to
the creation of artificial, rather than real, needs. The main problem, he
continued, was not so much the evils of advertising or styling *per se* but
the 'mind invasion' that living with so much obsolescence brought
about. Fourteen years later the writer Alvin Toffler isolated exactly the
same phenomenon as the central problem in contemporary society in
his book *Future Shock*, this time calling it 'information overload'. The
psychological dangers that Packard and Toffler both isolated, implied,
however, a very different threat from the physical one that Ralph
Nader pinpointed in *his* exposé of consumption and styling, *Unsafe at
any Speed*,[6] in which he focused on the dangers of the oversized US
automobile, designed for psychological fulfilment rather than safety
[12]. Nader's book had a tremendous impact upon automobile styling,
helping to encourage the return to the smaller, less ostentatious
automobile in the USA.

Design for Need

While Vance Packard saw the dangers of design as part of a much larger
picture, Victor Papanek, in his highly influential book *Design for the
Real World* of 1973,[7] focused on the particular role that design plays in
the modern world and on the need for the designer to come to terms
with the moral and social imperatives that working within mass
production and mass consumption necessarily imply. In the tradition of
alarmist literature that Packard and others had established, Papanek's
book was, in essence, an extended critique of the current ideological
status of design and a repeated exhortation for the designer to stop
occupying himself with 'toys for adults' and to start working instead,
independently of industry, on real human problems such as those
presented by the handicapped, the Third World, the elderly and the

45 Ergonomi Design Gruppen, dual-purpose cutlery for the disabled, 1980. The Swedish designers, Maria Benktzon and Sven-Eric Juhlin, who are the Ergonomi design team, have developed a range of utensils for the physically handicapped, including a bread-knife with a saw handle, manufactured by Gustavsberg, a glass with a wide stem for easy gripping, and a cutlery set, illustrated here, for people having the use of only one hand. Manufactured by RFSU Rehab, this set consists of two implements only, one which functions both as a knife and a fork, and the other which doubles as a fork and spoon. While performing these functions adequately these objects also look modern and attractive and avoid the institutional look traditionally attached to objects for the disabled. Ergonomi's objects are, in fact, also bought and used by people who have no physical disabilities but who are simply attracted by their confident appearance.

demands of world ecology. Papanek skilfully demolished all the highly regarded design achievements of this century one by one – from the Arts and Crafts Movement, to the Bauhaus, to the US industrial designer of the 1930s – in a tone that was rhetorical and moralistic. Like those before him, Papanek assumed a continued dependence upon advanced technology, although he put in a case for a responsible technology harnessed to alternative ends than those of nationalistic capitalism. Like Fuller, Papanek described his new designer as a generalist rather than a specialist, working with a team of people to a common goal which had a supra-national basis.

By the early 1970s a broadly defined alternative model of the industrial designer had, in theory at least, been made widely available which formed the basis of many debates held at that time about the nature and role of the industrial designer, not only in Western society but on a world scale. A crisis of conscience had been pinpointed and a number of efforts made, particularly in the curricula of a number of design educational institutions, [8] to put the theories into action. For the most part, however, no real threat was levelled at the role of the designer as a handmaiden to industry, and 'alternative' experiments, such as the work of the Swedish group, Ergonomi, for the disabled [45], remained on the periphery of mainstream industrial design.

Designing for Multilevel Production in India

One of Papanek's recurrent themes was the relevance of the designer to underdeveloped countries and he described the situation in a number of such places, including India: 'The ninety per cent native Indian population which lives "up country" has neither tools nor beds nor shelter nor schools nor hospitals that have ever been within breathing distance of a designer's drawing board or workbench.'[9] One attempt made to address this particular problem was the work of the National Institute of Design in Ahmedabad. Formed in 1961 following a decision by the Indian government to commission a report on design development from Charles Eames, the institute was established, fundamentally, as a training centre but it also comprised a design unit for client service and design cells outside Ahmedabad.

Since India's independence in 1947 much progress was made in the areas of science, technology and industrialization, but the gap

46 National Electric Company, visual display unit, Bombay 1980–1.
This visually unsophisticated design for a high technology product was undertaken by the National Electric Company's own design centre in Bombay. The crudeness of the forms and seams of the fabricated steel housing reflects the dated production machinery owned by the company. This object illustrates the fact that India, despite its problems of underdevelopment, feels the need to keep up with the West where high technology goods are concerned. This approach is in marked contrast to India's attitude towards design and production where goods for the rural home market, which are more closely geared to the idea of social need, are concerned.

between the urban elite and the rural poor remained enormous. Poverty was, and is, the norm for three-quarters of the population. It was against this background of economic inequality and unevenly distributed industrialization that the Institute developed its programme, determined to evolve a multilevel approach to design that would satisfy all the needs of India's mixed economy.

While Indian mass production of machine-tools and capital goods had expanded since the 1950s, providing one important aspect of the economy, local craftsmanship and batch production also remained wide-spread. Back in the 1930s Gandhi had encouraged skills like handspinning and weaving and the development of small-scale industry in his attempt to make India self-reliant, and the effects of his innovations lasted into the postwar period. Design in India could therefore follow the lead of Western industrialized countries in only one sector of its production and, in this, it followed meekly behind countries like West Germany and Japan in its 'styling for sales' approach to the design of goods such as calculators, film projectors, television sets and computer hardware, which were developed mostly for export [46].

On a domestic front, the continued need for traditional items for activities such as cooking or agricultural work put pressures on the designer and manufacturer to think out specific solutions to specifically Indian problems. The emergence of intermediate products like plastic monsoon shoes and buckets, and aluminium rice cake steamers, were examples in which both new materials and production techniques were used for the mass manufacture of traditional items, thus reducing costs and preserving natural resources.

The central problem for the Indian designer was to cater, in different ways, for different kinds and levels of production as a response to India's varying economic needs, as well as to work on products which were direct responses to social and cultural needs. Thus while one project at the Institute of Design involved designing a rapid radial drilling machine for a small-scale company which was aspiring, with the help of government aid, to break into the export market, another involved helping to develop symbols for medical use, including family planning for illiterate Indians. A similar, socially based project was one which involved designing an artificial limb which had to take into account specifically Indian constraints, such as the facts that rural Indians have to be able to climb trees, squat and spend a lot of time in water-logged fields which are a hazard to sponge-rubber. The project development for this design took a team of institute designers three years and the Jaipur limb which was evolved as a result of their research was soon put into wide use. On yet another project a group of Institute designers worked with some leather craftsmen in Jawaya, helping them to become economically self-reliant.

Design in India, therefore, has taken on special characteristics because of its function in fulfilling the requirements of multilevel production which includes mechanized mass production, decentralized small-scale production and handicrafts. The institute set out to encourage a multifaceted definition of design which varied according to the level of technology available and the nature of the market involved. This highly flexible concept was necessarily sophisticated in its application, requiring both breadth and specialization in its training programme.

The glaring clarity of the problems in India has forced it to address its own needs directly and to develop a more flexible and appropriate definition of design than the one that operates within Western industrialized society where the same problems exist but in different proportions and in a less obviously pressing form. As Charles Eames wrote of India in his report back in 1961: 'She need not make all the mistakes others have made.'[10]

Radical Design in Italy

While underdeveloped countries had a special reason for deviating from the 'good design equals good business' formula that the USA had pioneered in the 1930s, there was also evidence of dissatisfaction with that model in a number of countries in the Western industrialized world. In Britain, for example, the tastefulness of 'good design' came under attack in the mass stylistic revolutions initiated by the Pop Movement which was followed rapidly by a series of nostalgic revivals and an interest in kitsch and eclecticism. The Craft Revival[11] represented yet another attempt to reject industrialization, this time questioning the method of production rather than the aesthetic, and the values of hand-making were reasserted by many young craftspersons in a number of countries.

In Italy the movement called alternatively Radical, Counter- or Anti-Design had more revolutionary implications contained within it than mere stylistic innovation and it succeeded in putting forward, in theoretical terms at least, an alternative framework for design to that

199

provided by the mainstream. The movement grew out of the student revolutions of the late 1960s and the crisis of the architectural profession. Essentially utopian in nature, it took its inspiration and strategies from fine art movements like Neo-Dada and Surrealism, and presented a number of idealized projects which set out to ridicule the economic and cultural status quo and move towards a set of alternative premisses on which to base the definition of design. Overt references were made, in the work of the Florence-based architectural groups Archizoom and Superstudio, (qq.v.) to 'bad taste', nostalgia, eclecticism and popular styling as means of undermining both the aesthetic and the ethic associated with the twentieth-century tradition of Modernism, and 'good taste'. The fiercely anti-consumption stances adopted by such designers as Gaetano Pesce, Ettore Sottsass (qq.v.) and design groups such as Gruppo 9999 and Gruppo Strum (qq.v.) made it difficult, however, for them to incorporate their ideas into mass production and they relied on the communication of channels of exhibitions and specialist magazines through which to disseminate their ideas.

Like Victor Papanek and the Institute of Design in India, the Radical Italian designers placed the final responsibility on the shoulders of designers whose task it was, they claimed, to work towards humanitarian rather than economic ends, and to use their creative powers to improve the quality of life rather than simply assisting in the inevitability of the capital-accumulating process.

While the first phase of Italian Radical Design remained on the fringes of general design activity, the second phase, which occurred in the late 1970s and early 1980s, succeeded in reaching a much wider audience and in shaking the international design world, if not into action, at least into thought. Studio Alchymia (q.v.) was founded in Milan in 1979 and functioned like a fine art gallery as the mediating agent between the designer and the client. This implied a lessening of the power and function of the industrial manufacturer and a renewal of strength for the designer. Many of the designers associated with the studio had been involved in the first phase of radicalism – among them Ettore Sottsass, Alessandro Mendini and Andrea Branzi (qq.v.) – and they relied strongly on the strategies they had evolved in that earlier period, extending, for example, their visual references from popular styling of the 1930s to that of the 1950s and 1960s. Such tactics served as part of a search for a decorative aesthetic which would, at least theoretically, ally mass culture with high culture. As with all avant-

47 Ettore Sottsass, Carlton bookcase for Memphis, 1981.
Sottsass's dramatically shaped bookcase/room divider with two drawers is made of wood
and covered with plastic laminate, by Abet Laminati, in bright colours. The base is
covered with a Sottsass-designed print called 'Bacterio' which he designed in 1978 as one
of his decorative surfaces for the furniture range for Studio Alchymia. This piece
incorporates all the elements of the New Design which Sottsass and his friends promoted
as the successor to Functionalism, including the primacy of image over function, the need
for expression and 'sensoriality' in design, the importance of fashion and expendability
and the need for design to sidestep the ideology of industrial mass production. All
Memphis pieces, however, still perform their utilitarian function at the same time as they
attempt to renew the language and culture of design.

garde activities the products they designed remained exclusive and expensive, as did those of the important Radical Milanese design studio Memphis, which showed its first annual collection of furniture to the public in 1981 [47].

The new group was master-minded by Ettore Sottsass, now in his mid-sixties and heralded as the father of Italian Radical Design. In 1970 he had stated: 'I just thought that if there was any point in designing objects, it was to be found in helping people to live somehow, I mean in helping people to somehow recognise and free themselves.'[12] With Memphis, the direct role of industry was minimized and the designers involved could work directly with ideas, communicating them through objects which were both exhibited and made widely available through the design press.

The essentially intellectual and conceptual nature of Italian Radical Design prevented it from becoming more than a metaphorical knife in the back of the Establishment but it succeeded, none the less, in spreading its message widely and in inspiring wide discussion about the cultural implications of contemporary design and the social responsibility of the designer.

Unlike India, it has, within advanced capitalist economies, proved difficult for designers to break the link in the design-profit chain and to transfer their attentions to the immediate needs of man and society. Inevitably much work is undertaken with these aims in mind but its impact is small and its influence on mainstream design negligible. Much remains on the level of Utopian literature and projects, or within the context of avant-gardism or in educational establishments, and there are few indications that many of Papanek's radical proposals will be realized or that Sottsass's vision of mass culture asserting itself over high culture and elitism will ever be achieved.

The cultural function of all these various movements and ideas, which can be described collectively as Anti-Design, has been to provide, at least in theory if not in practice, alternative models of design activity removed from the economic determinism of manufacturing industry. It is an important phenomenon as reforming idealism has remained a constant theme in the story of modern design since the days of William Morris, defining the designer as, potentially, a free individual, and design as a concept which is capable of improving rather than impairing the quality of contemporary everyday life.

Notes: Chapter 12

1 Brochure for *Design for Quality in Life*, SIAD Conference, London, March/April 1973.
2 J. McCale, 'R. B. Fuller,' *Architectural Design*, no.179 (July 1961), p. 293.
3 R. Neutra, *Survival through Design* (New York: Oxford University Press, 1954), p. 74.
4 V. Packard, *The Hidden Persuaders* (Harmondsworth, Middx: Penguin, 1960).
5 V. Packard, *The Waste-Makers* (London: Longman, 1960).
6 A. Toffler, *Future Shock* (London: Pan, 1971); R. Nader, *Unsafe at Any Speed* (New York: Grossman, 1965).
7 V. Papanek, *Design for the Real World: Making to Measure* (London: Thames & Hudson, 1972).
8 The Design for Need movement has affected the curricula of a number of educational institutions all over the world. The Royal College of Art in London, for example, organized a conference on the subject in 1975.
9 Papanek, *Design for the Real World*, p. 56.
10 C. Eames, *India Report*, 7 April 1958, p. 3.
11 The Craft Revival was a movement which gathered its strengths in the late 1960s and early 1970s in the USA, Britain and a few other European centres. It favoured hand-making, 'quality' and 'variety' rather than mass production and standardization and it represented one of the ways in which a number of individuals sought an 'alternative' set of values to those perpetuated by the industrial status quo.
12 P. Sparke, *Ettore Sottsass Jnr* (London: Design Council, 1981), p. 63.

Conclusion:
Design and Culture
in the Twentieth Century

'I am collecting the history of our people as written into things their hands made and used . . . a piece of machinery, or anything that is made, is like a book, if you can read it.'[1] (Henry Ford)

The relationship between design and culture has taken many twists and turns throughout this century, as design is both a mirror of, and an agent of change within, twentieth-century culture. Thus modifications in the former's evolution both reflect and determine developments in the latter. All kinds and levels of cultural values, whether those manifested in, for example, political ideology, in various social and cultural activities, or in the economic status quo, find their way into the designed artefact by one means or another and those artefacts communicate those values in tangible and visual form.

A few designers, from Adolf Loos to Ettore Sottsass to Robert Venturi (qq.v.) [48] have realized the significance of design's umbilical link with culture in this century and have tried to make that recognition explicit in their work. Most practising designers have, however, defined their task less ambitiously and, by simply following the brief set them, have pursued the more passive path of sustaining, rather than challenging the cultural status quo.

Design inevitably perpetuates the ideology of the system it serves. In the twentieth century that system has been represented in industrial society almost wholly by the capitalist economic framework of mass production and mass consumption.' Design has, inevitably, served its ends and has, as a result, come to represent it in a major way. This is less a result of design's intrinsic characteristics than of its necessary rapport with the cultural system that sustains it. In its basic, acultural state, design is simply the creative act which determines the nature, appearance and the social function of useful objects. As such, like painting, sculpture, poetry, dance and music, it has the potential to

48 Robert Venturi, chairs for Knoll International, 1984.

In the 1960s, the architect, Robert Venturi, had already outlined his theories concerning post-modern 'complex and contradictory' architecture and he went on, in the 1980s, to apply his ideas to furniture. This resulted in a range of pieces, including nine chairs, a sofa and a coffee-table, which aimed to be 'historicist' and pluralistic. The chairs are manufactured on a semi-standardized, semi-batch-production basis and all have the same, Aalto-inspired, bent plywood silhouette but, from the front, communicate a number of different styles culled from the past. Pictured here are, on the left, Venturi's Art Deco chair and, on the right, his Sheraton version. The patterns and shapes he developed were 'representative' ones. They are all covered in plastic laminate and one version has an all-over pattern printed on it. Venturi is aiming to replace 'unity in variety' by 'variety in unity' in these highly adventurous designs.

improve the quality of life by rendering the material world both more beautiful and more efficient.

Where design diverges, however, from those areas of cultural activity which are related directly to self-expression and life improvement is the moment at which it enters the realms of mass production and mass consumption. From that point onwards it becomes harder for self-expression, whether that of the designer or of the consumer, to assert itself within the economic determination of the framework which defines their actions. Mass cultural values, reflected in mass taste and symbolized by mass-produced artefacts, are perpetrated by the mass manufacturer and absorbed wholesale by the mass consumer. Only within subcultures, or other 'alternative' cultural groups, are other values asserted and, once again, it is through artefacts, whether clothes or life-style accompaniments either made especially or appropriated, that these values are communicated.

Design is, therefore, an important medium of communication which expresses the values of the system within which it functions. This book has set out to describe twentieth-century design in as broad a cultural context as possible, indicating many of the different forces that have determined its evolution and describing a number of the more significant developments that have taken place. Many smaller, more self-contained histories could run parallel with this general work, serving to pull together many of the threads. The biography of any number of industrial designers, or the full story of any mass-produced object, such as the telephone or the chair, would, for example, touch and illuminate many of the themes that I have outlined. In the end this book is only a framework, but an important framework none the less. It serves to contextualize design not for academic purposes alone but also to allow designers themselves to see their task in perspective and to question some of the narrow assumptions they have inherited about their cultural role in this century.

The way forward for design remains difficult but exciting. Today's most dominant stylistic and philosophical tendency is an interest in pluralism. The demise of the 'black box' approach to design [49] has inspired both anarchy and thoughtfulness and there are numerous signs that the 'good design' movement was, in fact, not the final answer that it seemed to be for so many people, but merely the reflection of a temporary obsession with the machine and a taste set of middle-class values as major metaphors for design. It amounted in the end to little more than an interlude between two historical periods for which object

49 Marco Zanuso and Richard Sapper, Black 12 television for Brionvega, 1969.
Zanuso and Sapper's television design is the ultimate, sophisticated 'black box'. It is simply a cube of black acrylic with a TV screen inside it which is invisible when the set is switched off. As such, it takes modern design to the logical end of the tendency towards aesthetic reductivism which was implied by the ideas associated with Functionalism and the Machine Aesthetic in the early century. Philosophically, aesthetically and culturally, therefore, this product stands at one end of the spectrum, the other end of which is occupied by Venturi's chairs (Figure 48).

symbolism and consumer preference were, and are, much more important than form and good taste.

Within pluralism the weight of responsibility hangs increasingly on the shoulders of the designer. While still fulfilling manufacturing industries' needs for ever-increasing production and consumption, the designer is still in a unique position of being able to improve the quality of life in a number of ways, whether in terms of influencing the ergonomic and aesthetic quality of products, or of social and psychological fulfilment and cultural richness. This constitutes, in the end, design's positive contribution to twentieth-century culture and the reason for studying its history.

Notes: Conclusion

1 *Mechanical Arts* (Dearborn, Mich.: Henry Ford Museum, 1964), p. 1.

Glossary of Proper Names

The content of this glossary has emerged from the case-study material selected for this introductory book. It does not claim, therefore, to represent all the major individuals or companies involved with design in the twentieth century.

Aalto, Alvar   (1898–1976)
A Finnish architect-designer best known for his modern, yet humanistic buildings (for example, Viipuri Library, 1927–35 and Paimio Sanitorium, 1929–33), his furniture which resulted from experiments with moulded plywood bent into two-dimensional curves, his organic glass designs and his textiles.

Ahren, Uno   (1897–1977)
A Swedish architect and furniture designer who wrote about Le Corbusier (q.v.) in 1925 and was one of the people responsible for importing Modern Movement ideas into Sweden. With Sven Markelius he built a student union building for the 1930 Stockholm Exhibition and also designed Stockholm's first cinema in 1930.

Albers, Anni   (1899–   )
A student in the weaving workshop at the Dessau Bauhaus, the German textile designer, Anni Albers, went to the USA in the 1930s, where she taught at Black Mountain College and made a name for herself both as a teacher and practitioner of textile design.

Albers, Josef   (1888–1968)
German painter, theoretician and pedagogue who both studied and taught at the Bauhaus between 1920 and 1933, after which he took up posts at Black Mountain College and Harvard in the USA. Between 1950 and 1960 he was at Yale. Albers is best known for his ideas about colour.

Albini, Franco   (1905–1977)
An Italian architect-designer who worked on interior and exhibition design as well as town-planning, architecture and product design. He was professor of architectural design at Milan Polytechnic from 1963 to 1975 and, among other designs, is best known for his transparent radio, his elegant tensistructure book-shelves and his chair for Cassina.

Archipenko, Alexander   (1880–1964)
A sculptor who had worked with the Cubists in Paris in the years leading up to

the First World War. In the 1930s he was invited to Chicago by Moholy-Nagy (q.v.) to teach at the New Bauhaus.

Archizoom
The Italian Radical-Design architectural group Archizoom was formed in Florence in 1966. Its early members included Andrea Branzi (q.v.) and Paolo Deganello, and the group designed a number of visionary environments and some fantasy furniture as part of its attempt to move Italian design away from its preoccupations with consumerism and high style.

Arens, Egmont   (1888–1966)
The packager, Egmont Arens, was most influential in the 1930s through his writings in which he discussed the relationship between industrial design and the world of business and marketing. He edited, at different times, both *Creative Arts* and *Playboy* and established Calkins & Holdens' industrial styling division.

Arp, Jean (Hans)   (1887–1966)
A French sculptor, painter and poet who was part of the Dada group in Switzerland in 1916 and went on to work on sculptures, reliefs and collages which used abstract, organic forms. The aesthetic he developed was an inspiration to many designers after the Second World War who were looking for an alternative to the machine aesthetic.

Ashbee, C. R.   (1863–1942)
C. R. Ashbee was a member of the British Arts and Crafts Movement. He is most noted for his metalwork and his attempts to create a 'medieval style' workshop in Chipping Campden in the Cotswolds at the turn of the century.

Asplund, Gunnar   (1885–1940)
A Swedish architect-designer who was the creative force behind the Stockholm Exhibition of 1930. In the 1920s Asplund designed architecture and furniture in the neo-classical style which was immensely fashionable in Sweden at that time.

Banham, P. Reyner   (1920–   )
The British architectural and design historian and critic Reyner Banham wrote extensively in the 1950s and 1960s about the Modern Movement and its aftermath. A member of the Independent Group at the ICA in the 1950s he introduced discussions about mass culture and its relationship with design. He is at present Professor of Art History at the University of Los Angeles at Santa Cruz.

Barnsley Brothers
Sidney (1865–1926) and Edward Barnsley (1863–1926) were British furniture craftsmen-designers who set up a Cotswold workshop with Ernest Gimson

(q.v.) in 1895. Their work exhibits an interest in vernacular forms and traditional materials.

Barr, A. H.   (1902–81)
Director of New York's Museum of Modern Art from 1929 to 1943, Barr was responsible for introducing European art, architecture and design to the USA. He was responsible for mounting both Hitchcock and Johnson's International Style show of 1932, and the Machine Art Exhibition of 1934.

Bartnung, O.   (1883–1959)
A German architect who played a central role in the Expressionist Movement in Berlin. Among his best-known designs are those for the Schiester House (1921–4) and his House for a Director of the early 1920s, as well as for a number of Protestant churches.

Bayer, Herbert   (1900–80)
An ex-Bauhaus student, the typographer, Herbert Bayer, came to the USA in 1936 and became a consultant to Walter Paepcke's Container Corporation of America in 1946. From 1946 to 1976 he was a consultant to the Aspen Conference and he has played a central role in postwar US design.

Behrens, Peter   (1868–1940)
A German architect-designer who worked in Darmstadt, in an Art Nouveau style, before becoming a consultant to the AEG Company for whom he designed a complete corporate identity from 1907. Walter Gropius, Mies van der Rohe and Le Corbusier (qq.v.) all spent some time in his studio.

Bel Geddes, Norman   (1893–1952)
Bel Geddes began his career as a portrait painter before moving into stage design, shop-window display and, finally, consultant industrial design. His 'streamlined' fantasies for transport were the most expressive of the 1930s, but his work for production was more mundane by comparison.

Bellini, Mario   (1935–)
The Milanese architect-designer, Mario Bellini, is best known for his sensuous typewriters and office machinery designed in the 1960s and 1970s as well as for his furniture for Cassina. Bellini has also designed a tape-deck for Yamaha, and was much admired and emulated internationally in the 1970s.

Berg, G. A.   (1884–1957)
The Swedish furniture designer, G. A. Berg, renewed an interest in bentwood design in Sweden and opened a furniture shop in Stockholm at the beginning of the 1930s. Where furniture is concerned, he was one of the major forces behind the Swedish Modern Movement.

Bertoia, Harry   (1915–78)
Italian by birth, the sculptor Harry Bertoia came to the USA in 1930, studied at the Cranbrook Academy and began to work on furniture for Knoll (q.v.) in

1950. His famous steel-rod, grid chair of the early 1950s has become one of the best known and highly admired chair images of this century.

Bill, Max   (1908–   )

A Swiss architect who worked as a painter, designer and sculptor. An ex-Bauhaus student, he promoted the idea of 'gute form' in Switzerland in the 1950s and, from 1951 to 1956, was director of the Hochschule für Gestaltung in Ulm. Bill's wall-clock for the Junghaus of 1957 is among the best known of his products.

Bindesbøll, Thorvald   (1846–1908)

A Danish architect who also designed ceramics, furniture, metalwork and textiles around the turn of the century in a highly personal, expressionistic style. He was employed by the Copenhagen Lervarefabrik ceramics factory in the 1890s.

Bonsiepe, Gui   (1934–   )

The Italian designer critic, Gui Bonsiepe, studied at the Hochschule für Gestaltung at Ulm from 1955–9 and taught there from 1960–8. When it closed in 1968 he went to South America and in 1975 he published a book called *Teoria e practica del disegno industriale*.

Branzi, Andrea   (1938–   )

A Florentine architect-designer who was a member of Archizoom (q.v.) in the 1960s and moved, later, to Milan to play a central role in the second phase of Italian Radical Design at the end of the 1970s. He teaches at Domus Academy and edits *Modo* magazine.

Bredendieck, Hin   (1907–   )

An ex-Bauhaus student who came to the USA in the 1930s and worked with Moholy-Nagy (q.v.) at the New Bauhaus in Chicago where he led the foundation course. He encouraged experiments in cut paper thus repeating work done at the German Bauhaus.

Breuer, Marcel   (1902–81)

The Hungarian architect-designer, Marcel Breuer, was trained at the Bauhaus where he designed his well-known chairs in tubular steel. He went on to teach at that institution and, on its closure, came to Britain to work for Jack Pritchard's Isokon furniture company where he developed chairs in bent plywood. In 1937 Breuer went to the USA to join Walter Gropius (q.v.) at Harvard.

Brewer, Cecil   (1894–1972)

The architect cousin of Ambrose Heal (q.v.) who played a crucial role in the early years of the Design and Industries Association in Britain. Brewer designed Heal's shop in the Tottenham Court Road which was built during the First World War.

Brunel, I. K.   (1806–59)
The British engineer who was responsible for many feats of civil engineering in the nineteenth century, including the Great Western Railway and the Clifton Suspension Bridge. Brunel developed, unconsciously, an aesthetic which Modern Movement designers were to admire greatly.

Calder, Alexander   (1898–1976)
American sculptor whose 'mobiles' – abstract, metal sculptures – inspired many designers in the 1950s. He also worked on stage designs, graphics, jewellery and a number of household objects.

Castiglioni (Brothers)
Of the three Italian architect-designer Castiglioni brothers, Pier Giacomo (1910–68), Livio (1912–52) and Achille (1918–   ), it is the latter who, born in 1918, has had the greatest influence on design in this century. His designs for furniture, lighting and appliances, including the Tractor Seat for Zanotta and the Arco light for Flos, have won him numerous prizes since the 1950s and made him an important force within modern Italian design.

Chermayeff, Serge   (1900–   )
The Russian-born architect, Serge Chermayeff, came to Britain in the 1930s and played a central role in the architectural Modern Movement there. He is noted for his interior and display work for Waring & Gillow and for Broadcasting House and he pioneered modern industrial design in Britain with his bakelite radio housings for the Ekco Radio Company in the mid-1930s, a firm founded by Eric Kirkham Cole (1901–65) in 1921.

Clark, Paul   (1940–   )
A British graphic designer who made a name for himself in the 1960s with his designs for clocks, tiles and ceramic mugs which were decorated with targets and Union Jacks and which came to represent 'Swinging London'.

Coates, Wells   (1895–1958)
Born in Tokyo, Coates came to Britain in 1929 and became a major figure in the British Modern Movement in architecture and design. After working on shop interiors he went on to design an apartment block for the Isokon company of Jack Pritchard (q.v.) and pioneered modern industrial design with his work for the Ekco Radio Company.

Cole, Henry   (1808–82)
The civil servant, Henry Cole, was a major force in design reform in Britain in the mid-nineteenth century, both in his work with the Royal Society of Arts and

in his designs, executed under his pseudonym Felix Summerly. He was also influential in the establishment of the Victoria & Albert Museum.

Coray, Hans   (1907–   )
The Swiss designer, Hans Coray, is best known for his all-aluminium Landi chair which first appeared in 1939 and is still in production today.

Darwin, Robin   (1910–74)
In the 1940s Darwin was the Education Officer at the British Council of Industrial Design. He went on to become rector of the Royal College of Art in London in 1948 and was responsible for a programme of radical reorganization in that institution which was an attempt to bring it in line with contemporary industrial and technological developments.

de Carli, Carlo   (1910–71)
An Italian architect-designer who was responsible, in the period following the Second World War, for the design of a number of expressive furniture pieces which made use of the new materials, steel rod, bent plywood and foam rubber. The Cassina Company manufactured a number of his designs.

de Patta, Margaret   (1907–   )
An American jeweller who trained at the Institute of Design in Chicago and went on to make a name for herself for jewellery which relied on principles derived from abstract Constructivist Sculpture.

Deskey, Donald   (1894–   )
This American interior and industrial designer was a member of the group of pioneer consultants in the 1930s. From a background in advertising he visited Paris in 1925 and came back with numerous ideas about interior decoration which he applied to his many design projects, including the interiors of Radio City Music Hall in 1930.

Doblin, Jay   (1920–   )
After his training at New York's Pratt Institute, Doblin went on to work in Raymond Loewy's (q.v.) industrial design office in the early 1950s and subsequently succeeded Serge Chermayeff (q.v.) as the director of the Illinois Institute of Technology, formerly the Institute of Design in Chicago. He still works in Chicago as a consultant designer.

Dresser, Christopher   (1834–1904)
An English designer who began his career as a botanist but moved later into design. His metalwork and textiles were greatly influenced by Japan (which he visited in 1877) and he became one of the first British designers to work with manufacturing industry on a freelance basis.

Drexler, Arthur   (1917–   )
As director of the Museum of Modern Art in New York, Drexler has sustained the policies of Edgar Kaufmann Jnr (q.v.), by encouraging an emphasis on the

formal qualities of the objects bought for the museum's collection and ignoring their technological significance.

Dreyfuss, Henry (1902–72)

From a background in the theatre prop busines, Dreyfuss, like Bel Geddes (q.v.), was a stage designer before he set up, in the late 1920s, as a consultant industrial designer. His early clients included the Bell Telephone Company, the Hoover Company and the New York Central Railroad. He wrote about his attitudes to design in his book *Designing for People* published in 1955.

Eames, Charles (1907–78)

The American architect-designer Charles Eames first came to public notice when his bent plywood furniture, designed with Eero Saarinen (q.v.), won a competition at the Museum of Modern Art in New York. He had a one-man show there in 1946 at which he introduced furniture which combined bent plywood with steel rod and he went on to design a number of even more strikingly original furniture pieces throughout the 1950s and 1960s, as well as venturing into experimental film.

El Lissitzky (1890–1940)

Russian graphic designer who worked for various architects up to 1917 and then became involved with the artistic propaganda of the Revolution. His work displayed the style of Suprematism which the painter, Malevich, had pioneered and he is best known for his 'Proun' compositions of the early 1920s.

Estlander, C. G. (1834–1910)

Finnish art and design pedagogue who reorganized the Finnish Society of Arts and Crafts in Helsinki at the end of the nineteenth century.

Evans, Oliver (1755–1819)

Evans, an American engineer and inventor, built a grist mill near Philadelphia in 1787 in which the grain was passed mechanically through each stage of the milling process. His technique, which soon became accepted practice, was later imitated by the meat-packing industry. In 1800 he built the Columbian high-pressure steam engine.

Feininger, Lionel (1871–1956)

German Expressionist painter who worked as an illustrator and cartoonist from 1893 to 1907. He was one of the first group of individuals brought in by Walter Gropius (q.v.) to teach at the Weimar Bauhaus. Feininger's woodcut of a Gothic cathedral was used as the illustration on the Bauhaus manifesto.

Figini, Luigi and Pollini, Gino (both b. 1903)

The Italian architect-designers Figini and Pollini were part of Group 7, the Italian Rationalist architectural group of the late 1920s. They worked in that style through the 1930s, contributed to the Triennales of that decade, and, in

1934–5, designed the Olivetti building in Ivrea which was finally built in 1939–41.

Ford, Henry   (1863–1947)
The American industrialist, Henry Ford, established the Ford Motor Company in 1903 and introduced the moving assembly line into his automobile production in 1913. He also was a pioneer in standardizing his product. The Model T was replaced, however, with the Model A in 1927 and styling became an intrinsic element in Ford automobile manufacture from then onwards.

Frank, Josef   (1885–1967)
An Austrian Modern Movement architect who settled in Sweden in 1934 and became chief designer for a company called Svenskt Tenn. He modified his early purist ideas to include pattern and texture in his later furniture, lights and fabrics and became an early exponent of the Swedish Modern Movement. He remained with Svenskt Tenn until his death.

Fuller, Richard Buckminster   (1895–1983)
An American designer and visionary who wrote about design as an aspect of advanced technology at the service of mankind. He also designed his Dymaxion house in 1927, a Dymaxion car in 1932, and later a series of geodesic domes.

Gallen-Kallela, Akseli   (1865–1931)
A Finnish painter who changed his name to Axel Gallen in 1905 and worked as a designer across a range of craft media as part of the Finnish National Romantic Movement. Among his achievements was the award of the gold medal at the Paris Exhibition of 1900 for his furnishings for the Iris room.

Gate, Simon   (1883–1945)
The Swedish artist-craftsman who, along with Edward Hald (q.v.), brought modern ideas into his designs for glass for the Orrefors glassworks from 1916 onwards. He developed the 'Graal' techniques in the 1920s and did some exhibition work for the Paris Exhibition of 1925.

Gaudi, Antonio   (1852–1926)
The Spanish architect and designer who evolved his own idiosyncratic version of Art Nouveau. His buildings – including the Sagrada Familia of 1903–26, the Casa Vicens of 1878–80, and his Parque Güell, begun in 1900 – all display the same fantastic aesthetic as his furniture designs.

Giedion, Siegfried   (1888–1968)
A Swiss art historian who, under the tutorship of Heinrich Wölfflin, developed an approach to 'anonymous' history. This is best demonstrated in his major study, published in 1948, called *Mechanisation Takes Command* which has become an important design historical text.

Gimson, Ernest (1864–1919)

A British furniture designer-craftsman who set up a workshop with the Barnsley brothers (q.v.) in the Cotswolds in 1895. His wooden furniture represents the values of the British Arts and Crafts Movement at its most rural.

Giugiaro, Giorgio (1938–)

The Italian car designer who set up his own firm, Ital Design, in 1968. Since then Giugiaro has designed a number of very significant cars, including the Alfa Romeo Alfa Sud (1971), the Volkswagen Golf (1974) and the Fiat Panda (1980). He has also worked on a number of other products, including a camera for Nikon.

Grenander, Alfred (1894–1956)

An early member of the Deutscher Werkbund who did many designs for the Berliner Möbelfabrik and went on to design stations and rolling stock for the Berlin elevated tramway along highly rational lines.

Gretsch, Herman (1895–1950)

Dr Gretsch was a German product designer, engineer and architect who worked for, among other companies, the Arzberg Porcelain Works in the 1930s. Like Wagenfeld (q.v.), he continued to work in the modern idiom through the Nazi period in Germany. His work typifies the 'rational' quality of German design in this century.

Gropius, Walter (1883–1969)

The German architect, Walter Gropius, began his career in partnership with Adolf Meyer in 1910 – with whom he designed the Fagus factory in 1911 – and became the first director of the Bauhaus in 1919. He went on to become Professor of Architecture at Harvard in the USA in 1937.

Gruppo 9999

An Italian Radical Design group based in Florence which was interested in the role of theatre as applied to architecture and the other arts. In 1968 they instigated a 'Design Happening' on the Ponte Vecchio and created an interior environment for the Space Electronic discothèque in Florence in 1969.

Gruppo Strum

An architectural and design group based in Turin which played a role in the Italian Radical Design Movement of the late 1960s. The group (which called itself Group for Instrumental Architecture) worked in an experimental manner, concerned to use architecture as an active instrument for political propaganda.

Guild, Lurelle (1898–)

A pioneer American consultant industrial designer, Guild began his career in graphic design but went on, like so many of his contemporaries, to work in three dimensions. He is best known for his aluminium kitchen ware designed for the Ware-Ever Company.

Guimard, Hector   (1867–1942)

The French architect, Hector Guimard, is best known for his contribution to French Art Nouveau. He designed a number of buildings in Paris at the turn of the century, including the Castel Béranger, but is perhaps better known for his sensuous designs for the Paris Metro which made extensive use of wrought-iron.

Hald, Edward   (1883–1981)

The Swedish glass and ceramic designer who studied painting under Henry Matisse and went on to work with the glass company, Orrefors – where he was managing director from 1933 to 1944 – and the ceramics company, Rorstrand. With Simon Gate (q.v.), Hald introduced Modernism into Sweden.

Hansen, Fritz

The Danish furniture manufacturing company, set up by its founder, Fritz Hansen, in 1872 as a wood-turning business. It went on to introduce industrial processes into furniture-making and to bring in designers, including Mart Stam and Arne Jacobsen in the 1930s, and, more recently, Piet Hein, Verner Panton and Hans Wegner.

Harman Powell, David   (1933–   )

A British plastics designer who worked with Ekco and British Industrial Plastics in the 1950s and 1960s and helped bring 'modern design' into the production of plastic domestic utensils.

Heal, Ambrose   (1872–1959)

The British designer, Ambrose Heal, joined the family furniture business in 1893. He became attached to the British Arts and Crafts Movement and began showing his designs in 1896. The Heal's store was established in 1840 and Ambrose moved its emphasis from reproduction to simple, modern furniture. He became chairman of the business in 1913 and played a role in the formation of the Design and Industries Association in 1915.

Helion, Jean   (1904–   )

A French artist who was invited by Moholy-Nagy (q.v.) to teach at the New Bauhaus in Chicago but who was not finally employed because the school had to close due to lack of funds.

Henrion, F. H. K.   (1914–   )

Graphic designer of French origin who came to Britain in the 1930s and worked there, throughout the war and into the postwar period, as one of Britain's leading graphic designers.

Heritage, Robert (1927–)
A British furniture and lighting designer who set up his own office in 1953. He is best known for his lighting designs for Concorde. Since 1974 Heritage has taught at the Royal College of Art in London, and returned from there in 1985.

Hille
The British furniture company, Hille, developed from a small business set up in the early part of the century to a large company which sponsored modern design after the Second World War. Robin Day, Roger Dean and Fred Scott have all worked with Hille which was dissolved in 1983. Day's polypropylene chair of the 1960s is probably Hille's most influential product.

Hoffmann, Josef (1870–1956)
The Austrian designer who studied under Otto Wagner (q.v.) and, in 1879, was a founder member of the Viennese Sezession group. In 1903 Hoffmann founded the Viennese Werkstätte with Moser (q.v.) along British Arts and Crafts lines and was responsible for the design of many objects – furniture, fruit-bowls, tea-sets, and so on – in the first decade of this century.

Honda
The Japanese Honda Motor Cycle Company was founded in 1948. Its first important product was the Super-Cub step-through motor-cycle which, through aggressive marketing, succeeded in conquering the US market. Since then Honda has diversified into power appliances and motor cars. The Civic, Prelude and Accord are examples of successful Honda products in the latter field.

Horta, Victor (1861–1946)
A Belgian architect who in the 1880s moved from designing in a Neo-Renaissance style to becoming a leader of the Belgian Art Nouveau Movement. His best-known buildings include the Tassel House (1892), the Hotel Solvay (1895–1900) and the Maison du Peuple (1896–9). The last example had the first iron and a glass façade in Belgium.

Issigonis, Alec (1906–)
The British car designer who is best known for his designs for the Morris Minor of 1948, the Austin Mini of 1959, and the Morris 1100 of 1962. Of them the Mini was the most influential and made a significant impact on the world market.

Itten, Johannes (1888–1967)
Itten developed the preliminary course at the Bauhaus in Weimar. His ideas were too mystical for Walter Gropius (q.v.) who dismissed him in 1923. He went on to found his own school in Berlin and, later, to become director of the art schools in Zurich and Krefeld.

221

Jones, Owen (1809–74)
An architect by training, Jones was part of the group of British design reformers who circled around Henry Cole (q.v.) in the mid-nineteenth century. In 1856 he published his book *Grammar of Ornament* which approached pattern in a new, rational way.

Kåge, Wilhelm (1889–1960)
Trained as a fine artist, Kåge began working for the Swedish ceramic company, Gustavsberg, in 1917 and was responsible for encouraging it to use modern, democratic designs. In the 1930s he produced several ceramic ranges including Praktika and Pyro but returned to painting in 1949.

Kandinsky, Wassily (1866–1944)
A Russian painter who pioneered an expresive form of abstraction in the early twentieth century. In 1921 he was invited by Walter Gropius (q.v.) to work at the Weimar Bauhaus and his second major book *From Point and Line to Plane* of 1926 reflects his teaching approach at that institution.

Kaufmann, Jnr, Edgar (1917–)
Curator of Design at the Museum of Modern Art in New York in the late 1940s and early 1950s who was responsible for instigating the Good Design series of exhibitions in the early 1950s and in expanding the permanent collection by buying products from abroad, particularly from Italy and Scandinavia.

Kepes, Gyorgy (1906–)
A Hungarian artist and pedagogue who was invited by Moholy-Nagy (q.v.) to teach at the New Bauhaus in Chicago. He had been Moholy's assistant in Europe and, at the New Bauhaus, was in charge of the drawing and colour workshop as well as helping with photography. Kepes has written a number of books about art and design education.

Kiesler, Frederick (1896–1965)
Associated with the Viennese Sezession group, the Dadaists and the De Stijl Movement in Holland, Kiesler left Europe and came to the USA in the late 1920s and continued to work as an artist-architect-designer in that country. Among his numerous designs was one for a range of aluminium furniture in the 1930s.

Klee, Paul (1879–1940)
The Swiss-German artist who was, with Kandinsky (q.v.), a member of the Blaue Reiter Group in Munich in 1906. In 1930 he was engaged by Gropius to teach at the Weimar Bauhaus and his book *The Pedagogical Sketchbook* of 1925 describes his approach to teaching there.

Knoll
The Knoll furniture company was formed in the USA in the late 1940s by the German cabinet-maker Hans Knoll and his wife, Florence Schust, a graduate of

the Cranbrook Academy. From the beginning they used modern designers, among them Eero Saarinen and Harry Bertoia (qq.v.), and established a reputation for progressiveness where furniture design was concerned.

Larsen, Jack Lenor   (1927–   )
An American textile designer who trained at the Cranbrook Academy and opened his office in New York in 1952. Larsen has worked widely in the USA since that time. His designs include fabrics for airline companies and work for architectural projects.

Le Corbusier   (1887–1968)
The Swiss architect who, born Charles Édouard Jeanneret, became the leader of the Modern Movement in architecture and design. His buildings from the 1920s were typically white and flat-roofed in imitation of Mediterranean vernacular architecture, and he achieved a simple purity of form in all his work. He is best known, perhaps, for his Grand Confort chair and his chaise-longue.

Leland, Henry M.   (1843–1932)
Formerly the head of Leland & Faulconer, a machine-tools company, Leland set up the Cadillac Automobile Company in 1902.

Lethaby, C. R.   (1857–1931)
The British architect, C. R. Lethaby – one of the initiators of the Art Workers' Guild – founded the Central School in 1896. As head of the school he had a significant influence on modern British art and design education. He was also a founder member of the Design and Industries Association and wrote extensively on art, craft and design.

Levi-Montalcini, Gino   (1902–74)
The Italian architect and designer who worked in Milan in the 1930s in the Rationalist style. He is best known for his tubular steel and leather furniture.

Lichtwark, Alfred   (1852–1914)
Lichtwark was a German art historian and director of the Hamburg Gallery. His lectures on the subject of the English Arts and Crafts approach to design delivered between 1896 and 1899 were influential on German art education in the early twentieth century.

Lindig, Otto   (1901–   )
The German potter, Otto Lindig, was trained in the pottery workshop at the Weimar Bauhaus. He went on to teach along the same lines himself and was based in Hamburg in the years following the Second World War.

Loewy, Raymond   (1893–   )
Born in France, Loewy came to New York in 1919 and became one of the city's earliest consultant industrial designers. His first client was Sigmund Gestetner

for whom he restyled a photocopier in 1929 and throughout the 1930s, 1940s and 1950s he went on to design many products for a number of clients, including the Hupp Motor Company and Frigidaire, the 1940 Lucky Strike cigarette pack and the 1953 Studebaker.

Lonsdale-Hands, Richard   (1915–   )

A British designer-engineer who set up his design consultancy in Britain after the Second World War along prewar US lines. He worked on technical projects, including a number of designs for BOAC.

Loos, Adolf   (1870–1933)

An Austrian architect who worked with Otto Wagner (q.v.) and who wrote his famous article of 1908, 'Ornament and crime', in which he outlined the decadent nature of ornament as applied to modern building. His own designs include the Steiner House from the first decade of the twentieth century.

Lubetkin, Bernard   (1901–   )

Russian-born architect who came to Britain in 1930 and became a member of the Modern group Tecton. The influences of Russian Constructivism and of Le Corbusier (q.v.) were clear in his work of the 1930s which included a building for London Zoo and the High Point I block of flats.

McGrath, Raymond   (1908–77)

One of Britain's leading exponents of the Modern Movement in the 1920s and 1930s, McGrath wrote extensively on the subject – publishing his *Twentieth Century Houses* in 1934 – as well as styling numerous interiors in the then fashionable Parisian Style, including those for Broadcasting House.

Mackintosh, Charles Rennie   (1868–1928)

The Scottish architect who, working with a group of architects called collectively the Glasgow Four, worked on a number of buildings, interiors and pieces of furniture which created a special Scottish version of rectilinear Art Nouveau. Mackintosh's designs were very influential in Vienna.

Magistretti, Vico   (1920–   )

The Italian architect and furniture designer who was trained in Milan and who worked there, after the Second World War, particularly for the Arflex and Cassina furniture companies. Magistretti's brightly coloured plastic moulded chairs of the early 1960s were among the first of their kind and he has continued to design influential pieces since then for Cassina, including Sindbad of 1981.

Maldonado, Tomas   (1922–   )

Born in Buenos Aires, the design theoretician Maldonado was invited, by Max Bill (q.v.), to take over from him as the director of the Hochschule für Gestaltung in Ulm where he reigned until the mid-1960s. Maldonado favoured a systematic approach towards design. He is now Professor of Design at the University of Bologna.

Marcks, Gerhard (1889–1969)

The German sculptor, Gerhard Marcks, was a member of the November-gruppe in Berlin before he moved to teach at Walter Gropius's (q.v.) Bauhaus at Weimar. He became the *Formmeister* in the pottery workshop where he worked alongside the craftsman Max Krehan who was the *Lehrmeister*. Marcks left the Bauhaus in 1925.

Marimekko

A Finnish fabric company and shop, established by Armi Ratia in Helsinki in 1951. Marimekko (which means Mary's frock) is best known for its bold printed fabrics which are also made up into simple clothing.

Markelius, Sven (1889–1972)

A Swedish designer who was part of the Functionalist Movement of the mid-twentieth cenury. Among other things he designed simple wooden furniture and printed fabrics for Nordiska Kompaniet with Astrid Sampe.

Mathsson, Bruno (1907–)

The Swedish furniture designer who, with G. A. Berg and Josef Frank (qq.v.), was responsible for creating the Swedish Modern Movement in furniture. He used wood and hemp webbing rather than tubular steel and leather and his famous chair of 1934 is still produced today by Dux Möbel.

Mellor, David (1930–)

A British designer, based in Sheffield, who has established his own cutlery and product design and manufacture company. Trained at the RCA, Mellor is best known for his cutlery sets. Pride won a Design Council award in 1959 and was followed later by Chinese Ivory, a classic set of cutlery.

Mendini, Alessandro (1931–)

A member of the Italian Radical Design Movement, Mendini began his professional career working for the architectural group Nizzoli Associati. He went on to edit a number of design magazines, including *Casabella, Modo* and, currently, *Domus*. He masterminds the work of Studio Alchymia (q.v.).

Meyer, Hannes (1889–1954)

Meyer succeeded Gropius as director of the Bauhaus in 1928. He took a rigorously left-wing, systematic attitude towards architecture and design and did not remain in office long. Mies van der Rohe (q.v.) took over from him in 1930.

Mies van der Rohe, Ludwig (1886–1969)

The German architect who, with Walter Gropius and Le Corbusier (qq.v.), is one of the most renowned exponents of Modern Movement architecture and design. Mies was the least theoretical and most 'aesthetic' of the three. He was the last director of the Bauhaus in Germany, after which he went to the USA where he worked in Chicago and at the Illinois Institute of Technology. He is best known for the design of tubular-steel furniture, in particular his Barcelona chair of 1929.

Miller, Herman
The Herman Miller Furniture Company is based in Michigan in the USA. It first showed an interest in modern design in the 1930s, when it appointed Gilbert Rhode as its design director. It later went on to manufacture the designs of Charles Eames (q. v.).

Minton
The Minton Ceramics Company was founded in Stoke-on-Trent in 1976. It was one of the companies, along with Wedgwood and Doulton, to respond to the demands of the mass market and to develop a range of products aimed at different sectors of the market.

Moholy-Nagy, Laszlo (1895–1946)
Born in Hungary, Moholy-Nagy had moved to Berlin by 1920 and in 1922 joined the Bauhaus staff. Influenced by Eastern European Constructivism he worked as a painter and photographer and went to Chicago in the 1930s to set up the New Bauhaus which became the Institute of Design.

Mollino, Carlo (1905–73)
An Italian furniture designer who was based in Turin and who designed a number of furniture pieces in the late 1940s and early 1950s sculpted into organic shapes which he described as 'streamlined-surreal'. His work contrasts with the more rational design emerging from Milan in those years.

Moore, Henry (1898–)
The British sculptor whose organic forms have dominated British sculpture in the twentieth century. They also served to inspire a generation of designers after the Second World War, who wanted to move away from the geometric rigidity of the Modern Movement.

Morris, William (1834–96)
Father of the British Arts and Crafts Movement, William Morris was the nineteenth-century British craftsman-designer whose ideas about design, mechanization and society had a profound effect upon the philosophy of modern design in many countries. His designs themselves – for furniture, textiles, wallpaper, and so on – belong more to the nineteenth century.

Moser, Koloman (1868–1918)
Trained initially as a painter, the Austrian designer, Kolo Moser, moved from a curvilinear to a more rectilinear Art Nouveau style in his patterns and posters

by the end of the nineteenth century. He was a member of the Viennese Sezession group along with Hoffmann (q.v.) and Olbrich.

Mucchi, Gabriele (1899–)
An Italian artist, architect and designer who settled in Milan in 1934 and contributed to the Rationalist architectural movement. He also worked on furniture pieces in the same style.

Mumford, Lewis (1895–1972)
The American historian, Lewis Mumford, published a number of books which related technology to its cultural context, including *Technics and Civilization* (1934) and *Art and Technics* (1952).

Murdoch, Peter (1940–)
A British industrial designer whose fibreboard child's chair from the early 1960s produced by Perspective Designs earned him a reputation as a Pop designer. He went on to work on the graphics for the 1968 Olympics in Mexico City and later in the general area of graphics and corporate identity.

Muthesius, Hermann (1861–1934)
The German diplomat who travelled to Britain at the end of the nineteenth century and wrote his book *Das Englische Haus* (1905) about his findings. He was a major force behind the formation of the German Werkbund and did much to promote design for German industry in the early twentieth century.

Nizzoli, Marcello (1887–1969)
Trained as a graphic designer, Marcello Nizzoli was hired by Adriano Olivetti (q.v.) in 1938. He worked on the company's electrical machines and produced some highly elegant typewriters in the 1940s and 1950s – among them the Lexicon 80 and the Lettera 22. He also worked for the Necchi sewing machine company and produced the Mirella sewing machine in 1956.

Noyes, Eliot (1910–77)
An American industrial designer who, after working at the Museum of Modern Art in the 1940s, was hired by Thomas Watson, the son of the founder of IBM. From 1956 he worked with the graphic designer Paul Rand as the corporate design director of the company designing a number of pieces of office equipment.

Olivetti, Adriano (1901–60)
The son of the founder of the Olivetti Company, Adriano Olivetti took over in the 1920s and was responsible for bringing in the major designers who worked with them, notably Marcello Nizzoli and Ettore Sottsass (qq.v.).

Olivetti, Camillo (1868–1943)
The founder of the Olivetti Office Machinery Company in 1908, Olivetti

designed the company's first typewriter himself and manufactured it along the same lines as Henry Ford was doing with his automobiles in the USA.

Pagano, Guiseppe   (1896–1943)
The Italian architect who from 1931 worked with Eduardo Persico (q.v.) on the magazine *Casabella* and on a number of Rationalist buildings throughout the 1930s. He contributed to the Triennale of 1933 and to the Paris Exhibition of 1937.

Paul, Bruno   (1874–1954)
A German architect who taught at the Berlin School of Applied Arts in the early twentieth century and was an early and leading member of the German Werkbund. He later also became head of the Berlin Arts and Crafts Museum.

Paulsson, Gregor   (1889–1964)
The Swedish architect, Paulsson, was the first director of the Swedish Design Society – the Svenska Slöjdforeningen. He wrote a book about design in 1919 called *More Beautiful Everyday Things* which was highly influential in Sweden and contributed extensively to the 1930 Stockholm Exhibition.

Peach, Harry   (1874–1936)
A founding member of the British Design and Industries Association who during the First World War established Dryad Handicrafts in Leicester which later became the Dryad Furniture Company, well known for its production of cane furniture. Peach was a very active member of the DIA throughout the 1920s.

Pentagram
A British design consultancy which was established in 1971 on the basis of a graphic design consultancy from the 1950s called Forbes, Fletcher & Gill. The British industrial designer, Kenneth Grange, well known for his work with Kenwood, joined the group in the early 1970s.

Persico, Eduardo   (1900–71)
The Italian graphic designer who worked on a number of magazines, including – with Pagano (q.v.) in Milan in the 1930s – *Casabella*. He also collaborated with Marcello Nizzoli (q.v.) on a number of exhibition stands in the same decade, including the Aeronautical Exhibition in Milan in 1934.

Pesce, Gaetano   (1939–   )
An Italian architect-designer and sculptor who since the 1960s has worked in a highly individual, radical way, producing, among other things, nihilistic pieces of 'decaying' design. He has worked with the Cassina Company on several occasions and teaches architecture at Venice and in Brooklyn.

Pevsner, Nikolaus   (1902–83)
The German-born art historian whose writings about modern architecture and design have been very influential in this century. He supported the ideas of the

European Modern Movement and that commitment has coloured all his writings.

Pick, Frank (1878–1941)
A founder member of the British Design and Industries Association, Frank Pick's main contribution to modern design is as the man who masterminded the redesign of the London Underground in the 1920s and 1930s, and employed Charles Holden and Edward Johnston to work on the architecture and graphic design involved.

Pintori, Giovanni (1912–)
The Italian graphic designer and artist who was based in Milan from 1931 onwards and worked on a number of projects in the Rationalist Style before being employed by the Olivetti Company from 1936. In 1950 he became Olivetti's artistic director and worked there until 1968.

Poelzig, Hans (1869–1936)
A German architect and participant in the Expressionist Movement, Poelzig's work includes the Grosses Schauspielhaus of 1919 in Berlin. He also taught, working in Breslau (from 1903 to 1916), Dresden, and, finally, Berlin where he also set up an architectural office.

Ponti, Gio (1891–1979)
An Italian architect-designer and editor of *Domus* magazine from 1938, Ponti has worked since the 1930s on a range of products for a number of Italian companies, including Arflex and Cassina, and has been a central figure in the Italian mainstream design establishment since that period.

Porsche
The Stuttgart car company, named after Ferdinand Porsche, the designer of the Volkswagen. The Porsche car itself was designed by Erwin Komendo.

Pritchard, Jack (1899–)
A British furniture manufacturer who was influential in bringing Modernism to Britain in the 1930s. As well as inviting both Le Corbusier and Moholy-Nagy (qq.v.) to work for him he also established the Isokon furniture company which manufactured moulded plywood pieces designed by Marcel Breuer (q.v.).

Race, Ernest (1913–64)
Trained as an architect, the British designer Ernest Race went on to establish Race Furniture Limited in 1946 and to design some highly influential steel rod furniture for the Festival of Britain in the 1950s.

Rams, Dieter (1932–)
The German industrial designer who has made his name working for the Braun Company since 1955. He has designed for Braun many machines which have

come to typify the sparse, formal, geometric machine-style of much postwar German design.

Read, Herbert (1893–1967)
The English art and design critic who was influential in bringing European Modernism to Britain in the 1930s. His best-known book in this context, *Art and Industry* (1934), is still read widely today.

Redgrave, Richard (1804–88)
A painter who, as part of the Henry Cole group, became associated with the British design reform movement in the middle of the nineteenth century. In 1851 he wrote a *Supplementary Report on Design in the Great Exhibition* pointing out deficiencies in the design of British goods.

Reich, Lilly (1908–)
German Modern Movement architect-designer who worked closely with Mies van der Rohe (q.v.) after 1929 when she designed the interiors for his Weissenhof apartment block. In 1931 she exhibited a single-room flat in Berlin.

Reilly, Paul (1912–)
The son of the British architect Sir Charles Reilly, he began working for the Council of Industrial Design in 1947 and became its director in 1960. Reilly is largely responsible for bringing British design into an international context and for making Scandinavian ideas current in Britain in the 1950s.

Riemerschmid, Richard (1868–1957)
A German designer based in Munich who developed a range of standardized furniture for mass production in the first decade of this century. With Peter Behrens (q.v.) he became an early member of the Deutscher Werkbund.

Rietveld, Gerrit (1888–1964)
Born in Utrecht, the Dutch architect who trained as a cabinet-maker, became a member of the De Stijl group and developed a number of chairs, among them the Red-Blue chair of 1917/18 and the Zig-Zag chair of 1934 which have become modern classics.

Rodchenko, Alexander (1891–1956)
Russian Constructivist sculptor-designer who worked on interiors and street constructions at the time of the Russian Revolution with his wife, the textile designer Stepanova, and others. He moved increasingly towards Tatlin's (q.v.) idea of the 'artist-engineer' and began designing functional items like furniture and clothing in the 1920s.

Rosenthal
The German ceramics manufacturing company, founded in Bavaria in 1897. Through this century Rosenthal has encouraged designers, among them Tapio

Wirkkala, Raymond Loewy, Walter Gropius and Wilhelm Wagenfeld (qq.v.), to work with them on products presented within their Studio range.

Ruskin, John   (1819–1900)
The nineteenth-century British art critic who had a great influence upon British design, particularly in relation to the use of ornament and the relationship with mechanization. William Morris (q.v.) was directly influenced by Ruskin.

Russell, Gordon   (1892–1980)
Brought up in the Cotswolds, the British designer Gordon Russell formed a furniture manufacturing company in the 1930s working with his brother R. D. Russell. During the war he was in charge of the Utility Scheme and in 1947 became director of the Council of Industrial Design. He has played a major role in the British design establishment in this century.

Saarinen, Eero   (1910–61)
The son of Eliel Saarinen, the Finnish architect-designer, Eero came to the USA with his father in 1923. He studied architecture at Yale and in 1940 worked with Charles Eames (q.v.) on a range of moulded plywood furniture. In the 1950s his furniture, including the famous Tulip chair, was manufactured by Knoll (q.v.).

Saarinen, Eliel   (1873–1950)
The Finnish architect who was a leader of the National Romantic Movement in Finland before he emigrated to the USA in 1923. He designed the buildings for the Cranbrook Academy where he also taught and in 1937 he went into partnership with his son Eero (q.v.).

Sakier, George   (1893–1965)
Trained as an engineer, but having also studied painting in Paris, the American George Sakier worked as an illustrator and as an art director of *Harper's Bazaar* before becoming director of a Bureau of Design in the US Radiator & Standard Sanitary Corporation in the late 1920s. He was one of the few in-house industrial designers in the USA in the 1930s.

Sarpaneva, Timo   (1926–   )
A Finnish designer of glass, ceramics, textiles and metalwork who was employed by the Iittala Glassworks in 1950 and showed his work at the Milan Triennales in the 1950s, winning prizes at all three. He is one of the 'super-star' designers who emerged from Finland in the postwar period.

Sason, Sixten   (1912-69)
The Swedish industrial designer who trained as a silversmith and went on to work, on a consultancy basis, for Electrolux, Hasselblad and Saab Motors. For the latter company he designed the famous Saab 92 automobile.

Scarpa, Carlo   (1906–78)
Born in Venice the Italian designer, Carlo Scarpa, is best known for his work

for the Venini Glass Company executed between 1933 and 1947, and for his interior and exhibition designs, including that for the Frescoes from Florence Exhibition held in London in 1969. His son Tobia has worked with Gio Ponti at the Cassina company.

Scharoun, Hans (1893–1972)
A German architect who played a role in the organic, rather than the crystalline, school of German Expressionism. He set up as an independent architect in 1918 and his work includes an entry for the Friedrichstrasse skyscraper project.

Schawinsky, Alexander (1904–)
A Swiss ex-Bauhaus student who in 1933 was invited to work for the Olivetti Company. He worked there for three years designing graphics and helping on products. In 1936 he went to the USA where he taught for a brief period.

Schlemmer, Oscar (1888–1943)
A German stage designer and painter who taught at the Bauhaus. He produced his Triadic Ballet at the Bauhaus in 1923 and contributed to the work of Herbert Bayer's (q.v.) typography workshop in Dessau.

Schnaidt, Claude (1931–)
The design theorist Claude Schnaidt worked at the Hochschule für Gestaltung at Ulm and published a book on Hannes Meyer (q.v.), Walter Gropius's (q.v.) successor at the Bauhaus.

Schreiber, Gaby (1912–)
A German designer who began as an interior decorator and came to London in the 1930s. She was approached by the Runcolite Plastics Comapny in the 1940s and designed a range of modern plastic consumer products for them, including a cruet set.

Scolari, D'Urbino, Lomazzi and De Pas
Group of Italian architect-designers who worked with the Zanotta Company from the mid-1960s in producing Pop furniture pieces like the transparent plastic Blow chair of 1967 and the Joe Sofa chair in the form of a giant baseball glove in 1970.

Semper, Gottfried (1803–79)
The German architect, writer and educationalist who first came to Britain for the Great Exhibition of 1851 and contributed to the British design reform movement, along with Henry Cole and Richard Redgrave (qq.v.).

Sharp
The Japanese company, Sharp, began life in 1912 as a metalworks business. It took its name from the Ever-Sharp pencil which was developed in 1915 by

Tokiyi Hayakawa, after which it moved into electrical equipment and finally emerged after the war as a manufacturer of electronic consumer products.

Sinel, Joseph (1889–1975)
A commercial artist, born in New Zealand, who became one of the US independent consultant designers of the 1930s.

Sony
A Japanese manufacturer of electronic equipment which has gained a reputation for the design component of its goods. Formed just after the Second World War the company, called at that time Tokyo Telecommunications Engineering, produced the first tape-recorder in Japan in 1950, the first of many forays into new products.

Sottsass, Ettore (1917–)
The Italian architect-designer who, since setting up his practice in Milan, has been most closely associated with the Radical Design Movement in Italy. He has worked, publicly, with the Olivetti Company and, privately, on furniture and ceramics and masterminded the Memphis experiment.

Stabler, Harold (1890–1958)
The silversmith Harold Stabler was a founding member of the British Design and Industries Association and a director of Poole Pottery. He was one of the group which visited the German Werkbund Exhibition in Cologne in 1914. This encouraged him to form a British association which would promote links between design and manufacturing industry.

Studio Alchymia
The architect Alessandro Guerriero founded Studio Alchymia in Milan in 1979 as an outlet for the avant-garde ideas of designers like Ettore Sottsass, Andrea Branzi and Alessandro Mendini (qq.v.). It showed its Bauhaus 1 and 2 collections in 1980 and shocked the Milanese design establishment with its use of kitsch and popular imagery.

Sundahl, Eskil (1890–1974)
A Swedish architect who played a role in the Functionalist Movement in Sweden in the 1920s and 1930s and contributed designs to the 1930 Stockholm Exhibition. He worked closely alongside Uno Ahren, Sven Markelius and Gunnar Asplund (qq.v.).

Superstudio
Formed in Florence in 1966, Superstudio was one of the architectural and design groups that formed the Radical Design Movement in Italy in that period. They worked on Utopian architectural projects and some office tables which Zanotta produced.

Tatlin, Vladimir (1885–1953)
The Russian Constructivist sculptor who turned, after the Revolution of 1917, to working on functional projects such as workers' clothing. He is best known for his Monument to the Third International of 1919–20 in which he set out to work like an engineer in the service of the Revolution.

Taut, Max (1884–1967)
The brother of Bruno Taut, Max Taut was a German architect who played an important part in the Expressionist Movement. His work includes the Wissenger Tomb and a project for the Chicago Tribune competition of 1922.

Teague, Walter Dorwin (1883–1960)
A pioneer American consultant industrial designer of the 1930s, Teague is often called the 'dean of industrial design', implying his leadership in that profession. His team worked with Eastman Kodak for many years as well as with a number of other companies and Teague chaired the Board of Design for the New York World's Fair of 1939.

Terragni, Giuseppe (1904–69)
The Italian architect, Terragni, was a leader of the Rational Movement in Italy in the 1930s and a member of Gruppo 7. He is best known for his design for the Casa del Fasci in Como for which he designed a range of furniture in tubular steel and black leather.

Toyota
The Japanese company Toyota began in the late nineteenth century as a manufacturer of wooden automatic looms. In the 1930s it turned to automobile manufacture taking as its slogan 'cars for all the world', and has remained in that business ever since.

Van de Velde, Henri (1863–1957)
A Belgian Art Nouveau architect and designer who moved to Germany in 1900 and ran the Weimar School of Applied Arts. He wrote extensively about his theories of design, which owed much to William Morris (q.v.), and was a founder member of the Deutscher Werkbund.

Van Doren, Harold (1895–1957)
An American consultant industrial designer who, like his colleagues, worked with a number of companies throughout the 1930s, including Philco and Goodyear. He had moved from the museum world into this new profession and in 1940 published a book called *Industrial Design: A Practical Guide*.

Vassos, John (1898–)
John Vassos was Greek in origin but arrived in the USA in 1919 and became a commercial artist after studying at the Art Students' League. He moved gradually into designing labels, packages and the occasional small appliance.

Venturi, Robert (1925–)
The American architect who wrote, in 1966, his book *Complexity and Contradiction in Architecture* which heralded Post-Modernism. He worked on several Pop architecture products in the 1960s and early 1970s and has recently designed some eclectic furniture for Knoll (q.v.).

Vuokko
The name of the textile company owned by Vuokko Eskolin who trained as a ceramicist before working as a textile designer for Marimekko (q.v.) in the 1950s. She is well known for her dramatic, printed textiles and set up the Vuokko Company in 1964 which also produces clothing and accessories made from her own textiles.

Wagenfeld, Wilhelm (1900–79)
A German, ex-Bauhaus designer who worked at the Lausitzer Glassworks between 1935 and 1947 and who has, since 1954, run his own studio in Stuttgart. He has designed a great range of products, from glass to ceramics, cutlery and lighting and is considered to be Germany's leading industrial designer.

Wagner, Otto (1841–1918)
The Austrian architect-designer who worked on the edge of Art Nouveau in the early 1890s but who showed more classical tendencies by the end of that decade. His buildings include the Karlsplatz Stadtbahn in Vienna of 1897 and the Majolika Haus, also in Vienna, of 1898. His pupils, Hoffmann (q.v.), Olbrich and Moser (q.v.), formed the core of the Viennese Sezession group.

Walter Thompson, J.
The US advertising agency which was set up in the nineteenth century and which was highly effective in the 1920s in putting designers in contact with manufacturing companies. It has a world-wide network and is still a thriving concern today.

Wedgwood
The British ceramics company which was formed by Josiah Wedgwood who was one of the first manufacturers to turn to artists to style one of his ranges of goods. By the early nineteenth century he had invited John Flaxman and George Stubbs to design for him thereby creating a precedent which was emulated by many other companies.

Welch, Robert (1929–)
A British silversmith who was trained at the Royal College of Art in London in the 1950s and who set up a Cotswold metalwork workshop after he graduated, thus perpetuating the tradition of the Arts and Crafts designers of the previous century.

Wennerberg, Gunnar (1863–1914)

A Swedish painter who became artistic director of the ceramics company, Gustavsberg, in 1895. He brought to Gustavsberg products a new, fresh style based on direct observation from nature. Wennerberg left the company in 1908.

Whitney, Eli (1765–1825)

The American inventor of the cotton gin, Eli Whitney, is also regarded by some as the father of machine production of interchangeable parts in the manufacture of his fire-arms. It is probable, however, that he knew about the pioneering work by Blanc, a superintendent in the French Royal Arsenals, at the end of the eighteenth century.

Wirkkala, Tapio (1915–)

One of Finland's super-star designers of the postwar era who worked for the Iittala Glass Company from 1947. He exhibited his work at the Milan Triennales of the 1950s. More recently he has worked for both Venini and Rosenthal (q.v.).

Wolff Olins

A British design consultancy founded in 1965 which works on a range of products from graphics to interiors but which focuses on the corporate identity concept. Michael Wolff has designed trademarks for Bovis and Hadfields paint and the group has done corporate schemes for the British Oxygen Company and the Volkswagen/Audi company.

Wornum, Ralph N. (1812–77)

Wornum was keeper and secretary of the National Gallery, a portrait painter, a lecturer and an art critic. In 1856 he published his *Analysis of Ornament* in which he criticized the excessive ornamentation of much Victorian design.

Wright, Russel (1904–76)

The American designer who was best known for his dinnerware sets in the 1930s which were marketed under names such as American Modern. He also worked on furniture and aluminium products in that decade and became a very fashionable designer, his products selling in great numbers.

Introductory Bibliography

General

The only bibliography published to date which deals specifically with the subject of design is:

Coulson, A. J., *A Bibliography of Design in Britain 1851–1970* (London: Design Council, 1979) which, as its title suggests, is limited to the British Isles.

There are a number of books published, many of them in French and Italian – and, as yet, unfortunately, untranslated – which examine the meaning of modern design and which are useful introductions to that concept. They include:

Barthes, R., *Mythologies* (Paris: Senil, 1967). A text which analyses popular culture from a semiological perspective. The articles on the Citroën car and Plastics are most relevant in this context.

Baudrillard, J., *Le Système des objets* (Paris: Gonthier, 1968). A sociological analysis of consumer objects within a capitalist economy.

Bonsiepe, G., *Teoria e pratica del desegno industriale* (Milan: Feltrinelli, 1975). A general discourse on the nature of design in contemporary society.

Caplan, R., *By Design* (New York: McGraw-Hill, 1982). A series of essays which examine fairly lightheartedly the tradition of modern design in a US context.

Dorfles, G., *Introduction à l'industrial design* (Paris: Casterman, 1974). A general essay on the meaning of modern design.

Douglas, M., and Isherwood, B., *The World of Goods: Towards an Anthropology of Consumption* (Harmondsworth, Middx: Penguin, 1980). A study of consumption, which does not mention design by name, but which places consumer objects into a context of human demand rather than of economics.

Francastel, P., *Art et technique* (Paris: Editions Densel, 1956). A useful, but somewhat dated, study of the relationship between art and technology.

Hoffenberg, A., and Lapidus, A., *La Société du Design* (Paris: Presses Universitaires de France, 1977). A dense, sociological analysis of modern design.

Huisman, Denis, and Patrix, G., *L'Esthétique industrielle* (Paris: Presses Universitaires de France, 1961). A short analysis of the development and function of modern design.

Maldonado, T., *Disegno industriale: un riesame* (Milan: Feltrinelli, 1976). An account of the meaning and function of industrial design.

Nelson, G., *Problems of Design* (New York: Whitney, 1957). A dated but perceptive account.

Patrix, G., *Design et environment* (Paris: Casterman, 1973). A critical study of the role of design in contemporary society.

Pye, D., *The Nature of Design* (London: Studio Vista, 1964). An account of the meaning of design from a craftsman's perspective. A little dated now.

Read, H., *Art and Industry* (London: Faber, 1934). A discourse on the nature of modern design from an idealistic, Modern Movement perspective.

Selle, G., *Ideologie und Utopie des Designs* (Cologne: Dumont, 1968). An account of the social function of design in this century.

Wolf, L., *Idéologie et production: le design* (Paris: Editions Anthropos, 1972). A Marxist critique of contemporary design.

The number of introductory texts to the history of modern design and the decorative arts has expanded in the last ten or so years. Among the most useful are:

Bayley, S., *In Good Shape: Style in Industrial Products 1900–1960* (London: Design Council, 1979). A useful introduction which consists of a compilation of essays on modern design and notes on seminal products.

Benton, T., Benton, C., and Sharp, D. (ed.), *Form and Function: A Source Book for the History of Architecture and Design 1890–1939* (Milton Keynes: Open University Press, 1975). Excerpts from original texts by Modern Movement protagonists.

de Noblet, J., *Design: introduction à l'histoire de l'évolution des formes industrielles de 1820 à aujourd'hui* (Paris: Stock-Chêne, 1974). A general overview of the subject with useful appendices.

Doblin, J., *One Hundred Great Product Designs* (New York: Van Nostrand Reinhold, 1970). A pictorial introduction to modern design.

Drexler, A., and Daniel, G., *Introduction to Twentieth Century Design from the Collection at the Museum of Modern Art, New York* (New York: Museum of Modern Arts, 1959). A pictorial study with an emphasis on design as form.

Ferebee, A., *A History of Design from the Victorian Era to the Present* (New York: Van Nostrand Reinhold, 1970). A study in changing design styles. Useful but fairly superficial.

Garner, P. (ed.), *The Encyclopaedia of the Decorative Arts 1890–1940* (New York: Van Nostrand Reinhold, 1979). A collection of essays on various aspects of the decorative arts.

Garner, P. (ed.), *Contemporary Decorative Arts from 1940 to the Present* (New York: Van Nostrand Reinhold, 1980). Companion volume to the above text but less convincing.

Gay, B. (ed.). *Classics of Modern Design* (London: Camden Arts Centre, 1977). Catalogue accompanying an exhibition on British design this century.

Giedion, S., *Mechanisation Takes Command: A Contribution to Anonymous History* (New York: Norton, 1969. First published, 1948). The first, and best, account of architecture and design written from an anonymous perspective and which emphasizes the role of technology.

Heskett, J., *Industrial Design* (London: Thames & Hudson, 1980). The most thorough introductory account of the subject to date.

Hiesinger, K. B. (ed.), *Design Since 1945* (London: Thames & Hudson in association with the Philadelphia Museum of Art, 1983). A useful introduction to postwar ideas and objects.

Hillier, B., *The Style of the Century 1900–1980* (London: Herbert Press, 1983). A surface-deep account of limited use only.

Lucie-Smith, E., *A History of Industrial Design* (Oxford: Phaidon, 1983). A patchy account which starts with the Stone Age.

Pevsner, N., *Pioneers of Modern Design* (Harmondworth, Middx: Penguin, 1960). A reworking of the original 1936 *Pioneers of the Modern Movement* which revealed Pevsner's bias more clearly.

Pevsner, N., *The Sources of Modern Architecture and Design* (London: Thames & Hudson, 1968). A compilation of Pevsner's highly erudite essays on various subjects within this general area.

Pevsner, N., *Studies in Art, Architecture and Design. Volume 2: Victorian and After* (London: Thames & Hudson, 1968). Similar to title above.

Sparke, P. (ed.), *Reyner Banham: Design by Choice* (London: Academy Editions, 1981). A collection of essays by Banham on various modern architectural and design topics.

Two other main sources of material on modern design are the texts printed to accompany the Open University A305 course on Modern Architecture and Design which includes information on the following topics:

Art Nouveau
Europe 1900–1914
USA 1890–1939
The New Objectivity
The International Style
Design 1920s
English Architecture 1930s
British Design
Mechanical Services

and the Design Council publications of the proceedings of the Design History Society Conferences which include:

Design History: Leisure in the Twentieth Century, Middlesex Polytechnic, 1977.

Design History: Fad or Function?, Brighton Polytechnic, 1978.

Design History: Past, Process, Product, University of Kent, 1979.

Design History: Design and Industry, University of Keele, 1980.

Design History: Svensk Form, Victoria and Albert Museum, 1981.

From the Spitfire to the Micro-Chip, Polytechnic of the City of London, 1985.

Where the history of design in specific countries is concerned the following publications are among the most useful:

BRITAIN

Brutton, M., 'Review of postwar British design', *Design*, no. 251 (January 1970).

McCarthy, F., *A History of British Design 1830–1970* (London: Allen & Unwin, 1979). An essentially establishment-oriented account.

Introductory Bibliography

GERMANY

Selle, G., *Die Geschichte des Designs in Deutschland von 1870 bis heute* (Cologne: Dumont, 1978). A dense account of modern design in Germany.

ITALY

Branzi, A., *The Hot-House* (London: Thames & Hudson, 1985).
Fratelli, E., *Il disegno industriale italiano 1928–1981 (quasi una storia ideologica)* (Milan: Celid, 1983).
Gregotti, V., *Il disegno del prodotto industriale in Italia 1860–1980* (Milan: Electa, 1983). A very thorough survey of the subject.

SCANDINAVIA

McFadden, D. E. (ed.), *Scandinavian Modern Design 1880–1980* (New York: Harry N. Abrams, 1982). A collection of essays on various aspects of this subject written by experts in the field.

USA

Pulos, A., *The American Design Ethic* (Cambridge, Mass.: MIT, 1982). An account which stresses the social and technological contexts of US design.

It is essential to consult a few general books on modern economic, industrial, political, social, technological and cultural history in order to be able to put modern design into context. The books available are too numerous to list here but include:

Armytage, W. H. G., *Social History of Engineering* (London: Faber, 1961).
Ashworth, W., *A Short History of the International Economy Since 1850* (London: Longman, 3rd edn 1975).
Chandler, A. D., *Strategy and Structure: Chapters in the History of the Industrial Enterprise* (Cambridge, Mass.: Harvard University Press, 1962).
Floud, R., and McCloskey, D., *The Economic History of Britain since 1700*, 2 vols (Cambridge: Cambridge University Press, 1981).
Foster, H. (ed.), *The Anti-Aesthetic – Essays on Post-Modern Culture* (Port Townsend, Wash.: Washington Bay Press, 1983).
Fox, R. W., and Jackson, T. J. (eds), *The Culture of Consumption: Critical Essays in American History 1880–1980* (New York: Pantheon, 1983).
Galbraith, J. K., *The Affluent Society* (Harmondsworth, Middx: Penguin, 1962. First published, 1958).
Hudson, L., *Food, Clothes and Shelter: Twentieth Century Industrial Archaeology* (London: John Baker, 1978).
Jefferys, J. B., *Retail Trading in Britain 1850–1950* (Cambridge: Cambridge University Press, 1954).

240

Mumford, L., *Technics and Civilization* (London: Routledge & Kegan Paul, 1934).

Mumford, L., *Art and Technics* (London: Routledge & Kegan Paul, 1953).

Roberts, J., *Europe 1880–1945* (London: Longman, 1967).

Sabel, C. F., *Work and Politics: The Division of Labour in Industry* (Cambridge: Cambridge University Press, 1982).

Salter, W. E. G., *Productivity and Technological Change* (Cambridge: Cambridge University Press, 2nd edn 1966).

Singer, C. (ed.), *A History of Technology. Vol. V: The Late Nineteenth Century* (Oxford: Clarendon, 1958).

Waites, B., Bennett, T., and Martin, G. (eds.), *Popular Culture: Past and Present* (London: Open University, 1982).

Weiner, M. J., *English Culture and the Decline of the Industrial Spirit 1850–1890* (Cambridge: Cambridge University Press, 1981).

Williams, R., *Culture and Society, 1780–1950* (Harmondsworth, Middx: Penguin, 1958).

Williams, R., *Culture* (London: Fontana, 1981).

Williams, R., *Towards 2000* (Harmondsworth, Middx: Penguin, 1985).

The following books, articles and catalogues relate to the chapters in the main text:

1 Mass Production and the Mass Market

BOOKS

Adburnham, A., *Shops and Shopping 1800–1914* (London: Allen & Unwin, 1964).

Aslin, E., *The Aesthetic Movement: Prelude to Art Nouveau* (London: Studio Vista, 1969). A useful account of links between artists and manufacturers in the second half of the nineteenth century.

Bathe, G. and D., *Oliver Evans* (Philadelphia: National Publishing Company, 1935).

Borth, C., *Masters of Mass Production* (New York: Harper, 1945).

Church, R. A., *The Great Victorian Boom 1850–1873* (London: Macmillan, 1975).

Ferry, J. W., *The History of the Department Store* (New York: Macmillan, 1960).

Ford, H., *My Life and Work* (New York: Doubleday, 1922). This includes an account of Ford's early ideas about standardization and mass production.

Greenough, H., *Form and Function: Remarks on Art, Design and Architecture* (Berkeley, Calif.: University of California Press, 1947). Originally published in the nineteenth century, this is one of the earliest treatises on Functionalist aesthetics.

Habakkuk, H. J., *American and British Technology in the Nineteenth Century* (Cambridge: Cambridge University Press, 1962). A useful introduction to the subject.

Hamish Fraser, W., *The Coming of the Mass Market* (London: Macmillan, 1981). The most succinct and accessible account of mass consumption in nineteenth-century Britain.

Harvie, C., Martin, G., and Scharf, A., *Industrialization and Culture 1830–1914* (London: Macmillan, 1970). Excerpts from original writings on the subject.

Hounshell, D. A., *From the American System to Mass Production* (Baltimore, Md: Johns Hopkins University Press, 1985).

Klingender, F. D., *Art and the Industrial Revolution* (London: Paladin, 1972. First published, 1947). Still the most complete study of the subject to date.

Kouwenhoven, J. A., *Made in America* (Garden City, NY: Doubleday, 1948). A little dated but still useful.

McCabe, J. D., *The Illustrated History of the Centennial Exhibition: Philadelphia 1876* (Philadelphia, Pa: National Publishing Company, 1975). A reprint of the original catalogue.

Post, R. C., *1878: A Centennial Exhibition* (Washington, DC: Smithsonian Institution, 1976).

Raistrick, A., *Industrial Archaeology* (London: Paladin, 1973). A useful source of information about early mass-production machines.

Rolt, L. T. C., *Victorian Engineering* (Harmondsworth, Middx: Penguin, 1970).

Saul, S. B., *Technological Changes: The United States and Britain in the Nineteenth Century* (London: Methuen, 1970).

Veblen, T., *The Theory of the Leisure Class* (New York: Macmillan, 1899). The earliest, and still one of the most useful, account of mass consumption in the nineteenth century.

ARTICLES

Conway, H., 'The beginnings of product design? The American system of manufacture and design in America in the 1850s', in T. Bishop (ed.), *Design History: Fad or Function* (London: Design Council, 1977), pp. 34–7.

Samuel, R., 'The workshop of the world: steam, power and hard technology in mid-Victorian Britain', *History Workshop*, no. 28 (1977), pp. 21–37.

2 New Products for a New Life-Style

BOOKS

Byrn, E. W., *Progress of Invention in the Nineteenth Century* (New York: Harper, 1900). A book from the period which looks at the immediate past and provides an interesting account.

Cantacuzino, S., *Wells Coates* (London: Gordon Frazer, 1979). Includes information on his work with the Ekco Radio Company in the 1930s.

Cressy, E., *Discoveries and Inventions of the Twentieth Century* (London: Routledge, 1914). A view of the technological advances of the very early part of the century.

Davidson, C., *A Woman's Work is Never Done: A History of Housework in the British Isles 1650–1950* (London: Chatto & Windus, 1983). A fascinating account which includes information on labour-saving devices.

Delgado, A., *The Enormous File* (London: Murray, 1980). A general account of changes in the make-up of the office.

De Vries, L., *Victorian Inventions* (London: Murray, 1971). A pictorial account.

Fredgant, D., *Electrical Collectibles: Relics of the Electrical Age* (San Luis Obispo, Calif.: Padre Productions, 1981).

Griffith, C., *Women's Work: A Social History of Domestic Appliances 1851–1939* (London: Ash & Grant, 1978). An excellent account of the subject.

Hanks, D., *Innovative Furniture in America from 1800 to the Present* (New York: Horizon, 1981). A well-researched, scholarly study of the subject.

Hill, J., *The Cat's Whisker: Fifty Years of Wireless Design* (London: Oresko, 1978).

Hounshell, D. A., *Telegraph, Telephone, Radio and Television* (Washington, DC: Smithsonian Institution Press, 1977).

Katzman, D. M., *Seven Days a Week: Women and Domestic Service in Industrializing America* (Champaign, Ill.: University of Illinois Press, 1981).

Lincoln, E., *The Electric Home* (New York: Doubleday, 1936). A fascinating account from the period.

Palmer, A. J., *Riding High: The Story of the Bicycle* (New York: Dutton, 1956).

Rae, J. B., *The American Automobile: A Brief History* (Chicago: University of Chicago Press, 1965). The most complete account of the subject to date.

Taylor, F., *The Principles of Scientific Management* (New York: Harper, 1961. First published, 1911). Taylor sets out his ideas about the rational organization of work in this study.

ARTICLES

Forty, A., 'Wireless style', *Architectural Association Quarterly*, Vol. 6 (April/June 1972), pp. 26–32.

Forty, A., 'Electrical appliances 1900–1960', in *Design 1900–1960: Newcastle Polytechnic Design History Conference Papers* (Newcastle Polytechnic, 1976), pp. 104–5.

Giedion, S., 'Vacuum in the home', *Technology Review*, no. 27 (January 1947), pp. 157–60.

3   Theory and Design in the Twentieth Century

BOOKS

Barnard, J., *The Decorative Tradition* (London: Architectural Press, 1973). Useful section on nineteenth-century aesthetic theories.

Bill, M., *Form* (Basle: Karl Werner, 1952). A general survey of object appearance in the middle of the century.

Bøe, A., *From Gothic Revival to Functional Form: A Study of Victorian Theories of Design* (Cambridge: Cambridge University Press, 1957).

Braun-Feldweg, L., *Beiträge zur Formgebung* (Essen 1960). An essay on German 'good form'.

Brown, T. M., *The Work of Gerrit Rietveld Architect* (Utrecht 1958). The most definitive study of Rietveld's work which includes his forays into chair design.

De Zurko, E., *Origins of Functionalist Theory* (New York: Doubleday, 1957). A seminal work which places Functionalism into its philosophical context.

Durant, S., *Victorian Ornamental Design* (London: Academy Editions, 1972).

Gloag, J., *Victorian Taste: Some Social Aspects of Architecture and Industrial Design from 1820–1900* (Newton Abbot: David & Charles, reprint, 1972). A study which places taste and style into their social context.

Hitchcock, H. R., and Johnson, P., *The International Style* (New York: Norton, 1966). First published in 1932, to accompany the exhibition of the same name, this book shows how Modern Movement idealism translated itself into a particular visual style.

Jencks, C., *The Language of Post-Modern Architecture* (London: Academy Editions, 1977). A study of pluralism and eclecticism in recent architecture.

Madsen, S. T., *Art Nouveau* (London: Weidenfeld & Nicolson, World University Library, 1967). A thorough examination of the style's origins and manifestations.

Naylor, G., *The Arts and Crafts Movement* (London: Studio Vista, 1971). A thorough introduction to the ideas and objects of the movement.

Overy, P., *De Stijl* (London: Studio Vista, 1969).

Pevsner, N., *High Victorian Design* (London: Architectural Press, 1951).

Schaefer, H., *The Roots of Modern Design: Functional Tradition in the Nineteenth Century* (London: Studio Vista, 1970).

Schmutzer, R., *Art Nouveau* (London: Thames & Hudson, 1964).

Wilk, C., *Marcel Breuer: Furniture and Interiors* (New York: Museum of Modern Art, 1981). A useful study of the development of Breuer's ideas.

ARTICLES

Banham, R., 'Machine aesthetic', *Architectural Review*, no. 117 (1955), pp. 78–87.

Banham, R., 'Industrial design and popular art', *Industrial Design*, no. 124 (March 1960), pp. 47–51.

Beresford Evans, J., 'Good form', *Design*, (April, August and September 1956), pp. 62–5.

Konig, H., 'The Braun story', *Architectural Design*, no. 71 (March 1963), pp. 82–6.

McCullough, J., 'Rise and fall of the Functionalist style', *Industrial Design*, no. 124 (March 1960), pp. 42–6.

Moles, A., 'Functionalism in crisis', *Ulm*, no. 19/20 (1967), pp. 74–7.

Moss, R., 'Braun style', *Industrial Design*, no. 138 (November 1962), pp. 23–7.

EXHIBITION CATALOGUE

Rat für Formgebung, Munich, *Gute Form: An Exhibition of German Industrial Design* (1965).

4 Promoting Design

BOOKS

Banham, R. (ed.), *The Aspen Papers: Twenty Years of Design Theory from the International Design Conference in Aspen* (London: Pall Mall, 1974). A useful barometer of establishment design opinion since the 1950s.
Baynes, K. and K., *Gordon Russell* (London: Design Council, 1982).
Burckhard, T. L. (ed.), *Studies in the History and Ideology of the Deutscher Werkbund 1907–1933* (London: Design Council, 1980). A useful account which looks at its imitators in other countries as well.
Campbell, J., *The German Werkbund – The Politics of Reform in the Applied Arts* (Princeton, NJ.: Princeton University Press, 1978), The most complete account of the subject to date.
Carrington, N., *Industrial Design in Britain* (London: Allen & Unwin, 1976). A personal account of the history of the DIA.
Kaufmann, E., Jnr, *Introductions to Modern Design* (New York: Museum of Modern Art, 1950). A set of lectures in which Kaufmann sets out his criteria for 'good design' very clearly.
Lundahl, G., *Nordisk Funktionalism* (Copenhagen: Arkitektur Förlag, 1980). An account of Functionalism in Scandinavia.
Sieck, F., *Danish Arts and Crafts 1931–1981, Illustrated through Glimpses of the History of Den Permanente* (Copenhagen: Den Permanente, 1981).

ARTICLES

Clark, K. W., 'What is good design in industrial manufacture?', *Art and Industry*, no. 42 (January 1948), pp. 42–5.
'Five years of good design', *Industrial Design* (August 1954), pp. 16–18.
Pevsner, N., 'History of the DIA', in *Studies in Art, Architecture and Design. Volume 2: Victorian and After* (London: Thames & Hudson, 1968), pp. 226–41.
'Frank Pick', *Architectural Review* (August 1942), pp. 16–18.
Russell, G., 'What is good design?', *Design*, no. 1 (January 1949), pp. 3–4.
Shand, P. M., 'Stockholm 1930', *Architectural Review*, no. 16 (August 1930), pp. 23–7.
Sparke, P., 'Swedish Modern: myth or reality', in *Svensk Form* (London: Design Council, 1981).

EXHIBITION CATALOGUES

Fischer Fine Art Gallery, London, *Josef Hoffmann 1870–1956: Architect and Designer* (1977).
Kunstgewerkemuseum, Zurich, *Schweizerische Werkbund* (1960).
Die Neue Sammlung, Munich, *Zwischen Kunst und Industre: Der Deutsche Werkbund* (1975).
University of California, Los Angeles, *Connections: The Work of Charles and Ray Eames* (1976–7).

5 Democracies and Dictatorships

BOOKS

Bertram, A., *Design* (Harmondsworth, Middx: Pelican, 1938). An insight into the idea of design in Britain in the 1930s.
Gray, C., *The Great Experiment: Russian Art 1863–1922* (London: Thames & Hudson, 1982). An account of Russian design in the years before and after the 1917 Revolution.
Lane, B. M., *Architecture and Politics in Germany 1918–1945* (Cambridge, Mass.: MIT Press, 1968). A useful, well-researched text.
Muller, R. S., *Kunst und Industrie: Ideologie und Organization des Funktionalismus in Architektur* (Munich: Bruckmann, 1974). This provides an insight into German design activity between the wars.
Nelson, W. M., *Small Wonder: The Amazing Story of the Volkswagen* (London: Weidenfeld & Nicolson, 1967).
Pevsner, N., *An Enquiry into Industrial Art in England* (Cambridge: Cambridge University Press, 1937). An account of design as it happened in Britain in the 1930s.
Richards, C. A., *Art in Industry* (New York: Macmillan, 1922). A survey of US design education in the years following the First World War.
Zahle, E. (ed.), *Scandinavian Domestic Design* (London: Methuen, 1963). A thorough account of the ideas and objects which cover the interwar period. ·

ARTICLES

Benevolo, L., 'The beginnings of modern research 1930–1940', in Ambazz, E. (ed.), *Italy: The New Domestic Landscape* (New York: Museum of Modern Art, 1972), pp. 176–80.
Bowlt, J. E., 'The failed Utopia: Russian art 1917–1932', *Art in America*, no. 64 (July 1971), pp. 34–8.
Heskett, J., 'Modernism and Archaism in design in the Third Reich', *Block*, no. 3 (1980), pp. 17–20.
Woodham, J., 'British art in industry 1935', in N. Hamilton (ed.), *Design in Industry* (London: Design Council, 1980), pp. 39–44.

EXHIBITION CATALOGUES

Comune di Milano, Milan, *Annitrenta – arte e cultura in Italia* (Milan: Mazzotta, 1982).
Hayward Gallery, London, *'The Thirties'* (London: Arts Council, 1979).
Kunstgewerbemuseum, Zurich, *Industrieware von Wilhelm Wagenfeld* (1960).

6   The Professional Designer

BOOKS

Bel Geddes, N., *Horizons* (New York: Dover, 1977). Originally published in 1932 this was Bel Geddes's dramatic account of his own career to date.
Blake, J. and A., *The Practical Idealists* (London: Lund Humphries, 1969). A personal account of the story of the Design Research Unit.
Cheney, S. and M., *Art and the Machine* (New York: McGraw-Hill, 1936). A study from the period which outlines, in detail, the origins of the US industrial design profession.
Dreyfuss, H., *Designing for People* (New York: Simon & Schuster, 1955). Dreyfuss's personal manifesto.
Gloag, J., *The Missing Technician in Industrial Production* (London: Allen & Unwin, 1944). An attempt to persuade Britain to emulate the US model of the industrial designer.
Goslett, D., *The Professional Practice of Design* (London: Routledge & Kegan Paul, 1971). First published in 1960 this quickly became the 'bible' on this particular subject.
Holland, J., *Minerva at Fifty* (London: Weidenfeld & Nicolson, 1980). A personalized account of the history of the SIAD.
Loewy, R., *Never Leave Well Enough Alone* (New York: Simon & Schuster, 1951). An entertaining, autobiographical study.
Meikles, J., *Twentieth-Century Limited: Industrial Design in America 1925–1939* (Philadelphia, Pa: Temple University Press, 1979). The most thorough and dispassionate account of the subject to date.
Mercer, F. A., *The Industrial Design Consultant: Who He Is and What He Does* (London: The Studio, 1947). Transcript of a lecture on the subject.
Sparke, P., *Consultant Design: The History of the Designer in Industry* (London: Pembridge Press, 1982). A short introduction to the subject.
Teague, W. D., *Design This Day: The Technique of Order in the Machine Age* (London: Studio Publications, 1946). First published in 1940 this was Teague's personal statement about design.
Van Doren, H., *Industrial Design: A Practical Guide* (New York: McGraw-Hill, 1940). Provides many insights into attitudes towards industrial design at that time.
Wurts, R., *The New York World's Fair 1939/40* (New York: Dover, 1977). A pictorial survey with a short, but useful, introduction.

ARTICLES

'Both fish and fowl', *Fortune*, no. 2 (February 1934) pp. 9–13.

De Holden Stone, J., 'The Society of Industrial Artists', *Penrose Annual* (1951), pp. 333–42.

Goldsmith, M., 'DRU – An English Co-operative', *Graphics*, no. 3 (1948), pp. 97–104.

Gray, M., 'The design profession', in H. Read (ed.), *The Practice of Design* (London: Lund Humphries, 1946), pp. 54–62.

Guilfoyle, J. R., 'Raymond Loewy', *Mobilia*, no. 47 (October/November 1975), pp. 12–19.

Loewy, R., 'Selling through design', *Journal of the Royal Society of Arts*, vol. 9 (January 1942), pp. 226–34.

McConnell, P., 'SID – American hallmark of design integrity', *Art and Industry*, vol. 47 (1949), no. 27, pp. 262–9.

Pevsner, N., 'A century of industrial design and designers', *Designers in Britain*, vol. 3 (1951), no. 14, pp. 27–32.

Pulos, A. J., 'Consultant design: a retrospective view', *Industrial Design*, no. 65 (June 1966), pp. 64–71.

Sparke, P., 'From a lipstick to a steamship', in T. Bishop (ed.), *Design History: Fad or Function* (London: Design Council, 1978), pp. 43–7.

Teague, W. D., 'Building the world of tomorrow. The New York World's Fair', *Art and Industry*, no. 24 (April 1939), pp. 27–35.

Teague, W. D., 'Growth and scope of industrial design in the USA', *Journal of the Royal Society of Arts*, vol. 3, no. 7 (May 1959), pp. 27–32.

7   From Mass Taste to Mass Style

BOOKS

Bayley, S. (ed.), *Taste* (London: Conran Foundation, 1983). A compilation of essays, some useful, others less so.

Bourdieu, P. *Distinction* (London: Routledge & Kegan Paul, 1979).

Bush, D., *The Streamlined Decade* (New York: Braziller, 1975). A full account of the impact of Streamline style in the USA in the 1930s.

Carrington, N., *Design and Decoration in the Home* (London: Batsford, 1952). Provides an insight into the 1950s Contemporary style.

Dorfles, G. (ed.), *Kitsch: The World of Bad Taste* (London: Studio Vista, 1969). A compilation of essays of mixed usefulness. John McCale's article is interesting.

Grief, M., *Depression Modern – The Thirties Style in America* (New York: Universe Books, 1975). A description of US style in the 1930s with an emphasis on the 'decorative arts'.

Hillier, B., *Art Deco* (London: Studio Vista, 1968). A little coffee-table book which succeeds, none the less, in documenting Art Deco very fully.

Hillier, B., *Austerity/Binge* (London: Studio Vista, 1971). Hillier gives the

1940s and 1950s styles a similar treatment to the one he gave the 1930s in *Art Deco*.

Lynes, R., *The Taste-Makers: The Shaping of American Popular Taste* (New York: Dover, 1980). First published in the late 1940s this book suffers from its age but still makes some interesting points.

Melly, G., *Revolt into Style* (Harmondsworth, Middx: London, 1967). A light, but none the less very thorough, survey of the impact of Pop culture on design in the 1960s in Britain.

Moles, A., *Psychologie du Kitsch – L'art du bonheur* (Paris: Studio Vista, 1971). A heavy-going, psychological analysis of the phenomenon.

Perrealt, J., *Streamline Design: How the Future Was* (New York: Queens Museum, 1984). A useful essay which accompanied an exhibition of the same name.

Sparke, P., 'Theory and design in the age of Pop', PhD thesis, Brighton Polytechnic, 1975. Looks at the influence of Pop on architecture and design in Britain in the 1960s. (Unpublished).

Veronesi, G., *Style and Design 1909–1929* (New York: Braziller, 1968). A surface-deep, but useful survey with good illustrations.

Woodham, J., *The Industrial Designer and the Public* (London: Pembridge Press, 1983). A survey of the establishment's interaction with consumers throughout this century. Good section on Britain in the 1930s.

ARTICLES

Banham, R., 'The style "flimsy effeminate"', in M. Banham and B. Hillier (eds.), *A Tonic to the Nation. The Festival of Britain 1951* (London: Thames & Hudson, 1976), pp. 190–8.

Black, M., 'Taste, style and the industrial designer', *Motif*, no. 4 (March 1960), pp. 19–24.

Gebhard, D., 'The moderne in the US 1920–1941', *Architectural Association Quarterly*, no. 39 (July 1970), pp. 34–7.

Harrisson, T., 'Public taste and public design', *Art and Industry*, no. 34 (September 1943), pp. 17–21.

Kaufmann Jr, E., 'Borax or the chromium-plated calf', *Architectural Review*, vol. 6, no. 4 (August 1948), pp. 88–93.

Manser, J., 'Furniture: mainstream or throwaway', *Design*, no. 241 (January 1968), pp. 37–45.

Plummer, K. C., 'The Streamlined Moderne', *Art in America*, no. 51 (January/February 1974), pp. 35–41.

Reilly, P., 'The challenge of Pop', *Architectural Review*, no. 32 (October 1967), pp. 255–7.

Sontag, S., 'On style', in E. Hardwick (ed.), *A Susan Sontag Reader* (Harmondsworth, Middx: Penguin, 1983), pp. 137–55.

Spender, S., 'Things in everyday life', *SIA Journal*, January 1959, pp. 22–7.

Van Doren, H., 'Streamlining: fad or function', *Design*, no. 10 (October 1949), pp. 34–9.

Wolff, M., 'Life-enhancing', *SIA Journal*, January 1965, pp. 10–14.

8 New Materials, New Forms

BOOKS

Ashton, T. S., *Iron and Steel in the Industrial Revolution* (New York: Harper, 1923). An old but still useful account.

Burn, D. L., *The Economic History of Steel-Making 1867–1939* (Cambridge: Cambridge University Press, 1940). A solid account of that industry.

Dubois, J., *Plastics History USA* (Boston, Mass.: MIT, 1972). An account with a technical bias but useful as background.

Gloag, J., *Plastics and the Industrial Designer* (London: Allen & Unwin, 1945). Still among the best general introductory texts to the subject, although, inevitably, badly dated in places.

Hennessey, W. J., *Russel Wright: American Designer* (Cambridge, Mass.: MIT, 1983).

Katz, S., *Plastics: Designs and Materials* (London: Studio Vista, 1978). Good introduction from both a technological and a design point of view.

Plummer, A., *New British Industries in the Twentieth Century* (London: Sir Isaac Pitman & Sons, 1937). Contains a very useful section on aluminium.

Smith, P. I. (ed.), *Practical Plastics Illustrated* (London: Odhams, 1947).

Yarsley, V. E., and Couzens, E. G., *Plastics* (Harmondsworth, Middx: Penguin, 1941).

ARTICLES

Cahan, C. and R., 'The lost city of the Depression', *Chicago History*, no. 4 (Winter 1976/7), pp. 17–22

'Century of progress', *Architectural Forum*, vol. 17, no. 14 (July 1933), pp. 51–7.

Wren, J., 'Gaby Schreiber: designer for industry', *Art and Industry*, vol. 46, no. 42 (1946), pp. 25–30.

9 The Admass Society

BOOKS

Bigsby, C. W. E. (ed.), *Superculture: American Popular Culture and Europe* (London: Elek, 1975). A compilation of essays, some of which are useful.

Branzi, A., and De Lucchi, M., *Il design italiano degli anni '50* (Milan: IGIS Edizioni, 1981). The best book on Italian design in the 1950s – consists of reprints from *Domus*.

Fossati, P., *Il design in Italia 1945–1972* (Turin: Einaudi, 1972). The most thorough account of the subject.

Grassi, A., and Pansera, A. *Atlante del design italiano 1940–1980* (Milan: Fabbri, 1980). A useful general survey of design in postwar Italy.

Hard af Segerstad, U., *Modern Finnish Design* (London: Weidenfeld & Nicolson, 1968). A general introduction to the Finnish phenomenon.

Hebdige, D., *Subculture: The Meaning of Style* (London: Methuen, 1979). A very useful background book which deals with a hitherto undocumented subject.

Hirzel, J., *Kunsthandwerk und Manufaktur in Deutschland seit 1945* (Berlin: Hoffmann, 1953). A general and well-illustrated introduction to the subject.

Hopkins, H., *The New Look: A Social History of the Forties and Fifties* (London: Secker & Warburg, 1964). Invaluable as a background text to this period.

Kruskopf, E. (ed.), *Finnish Design 1875–1975* (Helsinki: Otava, 1975).

Stearn, G. E. (ed.), *McLuhan Hot and Cool* (Harmondsworth, Middx: Penguin, 1968). Varied opinions on McLuhan and his influence.

Thompson, D. (ed.), *Discrimination and Popular Culture* (Harmondsworth, Middx: Penguin, 1964). A useful book on the subject of popular culture with a good article by Michael Farr on 'Design'.

Toffler, A., *Future Shock* (London: Pan, 1971). A book in the tradition of alarmist literature which looks at the future of society. Design is frequently mentioned.

Williams, R., *The Long Revolution* (Harmondsworth, Middx: Penguin, 1965). An invaluable study in modern cultural history.

Williams, R., *Communications* (Harmondsworth, Middx: Penguin, 1968). Another invaluable study, as above.

ARTICLES

Hebdidge, D., 'Object as image: the Italian scooter-cycle', *Block*, no. 5 (1981), pp. 44–64.

Hebdidge, D., 'Towards a cartography of taste 1935–1962', *Block*, no. 4 (1981), pp. 62–9.

Reilly, P., 'Influence of national character on design', *Journal of the Royal Society of Arts*, vol. 104 (26 October 1956), pp 16–21.

Stevans, J., 'The romance of the scooter', *Scooter World*, February 1972, pp. 27–35.

EXHIBITION CATALOGUE

Smithsonian Institute, Washington, USA, *Design in Germany Today* (1960–1).

10 Educating Designers

BOOKS

Bell, Q., *The Schools of Design* (London: Routledge & Kegan Paul, 1963). A survey of nineteenth-century developments.

Design in America: The Cranbrook Vision 1925–1950 (New York: Harry N.

Abrams, 1983). A full account of the role of the Cranbrook Academy of Art.

Gropius, W., *The New Architecture and the Bauhaus* (London: Faber, 1935). A manifesto of Gropius's architectural and pedagogical ideas.

Kostelanetz, R. (ed.), *Moholy-Nagy* (New York: Praeger, 1969). A collection of essays about Moholy-Nagy and his contribution to art and art education.

Moholy-Nagy, L., *Vision in Motion* (Chicago: Paul Theobald, 1947).

Moholy-Nagy, S., *Moholy-Nagy: Experiment in Totality* (New York: Harper, 1950). In many ways this provides the greatest insights into this artist's work and ideas.

Naylor, G., *The Bauhaus* (London: Studio Vista, 1968). A short but thorough introduction to the Bauhaus.

Whitford, F., *The Bauhaus* (London: Thames & Hudson, 1984). A very readable account which brings many of the protagonists to life for the first time.

Wingler, H. M., *Bauhaus – Weimar Dessau Berlin Chicago* (Cambridge, Mass.: MIT, 1969). The fullest and most authoritative account of the Bauhaus to date.

ARTICLES

Arnold, D., 'Ulm in the flesh', *Industrial Design*, no. 124 (March 1960), pp. 50–4.

Darwin, R., 'The Royal College of Art today', *Design*, no. 17 (September 1950), pp. 22–7.

Frampton, K., 'Apropos Ulm: curriculum and critical theory', *Oppositions*, no. 3 (May 1984), pp. 34–41.

Giedion, S., 'Notes on the life and work of Lazlo Moholy-Nagy', *Architects' Year-Book* (1949), pp. 47–56.

Holmes, K., 'Design training in the US', *Art and Industry*, no. 73 (November 1953), pp. 14–22.

Kepes, G., 'Lazlo Moholy-Nagy: the Bauhaus tradition', *Print* (January/February 1969), pp. 51–62.

'Lazlo Moholy-Nagy and the Institute of Design in Chicago', *Everyday Art Quarterly*, vol. 17, no. 3 (1946–7), p. 24.

Maldonado, T., 'New perspectives on industrial design education', *Stile industria*, vol. 20, no. 27 (1959), pp. 37–45.

Schnaidt, C., 'Ulm 1955–1975', *Archithèse*, no. 15 (1975), pp. 19–27.

EXHIBITION CATALOGUE

Centre de Création Industrielle, Paris, *Lazlo Moholy-Nagy* (1974).

11 Design and the Company

BOOKS

Atterbury, P., *The Story of Minton from 1793 to the Present Day* (London: Royal Doulton Ltd, 1976). A short company history.

Atterbury, P., and Irvine, L., *The Doulton Story* (London: Royal Doulton Ltd., 1979). An account of Doulton's changing relationship with design.

Bayley, S. (ed.), *Art and Industry: A Century of Design in the Products We Use* (London: Conran Foundation, 1982). A short general summary which accompanied an exhibition of the same name and which looks at design in a number of companies including Gustavsberg, Olivetti and AEG.

Bayley, S. (ed.), *Sony: Design* (London: Conran Foundation, 1982). A full study of the role of design in the Japanese company which accompanied an exhibition of the same name.

Bayley, S., *Harley Earl and the Dream Machine* (London: Weidenfeld & Nicolson, 1983). The story of Earl's relationship with General Motors since the 1920s.

Buddensieg, T., and Rogg, E. H., *Industriekultur: Peter Behrens and the AEG – 1907–1914* (Cambridge, Mass.: MIT, 1984). A very thorough account of Behrens's relationship with AEG.

Japanese Industrial Designers' Association, *Structure of Dexterity: Industrial Design Works in Japan* (Tokyo: Rikuyo-Sha, 1983). A glossy, well-illustrated survey of Japanese industrial design.

Kelly, A., *The Story of Wedgwood* (London: Routledge & Kegan Paul, 1930). Still a useful introduction to that particular story of design in industry.

Larrabee, L., and Vignelli, M., *Knoll Design* (New York: Harry N. Abrams, 1981). A glossy account of Knoll's contribution to modern design.

Lyall, S., *Hille: 75 Years of British Furniture* (London: Elroon Press with the Victoria & Albert Museum, 1981). Accompanied an exhibition of the same name.

Naylor, G., *A History of Gordon Russell Ltd* (Broadway, Worcs: Gordon Russell Ltd, 1968). A short company history.

Sanders, S., *Honda: The Man and his Machines* (Tokyo: Tuttle, 1975). A fascinating story of the Japanese company, and its relationship with design.

Santini, P. C., *The Years of Italian Design: A Portrait of Cesare Cassina* (Milan: Electa, 1981).

Schmittel, W., *Design Concept Realisation* (Zurich: ABC Edition, 1975). A study of design in a number of companies including Braun, Citroën, Herman Miller and Olivetti. More promotional than academic in nature.

ARTICLES

Allen, D., 'Olivetti of Ivrea', *Interiors*, no. 34 (December 1952), pp. 25–37.

Hartland Thomas, M., 'Design policy begins at the top', *Design*, no. 14 (February 1950), pp. 31–9.

Mitarachi, J. F., 'Harley Earl and his product: the styling section', *Industrial Design*, no. 94 (October 1955), pp. 43–9.

EXHIBITION CATALOGUE

Carnegie-Mellon University, Pittsburgh, *Design Process Olivetti 1908–1978* (1979).

12 Anti-Design

Baacke, R. P., Brandes, U., and Erlhoff, M., *Design als Gegenstand: Der Neue Glanz der Dinge* (Berlin: Frölich & Kaufmann, 1983). A well-illustrated survey of international Radical Design.

Bicknell, J., and McQuiston, L. (eds), *Design for Need* (Oxford: Royal College of Art, 1977). Collection of papers from Royal College of Art Conference of the same name.

Fuller, R. B., *Utopia or Oblivion* (Harmondsworth, Middx: Penguin, 1970). A collection of some of Fuller's writings on technology and design.

International Congress of the Societies of Industrial Designers, *The Relevance of Industrial Design* (Edinburgh: University of Edinburgh, 1973). Papers from a conference of the same name.

Navone, P., and Orlandoni, B., *Architettura Radicale* (Milan: Casabella, 1974). The story of Radical architecture and design in Italy.

Neutra, R., *Survival through Design* (New York: Oxford University Press, 1954). Somewhat dated, but still interesting to read in the light of more recent developments.

Packard, V., *The Hidden Persuaders* (Harmondsworth, Middx: Penguin, 1960). One of the strongest attacks to date on built-in obsolescence.

Packard, V., *The Waste-Makers: A Startling Revelation of Planned Wastefulness and Obsolescence in Industry Today* (London: Longman, 1960). As above.

Papanek, V., *Design for the Real World: Making to Measure* (London: Thames & Hudson, 1972). A strong critique of contemporary indusrial design. The argument is a little simplistic, but well presented.

Radice, B., *Memphis* (Milan: Electa, 1984). The definitive account of that provocative group of furniture designers.

Sparke, P., *Ettore Sottsass Jr* (London: Design Council, 1982). A biography of Sottsass with a section on Italian Radical Design.

Vyas, H. K., *Design and Environment: An Introductory Manual* (Ahmedabad, India: National Institute of Design, 1984). A brochure describing the institute's syllabus.

Periodicals

There are many journals published throughout the industrialized world which either specialize in design or include it in their coverage. They are very useful sources for studying twentieth-century design and include:

Abitare (Italy est. 1960)
Architectural Review (Britain est. 1896)
Art and Industry (USA est. 1922)
Art and Industry (Britain est. 1936)
Art et Industrie (France est. 1926) (later *Design Industrie*)
Blueprint (Britain est. 1983)
Casabella (Italy est. 1925)
Design (Britain est. 1949)
Design Issues (USA est. 1983)
Domus (Italy est. 1928)
Everyday Art Quarterly (USA est. 1946) (later *Design Quarterly*)
Form (Sweden est. 1905)
Form (West Germany est. 1957)
Form and Function (Finland est. 1981)
Idea (International Design Annual) (Japan est. 1952)
Industrial Design (USA est. 1954)
Interior Design (USA est. 1932)
Japan Design Annual (Japan est. 1962)
Kontur (Sweden est. 1950)
Mobilia (Denmark est. 1955)
Modo (Italy est. 1977)
Ornamo (Finland est. 1936)
Ottagono (Italy est. 1966)
Product Engineering (USA est. 1930)
Stile Industria (Italy est. 1954)
Studio Year Book of Decorative Art (Britain est. 1906)
Ulm (West Germany est. 1958)
Werk (Switzerland est. 1914) (later *Werk und Zeit*)

Index

Icon Editions